The Thinking Heart

How do we talk about feelings to children who are cut off from feeling? How do we raise hope and a sense of safety in despairing and terrified children without offering false hope? How do we reach the unreachable child and interest the hardened child?

The Thinking Heart is a natural sequel to *Live Company*, Anne Alvarez's highly influential and now classic book about working with severely disturbed and damaged children. Building on 50 years' experience as a child and adolescent psychotherapist, Alvarez uses detailed and vivid clinical examples of different interactions between therapist and client, and explores the reasons why one type of therapeutic understanding can work rather than another. She also addresses what happens when the therapist gets it wrong.

In *The Thinking Heart*, Alvarez identifies three different levels of analytic work and communication:

- The Explanatory Level – the 'why–because'
- The Descriptive Level – the 'whatness' of what the child feels
- The Intensified Vitalizing Level – gaining access to feeling itself for children with chronic dissociation, despairing apathy or 'undrawn' autism.

The book offers a structured schema drawing on and updating some of her classic work. It is designed to help the therapist to find the right level of interpretation in work with clients, and provides particular help with the unreachable child. It will be of use to psychotherapists, psychoanalysts, clinical and educational psychologists, child psychiatrists, social workers, special needs teachers and carers of disturbed children.

Anne Alvarez is a consultant child and adolescent psychotherapist and is retired co-chair for the Autism Service at the Tavistock Clinic, London. She is currently a visiting teacher and lecturer for the Tavistock Clinic, and a lecturer on the San Francisco Psychoanalytic Society Child Program.

The Thinking Heart

Three levels of psychoanalytic therapy with disturbed children

Anne Alvarez

Routledge
Taylor & Francis Group

LONDON AND NEW YORK

First published 2012
by Routledge
27 Church Road, Hove, East Sussex BN3 2FA

Simultaneously published in the USA and Canada
by Routledge
711 Third Avenue, New York NY 10017

Routledge is an imprint of the Taylor & Francis Group, an informa business

British Library Cataloguing in Publication Data
A catalogue record for this book is available from the British Library

Library of Congress Cataloging in Publication Data
Alvarez, Anne, 1936–
The thinking heart : three levels of psychoanalytic therapy with disturbed children / Anne Alvarez.
p. cm.
1. Child psychotherapy. 2. Adolescent psychotherapy. 3. Behavior disorders in children—Treatment. I. Title.
RJ504.A48 2012
618.92'8914–dc23
2011048986

ISBN: 978–0–415–55486–2 (hbk)
ISBN: 978–0–415–55487–9 (pbk)

Typeset in Times New Roman
by Keystroke, Station Road, Codsall, Wolverhampton

For my children and grandchildren, who know better.

Contents

List of illustrations

Figures

Table

Acknowledgements

Some of the material from the Introduction and from Chapter 1 was first given to the San Francisco Center for Psychoanalysis in 2001. I am also grateful to the many other psychoanalytic and psychotherapy societies, including the Canadian Association of Psychoanalytic Child Therapists and the Association of Child Psychotherapists (UK), to whom I subsequently proposed the idea of the three levels, and whose discussions have greatly informed this book. A published version first appeared as: 'Levels of analytic work and levels of pathology: the work of calibration', in 2010 in the *International Journal of Psychoanalysis*, 91, 4: 859–878. I thank the reviewers who helped me to clarify my thinking. An earlier version of Chapter 2 was first published in 1997 in S. Reid (ed.), *Developments in Infant Observation: The Tavistock Model* (London: Routledge), pp. 123–139. I am grateful to Piera Fiurgiuele for permission to publish this revised version. An earlier version of Chapter 3 was published in 1995 as 'Fantasia inconscia, pensare e camminare: alcune riflessioni preliminare', in *Richard e Piggle*, 3, 2: 190–206. I am grateful to the editors for permission to use the material in this revised form. An earlier version of Chapter 4 was first read as the Annual Lecture for the *British Journal of Psychotherapy* in 1995. A version was published in 1998 as 'Failures to link: attacks or defects? Some questions concerning the thinkability of Oedipal and pre-Oedipal thoughts', *Journal of Child Psychotherapy*, 24, 2: 213–231. An earlier version of Chapter 5 was published in 1999 by myself, A. Harrison and E. O'Shaughnessy as 'Symposium on Frustration', *Journal of Child Psychotherapy*, 25, 2: 167–198. An earlier version of Chapter 6 was published in 1997 as 'Projective identification as a communication: its grammar in borderline psychotic children', *Psychoanalytic Dialogues*, 7, 6: 753–768. An earlier version of Chapter 7 was published in 1995 as 'Motiveless malignity: problems in the psychotherapy of psychopathic patients', *Journal of Child Psychotherapy*, 21, 2: 167–182. The following year, a version was published in M.O. de A. Franca and R. Almedia (eds), *Anne Alvarez in Sao Paulo: Seminars* (Sao Paulo: Sociedade Brasilei de Psicanalise de Sao Paulo). An earlier version of Chapter 8 was published in 2006 as 'Narzissmus und das dumme object- Entwertung oder Missachtung? Mit einer anmerkung zum Suchtigen und zum manifesten Narzissmus', in O.F. Kernberg and H.P. Hartmann (eds), *Narzissmus: grundlagen – Storungsbilder-Therapie*

(Stuttgart: Schattauer). I am grateful to Schattauer for permission to publish this material in a revised form. An earlier version of Chapter 9 was first presented as a paper at the Psychoanalytic Forum, Institute of Psychoanalysis, London, November 2006 in a series, 'Sexuality Throughout the Lifespan'. The present version was first published in 2010 as 'Types of sexual transference and countertransference in psychotherapeutic work with children and adolescents', *Journal of Child Psychotherapy*, 36, 3: 211–224. I am extremely grateful to Viviane Green for her comments and editorial help. An earlier version of Chapter 10 was first published in 2006 as 'Some questions concerning states of fragmentation, unintegration, under-integration, disintegration, and the nature of early integrations', *Journal of Child Psychotherapy*, 32, 2: 158–180. I am very grateful to Judith Edwards and Janine Sternberg for their dedicated help with and editing of what was an endless paper. An earlier version of Chapter 11 was first presented as a paper in June 2002 at the James S. Grotstein Annual Conference at the UCLA Faculty Center, Los Angeles. Some of the material had previously appeared in 1998 in A. Alvarez and A. Phillips, 'The importance of play: a child psychotherapist's view', *Journal of Child Psychology and Psychiatry Review*, 3: 99–103. I am grateful to Asha Phillips for permission to publish some of the material in this new version. A version was also published in 2003 as 'Sich die Realität vorstellen: Die Bedeutung von Spiel und positive Erfahrungen für geistiges Wachstum', *Analytische Psychologie*, 34: 156–172. I am grateful to Gustav Bovensiepen, and the editors at Karger Verlag, for permission to publish this material. Earlier versions of Chapter 12 were published in 2004 as 'Finding the wavelength: tools in communication in children with autism', *Infant Observation: The International Journal of Infant Observation and its Applications*, 7, 2/3: 91–106, and in 2007 as 'Trouver la bonne longueur d'ondes: les outils de communication avec les enfants autistes', in B. Touati, F. Jouly and M.C. Laznik (eds), *Langage, voix et parole dans l'autisme* (Paris: Presses Universitaires de France), pp. 239–260. For Chapter 13, where I make an excursion into some parallels with neuroscience, I was inspired by Lucy Biven to reread Jaak Panksepp's work on the 'seeking system'. This led me to think it might be worth drawing attention to a possible link with Bion's concept of K.

I am enormously grateful to Taylor & Francis for their generous permission to publish material from the journals cited above in Chapters 1, 2, 4, 5, 6, 7, 9, 10 and 12.

I am grateful to Britt Bonneviers, Janet Bungener, Tamsin Cottis, Judith Edwards, Caroline Freeman, Lucy Griffin-Beale, Soraya Lari, Pia Massaglia, Jo McClatchey, Motoyo Miki, Claudio Rotenberg, Marija Stojkovic, David Trevatt and many others for permission to use clinical and observational material.

I am extremely grateful to Joanne Forshaw, of Taylor & Francis, and Stephanie Ebdon, of the Marsh Agency, for their endless patience and help.

Special thanks to Erin Hope Thompson, who has not only formatted the whole manuscript and bibliography but constituted and reconstituted the three figures on the depressive, paranoid and schizoid positions. I also thank Sabine Dechent and members of a Tavistock Child Psychotherapy training group supervision seminar, 2010/2011, for their helpful comments. If the figures are still unintelligible, it is my doing and no one else's.

I owe a huge debt of gratitude, as usual, to Al Alvarez for his scrupulous editing of the earlier versions of the chapters in the book, and especially also to my dear friend and colleague, Judith Edwards, who has read, reread and made creative critiques and suggestions for virtually every page of the present book. I am also grateful for the helpful and clarifying suggestions made by the anonymous Routledge reviewer. If the idea of the three levels is still incomprehensible, not usable, or too simplistic, then the fault is mine.

Introduction

What we need more of is slow art: art that holds time as a vase holds water.
(Robert Hughes, 2004)

I love psychoanalysis, not least because it works. I think I can say that most of the children I have treated over the last 50 years have been helped by it. Nevertheless, two of my illest patients in my early years of work – a paranoid borderline psychotic boy and a boy with severe autism – challenged my methods in ways that baffled me. I found that some of my interpretations to the paranoid boy often made him more ill, more persecuted, desperate and dangerously violent. Many of my interpretations to the autistic boy, Robbie, often hardly reached him at all. In a previous book, I traced the origins of my accidental finding of a way through to him and my attempts to conceptualize this as a kind of reclamation. With both children, I learned what *not* to do, and to have some idea of methods somewhat different from the classical ones. Only much later have I begun to consider how these differing methods might fit into a wider schema of psychoanalytic interventions and priorities. This book attempts to describe and chart three points on this continuum.

In *Live Company* (1992) I tried to show the difference between a more neutral or containing psychoanalytic stance and the reclamatory one where I seemed to call Robbie into contact and to a more vital sense of being. *Live Company*, however, was not only a book about autism: the second half consisted of many chapters on technical issues that arise when working with borderline patients who have limited ego capacity and are too overwhelmed by despair or persecution to benefit from interpretations that seek to remove defences against painful truths. I learned that I needed to respond to, or even carry for them, their hopes and aspirations, and that such interventions need not encourage manic denial when thoughtfully applied. However, I was not clear at the time how those ideas and technical responses related to but also differed from the process of reclamation. I did observe, however, that many readers thought that the reference to liveliness in the title meant that we should be actively reclaiming all our patients, whereas I meant the title to relate only to the reclamatory moments with Robbie. I also began to observe in my own and others' work an intervention that, while not the same as the more positive reclamation, had a certain intensity in common with it. Now, with hindsight, I feel a little clearer that the idea of a continuum of different ways of ascribing and conveying meaning might shed some light on the subject by taking account of the patient's ability really to get what we are saying: that is, his capacity for introjection, together with his capacity for a complex level of cognition, called two-tracked thinking. The following experiences with Robbie when he was much more alive to feeling are what set me wondering about this. By now, he had his own source of liveliness, but at times it overwhelmed him.

I had seen Robbie – who was severely autistic and, I thought, cut-off – on a non-intensive and quite interrupted basis from the age of seven onwards. I eventually came to learn that, unlike some other children with autism, he was not hiding: he was lost. In any case, it was only at age thirteen that he came into five-times-weekly treatment. Some years later, when he was in his late teens, he had become more clear-headed, finally had a sense of time (a very anxious sense, however) and could orient himself spatially and geographically, so that he was able to travel by underground from his house to mine by himself. Furthermore, he now had, at times, an all-too-ready access to feeling. If there were delays on the underground, or if he himself had left late, and he was therefore even one or two minutes late for his session, he would ring the bell in a state of frenzied agitation and fury. I would open the door to a six-foot-tall man charging toward me with his arm outstretched, his clenched fist aiming straight at my chest. He was having boxing lessons at the time and the sight was quite frightening.

Primo Levi, in *The Search for Roots* (2001), his personal anthology of books that were vital to him throughout his life, explains why he includes some advice by Ludwig Gatterman on the prevention of accidents in laboratory work in organic chemistry. Gatterman advises:

> Work with *explosive substances* should *never* be done *without wearing goggles* . . . Care must invariably be taken with *ether* and other *volatile, readily inflammable liquids* that *no flame is burning in the neighbourhood*. If a *fire* occurs, *everything which may ignite must immediately be removed*. The fire should then be extinguished with moist towels or by *pouring on carbon tetrachloride*, but not water.
>
> (Cited in Levi, 2001, p. 75)

For months, whenever Robbie charged up the path, I think I was probably using water. I was clearly not removing ignitable substances!

I certainly tried to interpret quickly and aptly. I would say something like, 'You are very upset and angry because you [or the trains] were late. You feel as though it must be my fault, and you don't want to know what really happened, or what really caused your lateness.' This was a rather wordy explanatory 'why–because' and 'who–you' interpretation. He kept coming, still inflamed. A few months later, I shortened it: I simply said, sympathetically, 'You are very upset today.' This comment on the 'whatness' of his experience helped a little, slowed him down a little, but not much. Note, however, that I was still attempting to locate the experience in him by saying 'you'. Another few months later, I happened to say (not looking at him but into a space somewhere between us and off to one side), 'It is very upsetting when trains don't run on time,' or, simply 'It's so upsetting to be late.' This did help him to pause and think.

Beth Steinberg (personal communication, 1999), who worked with Bryce Boyers (1989), said the staff on an in-patient unit had learned never to say the word 'you' to a person in a paranoid psychotic state. I think this is because the simple word 'you' can sometimes flood or seem to accuse an already overwhelmed person, whereas 'it' can permit a modicum of perspective. The patient can then take as much or as little into himself as he can bear. In either case, *what* is being felt may, at certain moments, have to take precedence over *why* it is being felt, or even, on occasion, *who* is feeling it.

The act of reclamation, however – calling Robbie forth from his earlier far-gone and empty state – was certainly very different. It involved not a 'why', nor even a 'what', but a kind of 'hey!' This new book is an attempt to discover and make sense of possible links between these three therapeutic stances, and to examine more closely the states of mind in the patient that demand one response, rather than another, from the therapist. It identifies three points on a continuum of levels of analytic work and levels of meaning: in Part I, an explanatory level that offers alternative meanings (why–because); in Part II, a descriptive level that enlarges meanings (whatness and isness); in Part III, a more intensified, vitalizing level that insists on meaning (hey!). Many other contemporary authors have suggested that when explanatory interpretations do not reach the patient, a prior level (which I think involves, among other things, lending meaning via description or amplification) is more effective in helping them to think. The book stresses that this second method, where appropriate to the patient's developmental and psychopathological level, need not be seen as inferior to or less complete than the former type. When it meets a deep need for understanding, it may *feel right*. Some authors describe this as a feeling *on behalf of* others, as a feeling *with*. Either type of method of lending meaning, via interpretation, concerns the whatness, the isness of experience, and, I suggest, addresses issues concerning both the degree and nature of introjective processes and the level of the patient's capacity for symbol formation. It respects the patient's need for assistance at what Bruner (1968) has called the level of one-tracked thinking without pushing more demanding and possibly incomprehensible two-tracked ideas upon him. To repeat, I think that such a level of work is better defined in terms of what it is and what it provides, rather than what it is not.

I am not suggesting that we need not use words to convey our understanding, only that when we stay in touch with the deepest feelings the patient has evoked in us, we may manage to get the words and the tone and the tact right. This will involve close attention both to our own countertransference feelings and to the nature of the patient's transference, both positive and negative, to us. How we may use these observations in a variety of ways is the subject of the book. I once heard a Brazilian musicologist say that the aesthetic dimension slows down the every-day, utilitarian speed of speech to make us pay attention. The work of art, he said, stops time. In psychoanalytic work we may – very occasionally – manage to do the same.

The plan of the book

In Chapter 1 I outline and discuss the three points on the continuum.

In Part I: Explanatory level conditions (Chapters 2, 3 and 4), I shall try to show that the state of mind required to take in the higher levels of two-part explanatory interpretation involves a capacity for two-tracked thinking/feeling – that is, some capacity to think two thoughts (or hold two feelings) at the same time. The emotional preconditions are clear: there needs to be some capacity to tolerate anxiety and pain and to bear thinking – in other words, a state not too far from what Klein called the 'depressive position'. Yet there is also an element of cognitive functioning involved – that is, of already achieved ego development and symbol formation. Taken together, this may involve a neurotic or mildly borderline state of mind. It is worth noting that even a here-and-now transference interpretation – concerning a moment where a boy, say, is complaining about how a female teacher at school treats another boy – involves considering four thoughts simultaneously: that is, 'she', 'he', 'you' and 'me'. Yet I believe that thinking and feeling in the transference and countertransference continues to be absolutely central to this work. The question remains: how much and how often should we refer to this openly with the patient (Roth, 2001)? The three chapters (2, 3 and 4) describe, first, the emotional/cognitive conditions for the development of two-tracked thinking, and then various obstructions to it in children who nevertheless have some capacity to manage it.

In Part II: Descriptive level conditions (Chapters 5 to 10), I discuss a variety of situations with severely traumatized and neglected children that might require not the offering of alternative and additional meanings but the elucidation and enlargement of single meanings, one at a time, as it were. The six chapters in this section concern a variety of mental states and transferences in the patient which demand this more descriptive or amplifying level of work, sometimes via dramatization, but mostly through verbal, but emotionally informed, comments. These include states of overwhelming despair, bitter paranoid vengefulness, cold psychopathic cruelty and fragmentation. The chapters also illustrate ways of thinking about – and being sensitive to – brief, sometimes minuscule, signs of recovery. It may be worth pointing out in this regard that psychoanalysis has spent decades studying processes of projection, but that attention is now also being paid to patients' introjective processes (Williams, 1997). In this section I shall try to identify moments when it was useful for the therapist to slow down the work to a more purely descriptive level, in order to try to offer understanding that could be taken in. It is now accepted that work in the depths of the paranoid-schizoid position involves containment in the analyst's countertransference of the bad parts of the patient's self or object (Feldman, 2004). It is also important, however, to attend to the question of the underdeveloped good. I shall try to show, and shall illustrate further, that such containing functions can occur at this simple, empathic, descriptive level.

A particular element in descriptive work: attention to moments of gladness and curiosity

I have argued previously that I think we need a supplement to the theory of learning proposed by Freud and Bion that it is the experience of frustrating reality which wakes us from infantile dreams and makes us alert and able to learn. I suggested that pleasurable experiences – feelings of being liked or of liking, of aspirations recognized – can be equally as alerting as the more sobering ones, particularly in the case of children with little hope and low expectations. The deprived child may be alerted, not only emotionally but cognitively, by the discovery of the reliability, decency and countertransference responsiveness of his therapist. My experiences of these alertings are based on clinical phenomena, but it is interesting that brain research is now confirming that brain growth in infancy is facilitated by neurotransmitters such as opioids and dopamine, which are themselves elicited by such things as the caregiver's smiles, looks and voice (Gerhardt, 2004; Panksepp, 1998; Panksepp and Biven, 2011; Schore, 1994). (See Chapter 13 for a more detailed discussion of possible parallels with certain neuroscience findings.) Most of the clinical arguments and illustrations will appear in Chapters 5–10. We do, probably more often than we think, need to slow down our work so that it can truly hold time, as a vase holds water.

In Part III: Intensified vitalizing level (Chapters 11 and 12) I shall try to show that with certain autistic, despairing/apathetic, fragmented or perverse children, we may have to descend to another, even more prior, level of work which involves the containment *and intensified transformation* of internal objects perceived as useless and unvalued (not devalued), weak, or else too easily excited by perversion. I shall go on to add to my original ideas of reclamation as a vitalizing activity with patients (where the deficit or impairment was in the ego, the self *and* the internal object) by illustrating some additional ways of working at this third level of psychotherapy via an urgent insistence on meaning. The issue at this third level – with emptied-out or perverted patients – does not concern thinking about feeling, nor even identifying feeling, but gaining access to feeling itself. With perverse patients, it may mean opening a route to a very different kind of feeling from the deviant forms of excitement to which they are habituated.

These chapters will offer illustrations of a variety of intensified or vitalizing methods and of discouraging addictive or perverse preoccupations. It is not easy to strike a balance between being too intense and therefore intrusive, and being too remote or too weak. Yet, long before certain patients process their hatred and find their capacity for love, they may have to develop the ability to be interested in an object with some substantiality, life or, in the case of perversion, strength and a capacity to excite in a non-perverse manner. This vitalizing function involves work at the very foundation of human relatedness. Although we must draw attention to their lack of interest – or, for that matter, to their perverted interests – we may sometimes also have to find ways of demonstrating that other experiences can be interesting and even exciting. We may have to attract their attention, and then learn how to keep it. Once this is achieved, the work can move to 'higher' levels, sometimes in the course of a single session.

Throughout this book, I shall maintain that our work with very disturbed or autistic children and adolescents needs to be informed not only psychoanalytically but developmentally and psychopathologically. This book is no manual (witness the thousands of qualifications and exceptions), only an attempt to revisit some earlier cases and many new ones, and to calibrate the therapist's technical responses to a variety of states of mind into some sort of a hierarchy of priorities. Perhaps child and adolescent psychotherapists have learned enough by now to try to make some coherent theoretical and technical sense of our decades of experience with extremely disturbed and developmentally delayed children and adolescents. Like psychoanalysts from Freud on, we have had to learn from our mistakes.

Brief note on the table and figures

The table and figures in this book, like most charts, are over-schematic and over-simplified.

Table 1.1 (at the end of Chapter 1) attempts to put the concept of levels of work into a form of visualizable schema.

Figures A1, A2 and A3 (in the Appendix) attempt to conceptualize visually my elaboration and extension of the Kleinian theory of the development from the paranoid-schizoid to the depressive position. Figure A1 illustrates some features of the depressive position as described by Klein. Figures A2 and A3, however, differ from the Kleinian model by making a distinction between paranoid/persecuted and schizoid/empty states. They omit all sorts of questions regarding pathology, for example, when positive feelings escalate into manic defences, when negative feelings go on to addictive or even perverse sadistic destructiveness, and also when the empty, passive states described in the last graph are used or misused to get others to do the acting and living for us. And, of course, they do not do justice to the myriad complexities of the human mind with which we clinicians have to deal (and by which we are entranced) every day.

Chapter 1

Levels of therapeutic work and levels of pathology

The work of calibration

Introduction

There has been much discussion in recent decades about the relative importance, with borderline or very damaged patients, of two different levels of work: that is, of insight versus other, more primary, levels of understanding. In this chapter, I shall show that I agree with these authors, but will also suggest the need for a third level which is prior to both. I am also offering the idea that all three may be linked as points on a continuum of levels of meaning. At the third level (of psycho-pathology and, therefore, of technique) the question arises of whether feelings and meanings matter at all to patients in affectless states of autism, dissociation, despairing apathy or deviant states of excitement.

Discussions of the first two levels have been couched in a variety of terms: some concern the balance between the need for the patient to take responsibility for some feeling versus the need for its containment by the analyst (Bion, 1962b; Feldman, 2004; Joseph, 1978; Steiner, 1994). Other versions discuss insight versus mentalization (Fonagy and Target, 1998), and interpretation versus play (Blake, 2008). Still others stress the significance of something more than interpretation in terms of a 'procedural' mode of information processing during a 'moment of recognition' (Sander, 2002; Stern *et al.*, 1998). Schore (2003, p. 147) emphasizes the need for a 'conversation between limbic systems' in patient and therapist in the more severe levels of pathology. Botella and Botella (2005) describe the need for the analyst to carry out the 'work of figurability' with patients whose memory traces are not representational but more like 'amnesic traces'. More recently, Tuch (2007) has discussed how to facilitate the reflective function with pre-interpretive work.

Klein herself, the great scholar of the infantile levels of the personality, pointed out that when pre-verbal emotions and phantasies are revived in the transference situation, they appear as 'memories in feeling'. She went on to say that 'we cannot translate the language of the unconscious into consciousness without lending it words from our conscious realm' (Klein, 1957, p. 180). Child psychotherapists Lanyado and Horne have explored a variety of ways of working in the transitional area with extremely damaged and acting-out child and adolescent patients, while

Blake has illustrated the importance of humour in relieving impasses with aggressive deprived adolescents (Blake, 2008; Lanyado and Horne, 2006). In Parts II and III, I shall try to demonstrate that in order to reach – and communicate with – memories in feeling – or, worse, severe loss of feeling – we may have to go beyond words and consider the use of our emotional and even emotive counter-transference responses in ways which determine whether we choose the right words and especially the right tone.

Roth (2001) identified four levels of transference interpretation, ranging from comments about the meaning of relationships in the external world to enactments in the here-and-now of the analytic relationships. She suggested that while the latter level is at the epicentre of the analysis, the analyst has to be willing to follow the patient over quite a broad landscape of her experience in order to give a richer, more complete picture of her world. Roth does, however, comment on her patient's capacity to own some guilt at a point when she is making a particularly strong interpretation, which suggests that, at least at this point, she considers that the choice of level depends on the patient's capacity to hear something. But the main thrust of her argument is the usefulness and enrichment provided by working at all levels. Roth seems to suggest that all of this can provide insight. Most of the previous authors' primary concern, however, seems to be to identify the conditions under which insight-giving interpretations are inappropriate and something else is required first.

Anna Freud put the issue vividly, but in traditional one-person psychology terms. Returning to a discussion of the concept of defence with her colleagues at the Hampstead Clinic, she referred to the need for prior structuralization of the personality: she said that if you have not yet built the house, you cannot throw somebody out of it – that is, utilize projective mechanisms. Joseph Sandler added, 'nor throw him into the basement' – that is, utilize repression (Sandler and Freud, 1985, p. 238). A Kleinian object relations theorist treating very deprived children might agree, but might want to add that basically it is sometimes a question of building two houses – one for the self and the other for the internal object. Both A.M. Sandler (1996, p. 281) and Hurry (1998, p. 34) have gone further than Anna Freud, by maintaining that the distinction between developmental therapy and psychoanalytic work is a false one. Here, I will stress that the analytic work needs to be both developmentally and psychopathologically informed and therefore needs to take account of the patient's capacity for introjection.

Da Rocha Barros (2002) introduced the notion of a continuum when he pointed out that *steps toward* thinkability might be provided by affective pictograms in dreams. He claimed that at the earlier stages of their appearance, such visual and dramatized images are not yet thought processes, but may contain powerful expressive and evocative elements which lie underneath unconscious phantasies (p. 1087). He does not say whether the analyst should respond to such early steps with a different sort of interpretation: however, he does say that they may thus lead toward the transmutation and working through which then leads on to symbolic function and verbal understanding. Moore (2004) has demonstrated the tendency, in traumatized children, to create drawings that take the form not of symbolic representations but of re-presentations that are not genuinely symbolic. With psychotherapy, the children's drawings tend to become more free and genuinely representational. Moore likens this change to Hartmann's observations on the development, in traumatized adults, from night terrors in stage 4 sleep toward the REM dreams which signal that some degree of processing and digestion of the trauma has taken – and is taking – place (Hartmann, 1984).

Like Da Rocha Barros and Moore, I offer the idea of a continuum, but one which considers how to find the level of intervention appropriate to the level of disturbance and/or of ego development (and object development) in the patient. This will imply attention to his capacity for introjection. Da Rocha Barros offers the medium of dreams as a model for a particular step with his adult patients, whereas here I am considering how to make contact with the different levels of mental/emotional development in the child or adolescent patient during play or in the conversation between patient and therapist in ways that make sense to – and reach – the patient. How the therapist verbalizes and expresses his understanding, and processes his possibly very disturbing countertransference feelings, may facilitate or hinder moves toward symbolization. In the case of the patients described below, it is sometimes a question of steps toward working through, as Da Rocha Barros suggested. In other cases, however – where the question is not only of processing pain and anxiety but of introjecting possibly quite new experiences of relief, pleasure, or the interestingness and receptivity of one's objects – we might want to emphasize his other term – 'working toward' – or add another – such as 'taking in' – rather than 'working through'.

Questions of introjection, internalization and identification are at issue. Klein (1957, p. 90) wrote, 'There is no doubt that if the infant was actually exposed to very unfavourable conditions, the retrospective establishment of a good object cannot undo bad early experiences. However, the introjection of the analyst as a good object, if not based on idealization, has, to some extent, the effect of providing an internal good object where it has been largely lacking.' We now understand from Bion, developmentalists and neuroscientists that the capacity to think, and therefore to take in interpretations, involves both cognitive and emotional functions, or, as Urwin puts it, cognitive/emotional functions (Bion, 1962b; Panksepp, 1998; Schore, 1994; Trevarthen, 2001; Urwin, 1987). It depends, in part, on the level of ego, self and object development already achieved, but also on the level of emotional disturbance at any particular moment: when the disturbance is high, it can interfere with an already developed ego and symbolic function.

Neuroscientists have shown that social/emotional trauma or neglect in infancy affect not only behaviour and psychological development, but brain growth. The dissociation that arises after trauma – or possibly the inattention or withdrawal that arises in autism – can set the person on a deviant emotional and cognitive path of development, and it can interfere profoundly with growth in the feeling and relating parts of the brain (Perry, 2002; Schore, 2003). In fact, the orbito-frontal cortex, essential for empathic understanding of other people's minds and one's own emotions, develops almost entirely post-natally (Gerhardt, 2004) – via the infant's interactions with other human beings. When Robbie, who suffered from both autism and trauma, finally began to use his mind, it often seemed as though part of his mind/brain was behaving like a near-atrophied muscle – twitching suddenly and erratically into movement and life. At the time, the modern brain findings were not available, but current research leads me to believe that these events were happening in Robbie's brain as well as his mind. (See Chapter 13 for some reflections on the neuroscience parallels.)

In the Introduction, I described the steps I took toward finally finding a way to help Robbie with his frenzied panics whenever he was late, and how I eventually came to avoid the word 'you' when I tried to describe his feelings. I started pointing out with feeling that 'It is upsetting when . . .' and this seemed to permit necessary perspective. It seemed that he could then take as much or as little into himself as he could bear. In either case, *what* is being felt may, at certain moments, have to take precedence over *why* it is being felt (and, as I said earlier, even over *who* is feeling it).

I would suggest, therefore, that if we are engaged in building Anna Freud's house, or rather Melanie Klein's two houses (for the self and the internal object), we may have to start with the foundation of each house. Intersubjectivists have described the problem of deficit in the self, and the difference between defensive strategies designed to make up for a developmental arrest and true defences against conflicting desires (Stolorow and Lachmann, 1980). In Kleinian language, we might want to consider the difference between an attempt at 'overcoming' such a deficit and one that attempts to defend against it (Klein, 1937).

In this book, however, I want to add another dimension to the deficit issue by stressing the existence, in some patients, of a deficit or impairment in the internal object. This concerns objects experienced as uninteresting, unvalued (not devalued), useless and possibly mindless. It may also concern objects with a perverse, sometimes sado-masochistic, excitability. Some years ago (Alvarez, 1992, 1999), I suggested that an intensified level of intervention – termed 'reclamation' – responding to a countertransference sense of desperate urgency might be needed with patients such as Robbie in imminent danger of something like psychic death. As described above, the later experience – with a very much alive and almost psychotically frenzied Robbie – led me to wonder about the conditions under which he – and others like him in these differing states – could hear my attempts to reach them.

I suggest, therefore, that historical and chronological developments in theory and technique from Freud and Klein through to Bion, and then on to autism specialists – from the top down, as it were – may need to be reversed when we take clinical, psychopathological and developmental considerations into account. I shall work my way down from the top level of the house described by Anna Freud, through the ground floor, to the basement and its foundations by looking at three different ways in which an interpretation may ascribe meaning to experience or phantasy. Schafer (1999, p. 347) pointed out that the use of a hermeneutic model need carry no implication of 'mindless relativism'. And there is certainly no implication that the analysts or therapists quoted herein advocated only one level of work. I am citing some of their particular papers that have opened the way to extending technique. Furthermore, there is no implication that analytic work can be neatly divided into these three levels. There have been psychoanalytic maps before, notably Bion's grid (1963), but here I am hoping to link the level of symbolic development with technique. There are many points on the continuum between each of the three; nevertheless, they might be considered to involve recognizable steps from the foundation up, as it were, on the way to higher symbolic functioning. First, that is, certain patients need to be helped to be able to feel and to find meaning, sometimes via an experience that something matters imperatively to someone else; then, feelings can begin to be identified and explored; eventually, explanations, which bring in additional alternate meanings, may be heard and taken in.

The continuum of technique from the top level down

Explanatory level: offering alternative meanings

Freud (1893–1895) discovered the power of explanatory interpretations about the link between repressed, displaced parts of the personality and defences against them. (Your belief that your leg is paralysed is due to your unconscious guilt about your hostility to your dying father when you were nursing him.) This is a 'why–because' interpretation. Klein (1946) elaborated and amplified Freud's work on projection by emphasizing that whole parts of the personality could be projected into others. This may lead to another type of explanatory interpretation: that is, locating or relocating split off or projected parts of the personality. (You are trying to make me feel inferior in order to get rid of your own feeling of inferiority.) This is a 'who?–you' or 'where?–there' interpretation. Both types of interpretation tend to replace one meaning with another – the conscious with the unconscious, or the disowned with the re-owned. Bion (1962b, 1965) made the link between projective identification and countertransference: he pointed out that projective identifications emanating from the patient could be felt powerfully in the mind of the analyst and require both containment and transformation there before being returned to the patient.

Descriptive level: ascribing or amplifying meaning

Bion made a further point, however: he suggested that some projective identifications took place not simply for defensive or destructive motives, but for purposes of needed communication (Bion, 1962b). Joseph (1978) and Steiner (1993) went on to draw attention to this element of need: that is, the necessity, with certain patients, for the analyst to contain projections at certain moments without returning them to the patient. The analyst would explore the nature of the missing part of the patient as it resided in the analyst until the patient was able to own or re-own it. This more receptive attitude to the patient's need to project is similar to Winnicott's ideas on allowing the transitional object to carry meaning in its own (paradoxical) right, without being explained away too prematurely (Winnicott, 1953). Coming from the perspective of normal development, the researchers' study of parent–infant communication – and the consequences for infant mental health – has identified processes occurring in shared mental or emotional states which seem to imply that certain more simple empathic or amplifying comments may, by not overloading the patient with ideas, reach both the feeling and thinking parts of the mind at the same moment (Stern, 1985; Trevarthen, 2001). The Kleinians cited above are describing a phenomenon of 'feeling on behalf of' and the developmentalists are describing a 'feeling with'. Both seem to be central to the work of communicating understanding at very basic levels. Either method of lending meaning, when it is an interpretation, concerns the whatness – the isness – of experience and, I suggest, raises issues concerning both the degree and nature of introjective processes and the level of the patient's capacity for symbol formation. It respects the patient's need for assistance at the level of one-tracked thinking without pushing more demanding and possibly incomprehensible two-tracked ideas upon him. Perhaps such a level of work is better defined in terms of what it is, rather than what it is not.

An even more prior level of work – vitalizing level: insistence on meaning

Here, as I said, I want to add another dimension to the deficit issue by stressing the existence in some patients of a deficit or impairment in the internal object. This concerns objects experienced as uninteresting, unvalued (not devalued), useless, mindless or perversely excitable. The level of work required may need to precede both the explanatory and the descriptive levels. At the most severe level of psychopathology – and therefore most extreme level of technique – the question arises of whether feelings and meanings matter at all to patients in affectless states of autism, dissociation or apathy following chronic despair. There the deficit was even more severe: the object was so remote and faint it hardly existed. The question also arises of where dissociation and hardness has gathered perverse motivations to it, and here, also, the connection with a live internal object may atrophy.

This final level of work – at the foundations of mental and relational life – addresses the problem of being heard by patients who cannot listen or feel, perhaps due to autism, dissociation of a chronic nature due to trauma, or chronic apathy as a result of despair or neglect. This is not a question of one or two tracks. This is a question, first, of helping the patient to get on track, or back on track, in situations where he has been profoundly lost (not hiding). Or, to return to the house metaphor, to help our patients get on to 'solid ground', as a recovering autistic adolescent put it (Edwards, 1994). What is at stake is not simply a weak ego, or even major defects in the sense of self: it is a matter of defects in both self and internal object, where *both* are experienced as dead and empty or useless. There is often a chronic apathy about relating, which goes beyond despair. Nothing is expected. Green (1997) describes something similar in the case of patients who experienced sudden depression in their mother during infancy. He describes the 'decathexis of the maternal object and the unconscious identification with the dead mother' as a defence against the abrupt loss of the mother's love due to her own bereavement or loss (pp. 150–151). Here, however, I am thinking of cases where it seems likely that the mother's withdrawal was more chronic or the patient's withdrawal more like 'undrawal', sometimes for constitutional reasons. Bob Dylan describes something similar, but puts it more aggressively when he says that he is not looking for anything in anyone's eyes (Dylan, 1987). Dylan, however, knows what he is not looking for, whereas some children do not.

These clinical problems may arise in very different ways with a particular 'undrawn' sub-type of autism and also with some very deprived or abused and perverse children. I have suggested that the act of reclamation or claiming by a therapist responding to a powerful countertransference sense of urgency may be an extreme form of the mother's normal activity of awakening and alerting the normal, mildly depressed, or slightly distracted, infant (Alvarez, 1980, 1992). I later clarified that this technique seemed to be relevant only in cases of a particular sub-type of autism or deprivation where there is severe deficit in the sense of self *and of object* (Alvarez, 1999). Such work may involve waking the patient to mindfulness and meaning – or, in Bion's terms, at the very least, offering realizations to barely experienced preconceptions (Bion, 1962b). Where realizations have failed, preconceptions may have faded or even atrophied. I am writing here of work with children and adolescents, but Tiziana Pierazzoli (personal communication, 2002), John Mclean (personal communication, 2003) and Director (2009) have suggested that the activity of reclamation may also be relevant to work with certain chronically schizoid cut-off adults. Child psychotherapists have also made use of the concept (Edwards, 2001; Hamilton, 2001; Music, 2009), while Tanya Nesic (personal communication, 2005) has suggested that work with Asperger's patients involves a process of constant mini-reclamations.

Reid (1988) has described a similar more intensified intervention: whereas reclamation refers to instances of the therapist calling the child into contact with the therapist, Reid writes of how the therapist may try to fan a little interest in a toy or some other object in the room. She terms this the 'generation' or 'demonstration' of interestingness or meaning. She explains that she would use this method only with certain autistic patients, similar to Robbie, and only at certain moments.

It would, by the way, be essential to distinguish a despairing passive patient with a dead internal object from the sort of patient described by Joseph (1975) who projects interest and concern into the object, who is then pressured to carry liveliness and a capacity for activity that the patient appears to lack. (There is an example of a situation where both situations applied with a schizoid borderline patient. I managed, on a rare occasion, to respond to both, by returning part of the projected feeling to the patient, but holding and expressing some of it myself. See Alvarez (1992, p. 88).) It would also be essential to disentangle elements of the near atrophy found in something like a psychic desert from those involved in the 'psychic retreat' described by Steiner (1993). A psychic desert in infancy may gather defensive or addictive motives during the development to adulthood, and these motives would certainly need analytic attention. However, so also would the accompanying or underlying deficit where the object, rather than being avoided, is hardly found, due to its remoteness or weakness. In such states of mind, the patient is not hiding – he is lost. A retreat offers, at the very least, a place to go; a desert offers nothing.

Elaboration of the state of mind of the patient relevant for work at the three levels

Explanatory interpretations: a necessary precondition

Here is a brief example of more ordinary interpretations about anger, due to loss or jealousy, in patients who are not in a psychopathic, borderline or psychotic state of mind but functioning at a relatively well neurotic level, where it is positively helpful to say something like, 'You are cross, you are angry because . . .' This is in patients where there is some capacity for guilt, some capacity for love, some ego, which can process insight into their own aggression, but also some already established self-respect.

Recently, an adolescent girl came to the last session of the week in a great sulk. She explained that her sister had made her half an hour late for her session, but refused to say more and sat with her back to me, absolutely furious with me. Borderline patients or psychopathic patients might take weeks to recover from such a disappointment or disruption. In fact, they might not be feeling only anger or fury: they might be experiencing confusion or despair, or an icy increase in their cynicism. But, to Linda, I was able to say: 'You are absolutely furious with me because we've got such a short session today, especially as it's the last session of the week. It must be my fault.' She swung around and said, 'Yes, *and* I've got exams next week.' She calmed down quite quickly. It was enough to interpret her anger: it was not necessary to consider her desperation or to carry the sense of injustice for her because she was in touch with that herself. Some borderline despairing people need us to contain this for them (see Chapter 6 on moral imperatives), but Linda did not. She was capable of standing up for herself – what needed processing was her anger. Many important emotional and cognitive developments had taken place long before in this girl's life for her to get to this stage. (I go on to discuss these in Part I.)

These higher levels of interpretation involve a two-part interpretation, and therefore, I suggest, assume a capacity for two-tracked thinking: that is, a capacity to think two thoughts fairly fully at the same time (Bruner, 1968). The emotional preconditions are clear: some capacity to tolerate anxiety and pain and to bear thinking – in other words, a state not too far from the depressive position. Yet there is an element of cognitive functioning involved, too: that is, of already achieved ego development and symbol formation. Taken together, this may involve a neurotic or mildly borderline state of mind. Bruner (1968) has described a cognitive development, which he has called the capacity to 'think in parentheses' or to hold something in reserve. Bruner's study observed babies developing from a newborn state of what he called one-tracked attention, where they can either only suck or only look, to a coordinated capacity for two-trackedness at four months, where they can do both more or less at once. Bruner (1968, pp. 18–24, 52) calls this final stage 'place-holding' (like putting your finger on a line in a book while you listen to someone for a moment).

Others have described something similar to Bruner's two-tracked thinking. Bion (1950) described the psychotic patient's difficulty with binocular vision, and Segal (1957) suggested the importance of depressive position development in the achievement of symbolic functioning – a kind of thinking and feeling in parentheses on a deep emotional level, where love and hate are no longer separated but integrated, yet not blurred or confused. Bion (1955, p. 237) also described how thoughts can behave like people: that is, get on top of each other and, we might add, chase us, haunt us, chase each other and, in poetry and the other arts, occasionally conjugate in harmony. The normal child can hold a thought in reserve; consider the thought within the thought, and the thought beyond the thought. On the other hand, borderline patients (in their psychotic moments) are concrete, one-tracked, overwhelmed by the singularity of their state of mind, in danger of symbolic equations and massive splitting and projection. We may risk producing premature integrations when we try to leapfrog their urgent, imperative, single-minded states.

Bruner does not discuss the conditions under which the sense of a reserve may be facilitated or hindered, but psychoanalysts have suggested that the emotionality involved in the move from two-person to three-person (Oedipal) relationships may also play a major part in the development of this type of deep numeracy (Britton, 1989; Klein, 1932b, pp. 183–184; see Chapter 2 for additional examples of infants making use of this capacity). It seems likely that the capacity to register two different versions of the object – sometimes both positive (i.e. she can be near but also further away while yet present; or she is suckable but also seeable; or she is talking to him but also noticing me; or she waits for me in the background while I talk to him) – plays a part in the development of symbol formation and may be an important precursor of the depressive position capacity to hold together two far more different and opposed thoughts/feelings (love and hate or love and loss).

There is a further emotional factor in the capacity to hold thoughts in reserve, however, which I will consider in more detail in Chapter 2: namely, the element of pleasure and confidence and sense of agency, abundance and anticipation to be gained from experiencing more than one track of experience. There is an element of trust involved in expecting an idea to stay in the back of one's mind while you attend to something else. Equally, there is a large element of confidence and sense of adventure, which underlies the bravery involved in, for example, learning to walk and going forward to explore new ideas. All this can be seen to follow from Bion's (1967) great vision that the relations between thoughts seem to behave like the relations between people, or between the self and others. (Chapters 2–4 illustrate this notion in a variety of ways.)

Descriptive level: simple lending or amplification of meaning with patients with ego deficits

Many children are too ill or too learning disabled (due to autism, trauma or neglect) to be able to think two thoughts together, or even in close sequence. For them, the simple exploration of the qualities that surround an aspect of the object (its brightness, say) or of the self (my voice can be louder!) may be enough to be going on with if their mind is to grow. Many so-called learning-disabled patients can be found to have something more like an underlying 'wondering disability'. I should say that although I have implied that different levels of pathology correspond to the three levels, patients themselves refuse to stay put in neat diagnostic categories, so the levels refer only to different states of mind, which of course can occur in the same patient at different moments in the same session. Long ago, Glover (1928a, p. 18) warned that 'a transference interpretation of phantasy is incomplete' and that 'as a general rule our next transference-interpretation will be concerned with transference-indications of defence'. But he also advocated careful regulation and dosage of interpretation with borderline patients and warned against the dangers of premature interpretations with them (Glover, 1928b, p. 213).

Bion described two stages in the development of the capacity to think: first, a preconception had to meet with a realization for a conception to be born; and, second, a conception had to meet with frustration for a thought to be born. Interestingly, he neglected to say much about the first stage. He seemed much more interested in the second: he thought that real learning depended on the choice between techniques for evasion and techniques for modification of frustration (Bion, 1962b, p. 29) and he linked tolerance of frustration with the sense of reality. His concept of the preconception meeting with a realization seems to have some hints of the element of perfect fit implied in the theories of primary narcissism (Freud, 1938, pp. 150–151), symbiosis (Mahler, 1968) and illusion (Winnicott, 1953) and which can seem to imply a somewhat sleepy mindless state. Pleasant surprises, however, can be extremely alerting and cognitively stimulating, so perhaps Bion's first stage – that of the introjection of moments of contact or 'moments of meeting, or moments of recognition' (Sander, 2000) – deserves more study. The feeling of being understood may *feel right*, without implying a simple adaptation or gratification model. Indeed, such experiences may not involve meetings or recognitions exactly: because of the element of delighted surprise, they can be vitalizing and thought-provoking.

In any case, this level of work involves something more like simple ascribing or lending of meaning. Here, as I said, I suggest we are in the area of Joseph's (1978) ideas concerning the containing of projective identifications over time by and within the analyst and the avoidance of premature return of the projected, and Steiner (1994) on the importance of analyst-centred interpretations. This is related to Winnicott's (1953) ideas on respecting the paradox in the transitional area – that is, not identifying the transitional object too readily as belonging either to the object or to the self. Concepts of mental state sharing and attunement, offered by developmentalists such as Stern (1985), or the mindful companionship suggested by Trevarthen (2001), are relevant too.

Two of Schore's (2003, pp. 280–281) recommendations on technique with borderline patients are also apposite here: the recognition and 'identification of unconscious affects that were never developmentally interactively regulated' nor internally represented; and an approach that not only identifies discrete, automatic, facially and prosodically expressed affects, but one that also attends to the intensity, and especially the duration and lability of emotional states. The therapist of such patients may need, in Stern's terms, to be alert to his patient's 'vitality affects' – that is, the shaping, intensity and temporality of his patient's emotions – as much as their content and certainly more than their link with other emotions (Stern, 1983, pp. 53–60). That is, we might say not only, 'You are very upset today,' but, 'You are still terribly upset, aren't you?' Or, to a previously rigidly controlled and controlling child, 'You really seem to enjoy bouncing that ball, especially the way that it doesn't always come back to the same place.' To link the experience with other thoughts – for example, to its symbolic connections – may be at best redundant, at worst an interference with a new development. It is a question of whether we should think of descriptive or amplifying interpretations as partial, incomplete (Glover, 1928a, p. 18) and simply preparatory for the real thing, or whether we should think of a more complete experience as taking place at such moments. Is it necessarily a partial experience when something feels right?

A most helpful tool for working in this area is Bion's (1962b) concept of 'alpha function' – the function of the mind that makes thoughts thinkable and lends meaning to experience. As with Robbie, sometimes it may be better to avoid the whole question of who is having the experience. If the patient is very persecuted or desperate, or simply confused, it may be better to get an adjective or two attached to the noun, an adverb or two attached to the verb, and let it rest. An 'It is upsetting when . . .' may serve to place the feeling at some distance. Then the patient can choose whether to let it be his experience, owned by himself, or not. Naming and describing experience, I believe, has to have priority over locating it. Hopkins (1996) outlines Winnicott's views on the importance of simple naming via play: he supervised her work with a three-year-old child with no speech or attachment, or capacity to play. This level of work is important for psychotic patients emerging from states of severe dissociation and needing simply to identify and verify an emotional state well before they are able to acknowledge it as their own; it is also important with some traumatized or deprived patients who have little structuring of their emotional brain/mind. Schore (2003) has suggested that, when we are working with borderline patients, it is not a question of making the unconscious conscious, but of restructuring or even structuring the unconscious. I am speaking mostly here of patients such as borderline, autistic or psychotic, but in fact some verbally precocious people may also need much slowing down to attend to their actual experience. One adolescent, seemingly very keen to understand her difficulties, could say, 'I was very irritated with Matthew, and I know it is because I was jealous when he talked too long to that attractive girl last night.' I had to learn, however, not to be misled by the apparent insight, and sometimes simply to ask what she meant by 'jealous'. She needed help to slow down and examine her own experience, rather than to rush to swallow my interpretations whole and then feed me her rather undigested understanding.

Descriptive lending of meaning continued: an example of containment of projective identification

Bion's concept of projective identification as a communication described situations where the mother contains and transforms the projections of the infant in ways which make the unbearable bearable (1962b, 1965). He compared this to the containing function of the analyst, and there are many instances of this in clinical work where the patient is able to explore an unbearable experience via someone else. Joseph (1978) has drawn attention to the need for analysts to contain such often very powerful experiences within themselves, sometimes for long periods, without returning the projection to the patient, and Steiner (1994) has distinguished between analyst-centred and patient-centred interpretations. In child work such containment may occur through the therapist's willingness to enact (for a time), via the play, the part of the child's unwanted self. Freud (1911) and Bion (1962b) have stressed the importance of frustration in the learning process, but in certain cases it seems to be the freedom *from* frustration which promotes thinking – the opportunity to explore the experience in someone else who can feel it deeply and also think about it. Kleitman (1963) has shown that wakefulness from choice, states of lively curiosity, occur in newborn infants after a feed and a defecation, when the baby is comfortable, and not, as previously thought, when the baby is driven by hunger and discomfort.

A disabled and deformed girl, Jill, condemned to live life in a wheelchair, became desperate and suicidal when she moved from her primary school to a large secondary school. After a few months in therapy, she began to make her therapist sit in a chair with Sellotape wrapped around her legs. Jill told the therapist that she (the therapist) would never get out – she would have to stay there forever. The game was pretend (the therapist was not really trapped) but the tone was deadly – acidly – serious. Clearly this figure represented Jill, but from the clinical point of view it was important for the therapist to imagine – and describe – this extremely disturbing experience as belonging to herself and not to return the projection in the early stages. The patient not only wanted but needed to *try on* the identity of being the healthy one, while seeing someone else experience despair and bitterness on her behalf. She felt it ought to be *somebody else's turn*. The sense of urgent and rightful need is very different from a wish – even a passionate wish – that things be otherwise, and the therapist's words, countertransference responses and dramatizations can reflect that.

The game began sadistically, but as the weeks progressed it became more symbolically dramatized, and eventually – at moments – humorous. Returning the projection prematurely would only have increased the child's already unendurable frustration and despair and prevented the slow exploration of painful truths. Jill knew perfectly well how disabled she was and how deep was her despair. But somewhere she had a preconception of herself as a healthy able being, and here she found an opportunity for that to be realized, if only in phantasy. I am stressing here that the usefulness of such containment by the therapist need not only be seen as a step along the way to subsequent re-introjection of the sense of disablement, but rather also as a necessary step in the growth of hope and agency (and the desire for a decent, partially able life) in the self that has been left behind while carrying out the needed projection. Kundera (1982) described the way in which justice and even revenge phantasies could lead to the 'rectification' of a lifelong feeling of bitterness. Careful containment of projective identification seemed to enable Jill to recover from her despair and to begin to see herself as more able. Careful monitoring should warn us of the danger of going on too long and too passively with such receptivity, and of therefore denying reality, or, worse, feeding narcissism or sado-masochism.

Descriptive lending of meaning continued: an example of alpha function providing something like self-resonance

A little boy, David, had been born prematurely, and had breathing crises and hospitalizations throughout the first year of his life. He had also been emotionally abused and was severely delayed in his development. At first he did not know how to play or talk, but eventually he began to scold and shout at a teddy bear. Then he added a new game: he started asking the therapist to join him in dramatizing someone coughing and choking. He and the therapist coughed, retched and choked together, with David insisting on exact renderings of each detail. When his therapist, remembering the early history, at one point said, 'Poor baby!' David rejected this with desperate impatience. The therapist seemed to have to *be* David before David was ready for him to feel *with* him, and certainly before he was ready for him to feel *for* him. Perhaps companionship in identification of the experience has to precede empathy and empathy has to precede sympathy. Sympathy, after all, comes from an other. Perhaps David first needed to find and identify his traumatic experience, and to make the unthinkable thinkable. The exactness of the replay was clearly important to him. It is worth noting that this is not an example of projective identification: both the child and the therapist had to enact the part. It was a duet, not a solo, and the duet seemed to provide the necessary alpha function and resonance. When a child sees that someone other than himself *gets it*, as it were, I think we do witness the 'dyadically expanded states of consciousness' described by Tronick *et al.* (1998). I have seen traumatized patients be retraumatized and shocked by interpretations trying to link a current small phobia, say, to larger, more horrific events in the past: instead, they needed the therapist to treat recovery from trauma exactly like the mourning process as described by Freud (1917) – involving only a piecemeal step at a time. In 2004, the art critic Robert Hughes said,

> What we need more of is slow art: art that holds time as a vase holds water . . . A string of brush marks on a lace collar in a Velazquez can be as radical as the shark that an Australian caught . . . some years ago and is now murkily disintegrating in its tank on the other side of the Thames. More radical, actually.

Patients deep in the paranoid-schizoid position may need much help in getting alpha function around various minuscule elements within each side of the split, either the good or the bad, long before they are ready to integrate the two. The tiniest of brush strokes from us may suffice.

David's therapist lent meaning by taking part in a duet of actual coughing, but there are many verbal equivalents. My 'You are very upset' to Robbie offered some kind of sympathy, but the 'It is upsetting when . . .' had more to do with empathic identification. But, I suspect, David was at a level even more primary than the need for empathy: he needed to explore what *it felt like* nearly to choke to death; to get a handle on it, as it were. With an older patient, something like a 'How horrible!' might offer some needed alpha function, assuming that the therapist was truly able to imagine himself into the situation.

One obvious caveat: it is clear that the therapist needs to sense when the patient is able to take in higher levels of interpretation – that is, when he is sufficiently emotionally calm or intellectually able really to want to understand 'why' and 'who' questions. (We see such curiosity increasing in leaps and bounds in Little Hans and it is helpful to consider Pine's injunction about 'striking when the iron is cold' with borderline patients (Freud, 1909; Pine, 1985, p. 153).) Steiner (1994) has pointed out that the same patient at a better moment may be able to own the feeling and many fragmented child patients gradually begin to alternate between fragmented and more integrated states.

Steiner (1994, p. 421) points out that, in any case, it is not a simple question of an either–or dichotomy between containing the projection versus returning it. Clearly, tone of voice and grammar can convey different levels of receptivity on a continuum of levels of receptivity to projective identification. (And, of course, the tone of voice accompanies the grammar – this is not a mere question of words.) A 'You want me to feel . . .' is very different from a 'You feel I should feel . . .'; both are different from 'I think I should feel . . .'; and all three are different from Searles' open confession of his jealousy about his borderline and schizophrenic patients' relationships with idealized figures, parts of themselves, or even their hallucinations (Searles, 1961, p. 438). Such calibration of degrees of receptivity may be closely correlated with the degree to which the patient has experienced himself as previously projected into and the consequent need to make use of projective identification, not as a defence, but as a necessary communication (Bion, 1962b). Moving to the other end of this particular spectrum, we must ascertain how long we should go on playing the part of the victim that the abused child once was (and for a while needs us to be), and when we should start showing the resistance he was unable to muster.

Intensified and vitalizing levels of work: reclamation and getting the right band of intensity with patients with deficits in ego, self and internal object

At stake here is not simply a weak ego, or even major defects in the sense of self: it is a matter of defects both in self and internal object, where *both* are experienced as dead and empty, useless or capable of deviant excitements. There is often a chronic apathy about relating, which goes beyond despair. Nothing is expected. If it has any connection with Bowlby's (1988) observations on the descent from protest to despair and then detachment, I am here thinking of situations that start *so early* that detachment has led to unattachment. In more severe cases, the child, for reasons of autism or severe neglect, may never have become attached (see Perry, 2002).

An example of reclamation

I now want to return to the autistic patient, Robbie, at an earlier phase of his treatment. He differed considerably from other children with autism I had seen – those whom Tustin (1992, pp. 23–30) describes as of the 'shell-type' and Wing and Attwood (1987) term 'aloof'. Robbie seemed more undrawn than withdrawn, more lost than hiding. I have previously described (Alvarez, 1992) how I gradually came to the conclusion that his passivity was not the result of a defensive retreat: he had given up rather than turned away. Nor was it the result of a massive projection of intensified parts of his ego into the object: his internal object seemed as emptied out as he was. He eventually termed it 'a net with a hole in it' – not a very human, containing, nor, for that matter, attractive or interesting object. Receptive containment of a too passive nature on my part seemed not to be helping him, and in any case I believe his capacity for projection was very weak. I despaired for years about how I was to become dense enough, substantial enough, condensed enough, to attract his attention and concentrate his extremely flaccid mind.

At one point, when Robbie was 13, I had to stop his twice-weekly therapy for some months due to the birth of my baby. During the same period, his mother also had a new baby, and when Robbie returned to what was only a series of monthly reviews, he seemed to have given up completely. He seemed to have died psychologically. In the last session before the summer break, I felt in my counter-transference a desperate sense of urgency: I was talking about the coming break, the need to say good-bye, and the possibility of his considering us remembering each other. Nothing reached him and I felt more and more worried that I had lost him for good. I then found myself moving my head into his line of vision and calling his name. He suddenly looked at me in surprise, like someone surfacing from the deep, and said, 'Hello-o-o . . .' wonderingly and sweetly, like someone greeting a long-lost friend. (Note that, unlike a defended patient, he showed no resistance to his emergence, only surprise.) The next day, he had something like a depressive breakdown, or rather a breakout from his autism. He sobbed for several days to his parents about a traumatic separation he had had from them at the age of two, when his mother had been rushed to hospital. A few months later, after an increase to five-times-weekly sessions, he told me with great excitement, but quite coherently, that he had been down a deep well and someone had thrown down a long, long, long stocking and pulled out him and all his loved ones. One by one, they had all gone 'flying over to the other side of the street'. He normally spoke in tiny wisps of phrases – listless utterances that he seemed to feel had no importance, and that were all too easy to ignore or forget. But here Robbie came verbally, musically and dramatically to life as his voice rose and fell with the story of the characters' rescue and flight. Judith Edwards has pointed out that, for Robbie, not only his self but his internal objects were coming to life at this moment (personal communication, 2010).

The implication seemed to be of some sort of lifeline, and the *length* of the stocking corresponded exactly to my feeling that my emotional reach had had to be long because Robbie was a long way off and he had been there a long time (he was now 13). I had spoken more loudly, with more emotional urgency, and had unconsciously placed my face so that it caught his gaze. All in all, I was demanding his attention in what seemed to me at the time an unusually active manner; and, to my surprise, I got it. Later, of course, I had also increased his sessions from once-monthly to five times a week. I believe that Robbie needed to be recalled both to himself and to the human family and that the process did seem to involve a kind of awakening from autism or lifelong dissociation – or both. (It is possible that an autistic constitutional weakness was accompanied by a dissociation triggered by his sudden separation from his parents under frightening conditions. Reid (1999a) has described the effects of trauma on a small sub-group of children with autism.) I originally thought of Robbie's psychic near-death as a kind of withdrawal, but I came to think it was closer to a despairing giving up than a defensive cutting-off. In any case, the chronicity of any condition needs to be carefully distinguished from the original defensive use of it, or, for that matter, from the deficit that may have started it off. And analytic technique can take account of this.

Susan Reid (personal communication, 1989) has pointed out that one would not want to advocate such a technique with the shell-type autistic child, with whom we must not be intrusive. For that matter, it would have been counter-productive with Robbie at later stages when he exploited his passivity often simply because it was comfortable to leave the work of feeling and thinking to everyone else. We talked a lot about the difference between his misuse of help and his genuine need for help in the early days. This intensified vitalizing technique would of course not be necessary with a patient who had sufficient ego, sense of self and interest in life to struggle with his habit of withdrawal. It is interesting that my emergency rescue operation did not need to be repeated after that rather dramatic day, his subsequent breakdown, and the change to intensive treatment. What I learned from it, however, was that I had to do much work on myself to provide a tauter, tighter, less slack ongoing attention. Work in the casualty department of my mind had to be replaced by work in its intensive-care ward. An almost hypervigilant attention is required with some autistic patients if contact is to be maintained – until, that is, they discover their own motivation for relationship. In fact, infant observation and research suggest that certain babies do require a firmer pull on the lifeline of contact than others (Brazelton and Nugent, 1995, pp. 65–66, 73). Certainly, it was also important to take note of, and interpret, the consequences when I slackened. Later, when Robbie had more language, he described an image of two boats slowly drifting further and further apart. One day he also told me that, long ago, his uncle had helped him out of a deep freeze, where he had been stuck and 'left to be dead for ever and ever with no eyes, no ears, no mouth, and no penis'. He demonstrated what it had been like to struggle out of the ice, with his legs moving terribly slowly at first. It seemed to me a vivid illustration of the difficulties of overcoming chronicity, and is a reminder of the *practice* it takes, once the patient is more alive, to stay alive. Robbie became much better at catching himself drifting off or, for that matter, sinking.

Greenspan (1997) has discussed technique in managing extremely disordered (very high or low) levels of arousal in certain patients, many of whom, but not all, are autistic. Greenspan's ideas on how to down-regulate over-aroused patients would probably accord with the Bick model of containment (different from Bion's – to do with fostering integration, in the sense of a coherent sense of self and the object world, and even offering soothing to frantically hyperactive agitated children; see Miller (1984)). But Greenspan (1997, p. 282) also suggests that for under-aroused patients, clinicians can create 'a more compelling personal environment', by up-regulating: that is, by, among other things, energizing their voices to reach them. Greenspan's method, which seems to follow from a one-person psychology, may therefore seem a bit thin to those versed in object-relations thinking, and in the whole rich complexity of the inner world with its ebb and flow of projective and introjective processes, but I suggest that this area of unawakened or un-aroused states of mind, were it to take account of the existence of internal objects which may also be dead, unvalued and uninteresting, might require more study of the methods of introducing meaning and significance to – and making emotional contact with – patients in such depleted states.

There is a third type of intensified use of the countertransference, which is different from the desperate urgency I felt with Robbie when I felt he had nearly died psychologically. It sometimes arises where there is a feeling of empty bore-dom and meaninglessness in the countertransference. Bergstein (2009) has pointed out that it is important for the analyst to experience the boredom and emptiness with his patient, and not to rush into premature filling up of the hole. However, he also distinguishes between different kinds of emptiness, and here I am stressing situations where the patient's emptiness at such moments is neither out of despair nor defensive in the sense of projecting the alive parts of the self into the object, but that it has become an addictive solution. Here one may have to help the patient to get a move on, as it were. Or, in another situation of a fourth type, there may be a feeling of vast impatience, if not outrage, with the perversely repetitive nature of sado-masochistic activity. I shall discuss the use of such types of countertrans-ference in Chapter 7, on working with psychopathic children, and the more inten-sified use in Chapters 11, on play, and 12, on finding the wavelength.

Conclusion

Psychoanalysis has spent decades studying processes of projection. Attention is also beginning to be paid to patients' introjective processes (Feldman, 2004; Williams, 1997). I have tried to identify moments when it was useful for the therapist to slow down the work to a more purely descriptive level, in order to try to offer understanding, which manages to 'hold time as a vase holds water'. I have also suggested that with certain autistic, despairing/apathetic or fragmented

Table 1.1 Levels of interpretation

Interpretation/ types of meaning	Theory and technique	Cognitive capacity	Grammar of interpretation	State of mind (not diagnosis)
Explain, locate (offer alternate meanings)	Freud, Klein Wishes/defences, Returning projections	2 tracks	Why–because, Who–you	Neurotic, Normal, Mild borderline
Describe, name (lend and enlarge meanings)	Bion, Winnicott, Stern Needs, Protections, Contain projections, Facilitate introjections	1 track	Whatness, Isness	Borderline, Autistic, Psychotic, Developmental delay, Addiction, Perversion
Vitalize (insist on meaning)	Tustin, Reid, Alvarez Reclaim, Generate, Discourage addiction or perversion	0 tracks or deviant tracks	A call – Hey!	Autistic, Psychotic, Despair, Developmental delay, Addiction, Perversion

children, we may have to descend to another, even more prior, level of work which involves the containment *and intensified transformation* and vitalization of internal objects perceived as useless and unvalued (not devalued), weak or too easily excited by perversion. It is not easy to strike a balance between being too intense and therefore intrusive, and being experienced as too remote or too weak. Yet, as I said in the Introduction, long before certain patients process their hatred and find their capacity for love, they may have to develop the ability to be interested in an object with some substantiality and life. Something and someone have to matter. This is work at the very foundation of human relatedness. That is, although we must draw attention to their lack of interest, we may, as I said in the Introduction, sometimes also have to find ways of attracting their attention, and then to find out how to keep it. Once this is achieved, the work can move to higher levels, sometimes in the course of a single session. What I am certain of, however, is that our work with very disturbed or developmentally impaired children needs to be not only psychoanalytically but developmentally and psychopathologically informed. This book is an attempt to calibrate some of these thoughts into a hierarchy of priorities.

Part I

Explanatory level conditions

Chapter 2

Some emotional conditions for the development of two-tracked thinking

The sense of agency and the sense of abundance

Anne Alvarez with Piera Fiurgiuele

Introduction

I suggested in Chapter 1 that certain cognitive/emotional skills might be necessary to the capacity to understand an explanatory interpretation such as 'You are angry with me today because of the pending break from treatment and the way it invokes your very strong feelings about separation' or 'Your sudden feeling of outrage about the way that teacher treated a boy at school may be connected with some feelings of irritation and injustice concerning what I just said about the way you tend to . . .' I suggested that Bruner's (1968) study of the development of a capacity for two-tracked thinking may be a useful way of conceptualizing one set of elements in these skills. However, Bruner entirely omits the possibility of emotional components in the development from one-tracked to two-tracked thinking.

In this chapter I would like to extend and augment Bruner's findings with some evidence from naturalistic infant observation. I shall therefore look at the emotional and object-relations elements in what has been termed the infant's sense of agency and see how these might relate to the capacity to 'think in parentheses' identified by Bruner. The normal infant is, in many ways, helpless and dependent; but he is also competent, thoughtful, alert and, when conditions allow, full of passionate curiosity about his world.

Developmental researchers have spent decades attempting to analyse the separate elements in the conditions essential for healthy cognitive/emotional development. The sense of efficacy – or agency – is one such element identified by Broucek (1979). He has suggested that this sense of efficacy – and the pleasure associated with it – are the foundations of self-feeling. Broucek (1991) cites Jonas (1974), who thinks that the source of the concept of causality is in the experience of the body exerting itself in action. Broucek (1991, p. 28) also describes Tompkins' (1981) observation that infants, soon after birth, replace reflex sucking with voluntary sucking and reflex visual tracking with voluntary visual tracking. Broucek points out that Tompkins insists that from the first moments of life, infants are engaged in making good scenes better by *doing it themselves*. Broucek thinks this is one of the first manifestations of intent and of the will – a fascinating theory on the origins of basic self-feeling. Yet Broucek is clear that the infant is usually acting on some*one* and we might need to add, therefore, the equal importance of object-feeling: that is, feelings about the nature of the human beings or – in the language of attachment researchers – internalized representational figures upon which the baby sees himself acting. Clearly, causal experiences are not purely physical; they are also mental. The baby has plenty of experiences of his mind exerting itself in action and producing effects on another mind. There may be more, by the way, to the sense of agency than pure power or mastery, even though this latter element may not be negligible. I do not think this can any more be understood simply in terms of 'infantile omnipotence' (Klein, 1946, p. 7) or of Winnicott's (1945) 'illusion': babies may be physically helpless, but they are anything but helpless emotionally and socially – that is, if the caregivers allow them to be (Reddy, 2008).

In his 1979 paper, Broucek reviewed a number of research studies on 'contingency'. He described the baby's joyful delight in discovering that he himself can be a causal agent of events. The infant shows much pleasure – smiling, excitement and cooing – at the discovery that there is a contingent relationship between his own initially spontaneous behaviour and an event in the external world and 'the subsequent ability to produce *at will* the external event through repetition of the antecedent act. The conclusion seems inescapable that the infant's pleasure in this situation is pleasure in being the cause' (Broucek, 1979, p. 312). Broucek stresses the importance of the will – a relatively unexplored subject in psychology and psychoanalysis – and describes what happens when babies are denied adequate opportunities for the experience of efficacy: if the baby is very young, the capacity for initiative may atrophy.

Papousek and Papousek (1975), in a laboratory experiment, first gave babies the opportunity to cause an event to take place. The babies' pleasure was, apparently, insatiable. (The experiment showed that there was nothing special about the event itself that was rewarding – it was the ability to make it happen that mattered to the babies.) The experimenters then deprived the babies of this satisfaction, and found that the first reactions were intensified respiration, pulse rate and perspiration. However, an even more worrying situation arose: some of the babies began to 'play possum'; they lay motionless with non-converging, staring eyes and sleep-like respiration. Papousek and Papousek (p. 313) suggested that this passive state of a sort of 'total inner separation from the environment' was more likely to appear in babies under two months of age; infants older than three months placed in similarly frustrating situations seemed more able actively to avoid everything connected with the unsolvable problem. Active avoidance and passive unresponsiveness were thus seen as very different ways of reacting to a feeling of inefficacy; the result in both cases was a lowering of attention and orientation. (There may be some interesting issues here for diagnostic and clinical consideration. Clinicians have sometimes considered it to be an achievement and a development when the withdrawal of an autistic child changes from being more automatic and helpless to more actively intentional – when, for example, dull eyes are replaced by a deliberately averted gaze (Alvarez, 1992, p. 98; Susan Reid, personal communication, 1989).)

Psychoanalytic writers have discussed issues similar to, but slightly different from, the sense of agency or efficacy. Freud (1920) wrote of mastery, Kohut (1985) of the need for self-objects. Melanie Klein (1961, p. 465) made it clear that she distinguished between omnipotent defences and genuine potency. Alvarez (1992) has stressed the danger for the therapist of confusing the child's triumph in his sense of omnipotence with his pleasure and shared pride in the sense of potency – and the importance of the latter in the recovery from certain types of severe depression in childhood.

Broucek (1991) makes it clear that the efficacy of the infant's efforts vis-à-vis the world depends on sensitive and 'good enough' maternal responsiveness. He had previously posited, 'I cause and I intend, therefore I am' (Broucek, 1979, p. 313), but he also points out that young babies are mostly interacting with human caregivers, not with the flashing lights of laboratory experiments. One might therefore need to expand his statement to read: 'I cause things to happen in her, therefore I begin to feel that I am, and I also begin to feel that she is.' More recent work by researchers such as Reddy (2008) and Trevarthen (2001) demonstrates the pleasure even very young infants of seven or eight months take in showing off when it elicits delighted responses from caregivers (Reddy, 2008, pp. 136–144, 148–149). Reddy describes the dramatic or silly things babies will do to gain and manipulate attention in order to 'heighten their visibility' to others who are attending to them (p. 136). She also points out that two things are important about these findings: first, babies have self-consciousness far earlier than is posited by cognitive psychologists, who think it has to wait for a fully developed concept of self at 18 months (p. 128); second, the phenomenon should not be defined as self-consciousness – it is always in the context of another person, and should therefore be termed 'self-other consciousness' (p. 149).

This chapter attempts to identify two possible components in this causal relationship. The first is the willingness of the caregiver to respond with thoughtful interest to the baby's initiatives and the baby's related sense of being a causal agent in evoking such responsiveness. This component concerns moments when the baby is in the foreground of the caregiver's interest, as implied in Broucek's argument. The first component (1) thus concerns a two-object relationship where the baby may feel a sense of agency toward one object. The second component, or rather set of components (2), concerns a tripartite relationship, where the caregiver or baby is an agent in relation to two objects and engages in something Bruner (1968) has called 'two-tracked thinking'. Two slightly different behaviours of caregivers in the first and third observations below may help to facilitate the baby's development of this capacity. The first behaviour (a) concerns the caregiver's capacity to keep the baby in the background of her mind at moments when some other object is in the foreground. It is possible that the baby's confidence in expecting this facilitates his consequent identification with an object capable of such two-tracked thinking. The second behaviour (b) concerns the willingness of the caregiver to step aside *and wait* (interestedly) while the baby's attention is elsewhere. Thus, to repeat, in the first situation (as in Broucek's examples), the baby may experience agency in relation to one object; in 2a, he may experience himself as held in the back of someone's mind and so come to identify with that two-tracked capacity; in 2b, he may be able to experience agency in relation to two objects (one in the foreground, the other 'on hold' in the background).

In the three babies described below, both the first and second type of agency were seen to contain both emotional and cognitive features: first, the object acted upon was responsive, reactive *and* interested mentally; second, emotional richness, a sense of abundance, in both the caregivers and the baby, was accompanied by an easy access to a wealth of ideas. A sense of the world's plenitude and replenishment seems to have connected with the feeling of being full of ideas – not ideas which crowd demandingly and confusedly for equal attention, but ideas which wait their turn in the queue and do not disappear. (See Chapter 3 for an example of a child whose thoughts would not wait their turn in the queue in his mind.) This may be related to what Bruner (1968) calls the capacity to 'think in parentheses' – to manage two or more trains of thought at the same time. The three babies will serve to illustrate these phenomena. Alice, the first, and Angela, the third, were rich in both senses of agency; Paul, the second, was impoverished in both.

The development of two-tracked thinking and observation of Alice

Beverley Mack, an observer in an infant observation seminar at the Tavistock, was impressed by an incident where Alice, a girl aged one year and one week, had displayed a capacity for an interesting piece of two-tracked thinking. The observation took place on a day when the family's sitting room was full of people. Her very fond paternal grandparents were visiting, her father had returned from work, and her mother and four-year-old brother George were also present. At one point, in the middle of a peek-a-boo game, Alice fell over and hurt herself. Her mother comforted her, made her a drink and then carried her back into the sitting room:

> Mother sat next to father and Alice sat enveloped by the contours of her mother's body, drinking her squash. She still had tears in her eyes and on her cheeks but was regaining her spirits. She sucked quietly at her drink and watched George's activities. After a few minutes, Alice placed her cup on the ledge of George's large toy car (almost the size of a large table), rested for a few minutes and – without looking – reached for the cup (accurately), grabbed it and began drinking again.

The observer was struck by Alice's capacity to remember, without looking, exactly where she had left the cup, while she seemed to be attending to something else.

Another recent observation may serve to demonstrate the mindful attention both father and mother gave to Alice. It also illustrates some interesting two-tracked thinking on the part of her mother, who showed a capacity to keep her in mind, just as Alice had kept the cup, while also attending to something else.

> Mother had placed a toy truck full of milk churns in front of Alice. The milk truck obscured my view but I think she removed a milk churn and put it in a little car. Father and George then joined us. Mother noticed that Alice had a runny nose and wiped it. Alice moved her face sideways, as though trying to avoid being wiped. Mother then proudly said to father that Alice can blow her nose and commented on how clever she is to be able to distinguish between her nose and mouth. Mother asked her to blow her nose, holding the tissue to her face. Alice smiled, obliged, and toddled off looking pleased with herself. Father said, 'She knows when she's being clever!' Alice continued to play, pushing her little car along the ground and following it, on her knees. She then removed another milk churn from the truck but dropped it, as George caught her attention. Alice began to look around on the floor, seemingly in search of her milk churn. Mother, who had been in conversation with father, suddenly said to Alice, 'Are you looking for your milk churn?' at which Alice got up and walked over to mother.

Note how both mother and father underline Alice's new achievement; father then goes even further to show that he is interested not only in her clever new learning but in her state of mind *concerning* her cleverness. He knows she is being clever, but he also knows that she knows she is being clever (mental agency in the first sense). These are interested, responsive parents, but what particularly struck the observer as an additional element was mother's capacity to know that Alice was looking for her milk churn, even though mother's attention was on her husband at that point. She was able to keep her mind on both her husband *and* her daughter. It seemed likely that Alice's impressive capacity to learn – and, in particular, her capacity to manage two trains of thought at once – owed a lot to her parents' capacity to lend her mindful attention when she was fully in the foreground of their minds but also to their capacity, when other objects demanded their attention, to keep her in the 'back' of their minds (mental agency in the second sense).

As I said, Bruner (1968) has described a cognitive development that he has called the capacity to 'think in parentheses', or to hold something in reserve. It is fascinating to watch this capacity develop in previously mindless psychotic and autistic children, and also in chronically depressed, deprived children, as they begin to be able both to think and to believe in thinking. This achievement, however, is not purely cognitive and may bear some relation to the development in the infant of a phantasy or expectation of an available, enduring, even abundant world. That is, the infant's sense that 'I can do or have something' may be related to the sense that 'I am in the company of a doable to or haveable object'; and even, perhaps, an object which will *wait* for me to have it fully or explore it fully and is furthermore content to wait – in parentheses, as it were – while I interest myself in something else.

Bruner's strictly cognitive but fascinating study observed babies developing from a newborn state of one-tracked attention – where they can either only suck or only look – to a coordinated capacity for two-trackedness at four months, where they can do both more or less simultaneously. (Early on, at the first stage, they shut their eyes while sucking; at the second stage, they begin to be able to alternate sucking with looking; at the third stage, they 'soft-pedal' the sucking by engaging in non-nutritive sucking while looking at something. (One imagines that this something is likely to be the mother's face.)) Bruner (1968, pp. 18–24, 52) calls the third stage 'place-holding', and describes an observation on the later move to threeness and to even greater conceptual multiplicity: the experimenter hands the infant one toy and then immediately hands him a second. At about seven months, the baby drops the first toy, picks up the second with the same hand, moves it to his mouth, and forgets the first. By about 12 months, the child is able to put the second toy in his free hand, but if he is offered a third, he drops one of the first two. He can therefore manage two but not three. At about a year and a half, when offered the third toy, he no longer drops one but puts one in the crook of his arm, so he has a free hand to take the third. He will then take more in the same manner. Bruner points out that the child has gone from a limit of one – defined by the mouth – to a limit of two – defined by the hands – to a limit of many – defined by a reserve.

Bruner does not discuss the conditions under which this sense of a reserve may be facilitated or hindered, but psychoanalysts have suggested that the move from two-person to three-person relationships may also play a part in the development of this type of deeper numeracy (Britton, 1989; Klein, 1923). Trevarthen and Hubley's (1978) brilliant work on the developmental steps involved in the move from primary to secondary intersubjectivity – where the baby becomes able to take turns with his caregiver in playing with a toy – is relevant, too. Here, mother and baby can be interested in a third object, a toy or a person *together*.

Clearly, as infant observation and infant research has shown, the relationships between the baby's mother and father, and the degree of support for mother from grandparents and internal figures, are vital. An emotionally impoverished child, however, may be impoverished on the microcosmic as well as the macrocosmic level, so we may also need to study very early and minute temporal patterns of interaction between mother and baby. How steady, for example, is the mother's gaze-holding while her young baby takes fleeting glances at her and away (Fogel, 1977)? That is, how is the sense of a durable object built up? How willing is the caregiver to follow the trajectory of the baby's gaze and interest herself in his interests? For how many seconds can she sustain her interest in him *and* his interests? Research has suggested the conditions under which a baby's attention span to a single object may be prolonged (Brazelton *et al.*, 1974; Stern, 1977). One could speculate that his attention to two objects at once (i.e. to his mother's background interest and the new object's foreground magnetism) may be facilitated by his mother's ability to wait for her baby's return of his attention to her – that is, by her acceptance of his two-trackedness. He learns to accept her interest in other objects – father, siblings, household chores, the telephone – while she learns to accept and respect his curiosity in things and people other than herself.

Bruner himself (1986), some years after this study, said that David Krech used to urge that people 'perfink' – perceive, feel and think at once. Urwin (1987) has criticized cognitive researchers for seeing emotion as slowing down or speeding up cognition, whereas she, like the psychoanalyst Bion (1962b), suggests that emotion enters into the structure of cognition itself. Can the sense of being able to hold something in reserve imply a mental phantasy of an object that will stay put there in the crook of the arm of your mind, as it were? Will that toy, person or thought wait for you to get back to it? Or will it disappear? This capacity for holding firmly on to several strands of thoughts at one time must also depend, to some extent, on a prior phase – the one-tracked one, where each thought or experience is given time to be explored fully by both baby and caregiver. (See the chapters in Part II, which illustrate the clinical efforts to develop this capacity in children with delayed cognitive or emotional development.) The will is, to a large extent, exercised on a willable – and (to be hoped, eventually) willing – object. (It would be wrong, of course, to suggest that the role of the actual caregivers is the only factor in this development. It is well established that some babies are born with a far greater capacity to shape their universe, and to hold their caregiver's attention, than others. However, it did seem that the mothers of the two babies described below had very different notions of a reserve. Selection of material has meant some drastic over-simplification.)

Both babies described below, firstborns, were observed by female observers. They were observed for one hour a week at home with the major caregiver for a period of two years. (See Miller *et al.* (1989) for a description of this type of naturalistic observation.)

Observation of Paul

The parents of Paul were professional people in their mid-thirties. Father and both sets of grandparents gave mother considerable support with the baby. During the first observation at home, Mrs J spoke at length to the observer about her anxiety and uncertainty about her capacity to be a good mother. She seemed sensitive and very concerned for her baby's wellbeing. At the two-week observation, she voiced a worry common to many new mothers as to whether she had enough milk. She added, without apparent awkwardness, that her sudden decision to supplement the breastfeeds with bottles had probably been the result of her panic. This forgiving attitude to her own anxieties soon faded, unfortunately, and she began to be critical of everyone, including the baby, who dared to raise feelings of anxiety or failure in her. She could still be tender and affectionate when Paul's state of wellbeing gratified and reassured her, but at other times she began to regard him with distaste. Later, she often warned him not to 'pull a face' when he was concentrating hard on sucking or defecating. When his lip drooped or his head lolled, she told him he was 'ugly'. His perfectly ordinary and natural degree of infantile helplessness seemed to remind her of something or someone, but we never established what or who.

Paul began to refuse to have the breast before the bottle and was weaned fully to the bottle at two and a half months. 'He turned his head away and there was nothing I could do about it,' his mother told the observer disappointedly. Then she added, 'It doesn't matter. It is even easier now. I am more free, because anyone can give the bottle to him.' But there were signs that it *did* matter to this mother. It affected her view of herself and made her even more critical. Paul, however, seemed determined to work hard to hold his mother's attention and to please her. He had a strong capacity to seek his mother's eyes, and to engage with her in a smiling way. She did, at times, respond to his loving communications deeply, but always fleetingly: she would suddenly cut off, look a bit lost, saying, 'What shall we do?' or 'What do you want?' as though the world which for a second had seemed full of possibility for both of them had suddenly emptied. Her own belief in an object, which could be of lasting interest, seemed to be tragically impaired. In later months her sudden turning away became more active and decisive: she would simply go and make a phone call. She almost always held the baby facing away from her when she gave him his bottle, in spite of her own mother's pleas and protests about this.

When Paul was around three months, Mrs J seemed to harden up even more: she developed a sarcastic and at times cruel attitude to his by now slightly stronger vocal protests and greater bodily motility. The observer began to describe Paul as frequently being in a state of floppiness, with his eyes glazing over. He would begin to protest at being lain on his back in his pram for the umpteenth time, but he would quieten when he heard the icy threat in his mother's voice as she stared down at him and half held him down. What had started as a frightened inhibition on his part changed to a more listless apathy, as though he were giving up. In the seminar where the observations were discussed, we began to fear that Paul was in danger of a kind of psychic death.

By four months, Paul had taken to biting his hands ferociously and trying to stuff toys all the way down his throat. It was very painful for the observer and the seminar group to witness his mother's depression, cynicism and difficulties in seeing Paul's needs. Paul desperately needed to be entertained. He wanted attention, some conversation, some play. But Mrs J often felt empty and at a loss. She seemed not to be able to believe that she herself could be the main object of interest – and one of lasting interest – for the baby. She ended up actively preventing Paul from remaining in contact with her. She held him with his back to her and seemed unaware of his struggle to regain her face, her eyes and her attention. The observer's comments, frequently aimed at helping to re-establish communication, went unheeded. The mother seemed to feel disappointed and irritated, and often mocked the baby's achievements (his 'squeaks'). However, in one session, perhaps helped by the fact that the baby's call conveyed more life and interest to her – and perhaps because she had been able to identify a little with the observer's 'conversation' with the baby – Mrs J was able to be kinder to Paul: she wanted to seat him more comfortably. She looked after him for a while and mentioned his nightmares. Later in the same observation, mother was speaking to the observer about the fact that chatting with Paul was amusing and he seemed to reply nowadays; there were real dialogues. However, when he called a little because he was slipping sideways on the sofa, she responded harshly with considerable irritation, and eventually sat him on her lap facing away from her, holding him with her hands on his tummy to stop him moving. The baby became quite immobile, and his eyes were dull and blank.

This session was almost unbearable to hear. Paul's mother wants a lively, intelligent baby, but she cannot resist discouraging his initiatives. She rejects his interest in her, and almost forces him into physical immobility and mental emptiness. The result seems to be a terrible loss of initiative and efficacy, a kind of sapping of his will. During the whole observation, a depressed and persecutory atmosphere hung in the air, making it very difficult for the mother to do the right things and for the observer to be of help. The observer felt that anything – silence, words, doing, not doing – could be felt as persecutory. The seminar group encouraged the observer to engage in some degree of 'participant' observation (more actively therapeutic) but the mother rejected this. We also discussed the question of child protection issues with legal experts, and it was clear that what we were seeing was too subtle to be considered child abuse by anyone but a careful observer. It was very painful for the observer to see Paul's dazed expression, and this mother making efforts to find a way into her baby, failing, and then seeming to harden herself. This led to even more disdainful and even cruel behaviours with the baby, in which Mrs J often sought the observer's collusion. The observer sometimes felt a mute request in the sad expression of the baby to which – given her role as observer and in light of mother's competitiveness and touchiness – she could respond in only minimal ways. She tried, in a variety of tactful ways, to help this depressed but also controlling mother to get together with her baby, including, when even mother eventually acknowledged concern about Paul's mental development, suggestions about where she could get information and help. But these were rejected. We were aware that Paul was losing his will to make an impact on his world, but we began to fear that he would lose his mind, too.

Yet all was not lost. Mrs J sometimes seemed able to find relief in the fact that someone else, in her presence, was looking after the baby and the relationship with Paul was therefore mediated at some distance. The baby seemed a little happier, too. In the same observation, for example, we see things going better with the arrival of the father:

> At first the father speaks with the mother, and the baby, left to himself, leans forward with a sad dazed look and with saliva dripping down. Then the father picks him up, walks with him and talks to him. He sings him nursery rhymes, which he usually makes up especially for him. Paul seems to start to feel that

he exists again; he comes back to life, says 'ghee'. Little by little, he begins to explore his surroundings with his eyes again. The mother is now more relaxed. She smiles at him from the sofa and says 'hello' in a loving tone. After an initial moment, when he refuses to look at her, encouraged by his father, Paul turns and smiles back. The mother is content and greets him again. The father is relieved and exclaims, 'Oh, there, a smile at last!'

Similar recoveries were observed when the grandmother was present. Unfortunately, even though there were two parents present for Paul, there was rarely little sense that both were fully present for him together. At least during such episodes with his father or a grandparent he had, finally, the care of one, with his mother as a not unfriendly witness. Such threeness as existed was a pale shadow of what we shall see in the next observation. Mother's personality difficulties seemed to have been profound and the help of relatives did little to reduce her cynicism and boredom. She soon began to look back with regret on her former life. She complained it was 'no fun' being a mother and said she could do it only 'in small doses'. Paul was often placed on the floor to play alone, and here he engaged in activities of an ominously repetitive quality: he would sit and simply shake a toy monotonously. He also had many moments of immobility and passivity.

At seven months, mother's anxious need to control and limit Paul's initiatives extended to his attempts to handle his feeding cup, and also to his tentative attempts at physical adventure and exploration. She complained that he was at the bottom of the class developmentally and tried to 'teach' him to roll over. (Most babies teach themselves to roll over because the world beckons from the other side. Paul had relatively little to strive for and, anyway, little belief in his own capacity to attain it.) His mother interpreted his reaching for a bright red cube in a tower she set up for him only as a wish to knock it over. She was often frustrated by his apathy, but could not help engendering it. Any sense of himself as an active agent in his world seemed terribly impaired. In many ways, he seemed to have given up on such ideas. He was becoming a little Oblomov.

Yet, at around nine months, after a family holiday and some improvement in Paul's motor skills and ability to understand (or, rather, in his mother's belief that he understood), Mrs J did seem somewhat more interested in him – as a sort of little pupil. Her husband was helpful and easier with Paul than was she, but he was very busy himself, and they tended to take turns in his care, rather than being together with him. Also, father, and the grandparents, treated his fragile but demanding wife with great caution and never crossed her. In fact, they all seemed afraid of her. On one occasion, when Paul was 16 months, he indicated that he wished to get close to some flowers in the sitting room. Mother took him to them in her arms, insisting, 'Don't touch, just look!' and then immediately tried to get him to name the colour of the bright yellow mimosa flower. As usual, she was bent on pulling the response she wanted from him, rather than respecting his spontaneous but, as usual, only very gently demanding request. When he did manage, at the next vase, to reach out and touch a peach blossom and inadvertently to knock one off, she said, 'Don't knock all the flowers off – the bare twigs will be so ugly!' There is, possibly, a glimpse here of what may have lain behind her cruelty and hard impatience. The world was un-replenishable. There was no reserve: it really seemed as though she felt there could never again be more peach blossoms in the universe. At this stage, she could not let herself be a patient witness to Paul's explorations: she either interfered impatiently or abandoned him to get on with it himself.

Soon after her return to work, however, Paul's mother seemed to recover somewhat from her depression: she became more animated and able to enjoy some of Paul's independent explorations around the house. For example, she permitted him to take books off the shelf and look at them. She liked 'teaching' him and he mostly learned to name things, always looking up immediately to her for praise. She worked hard to make him numerate. There may be a painful lesson here in the difference between numeracy and the sense of a deeper multiplicity and of a something available in reserve, of a replenishable abundant universe.

Yet it was clear that Paul had managed to emerge from his previous listlessness and had not become severely withdrawn. He had found a way through to his mother and she to him – up to a point. It was hard to find evidence that he ever learned much for its own sake or for his own. By now, he was almost always on the move, and his anxieties, at times, were overwhelming. He was regularly distraught when his mother would tiptoe out to work. He would grab desperately for his cup at mealtimes, as though he could not believe it was really coming toward him and would be his for a while. We never heard of the kind of exploratory play that occurred during the observation of the next baby. And there was certainly little time for reflection.

When sent to a day nursery, at ten and a half months, Paul was anguished and often physically ill. But he found a way through, however narrow and single-tracked its quality: he learned to name objects and to count, and he worked hard to please. Although he clearly benefited considerably from the care of his loving grandparents, he did not seem to feel rich and blessed in the sense of feeling he had, as did Angela (see below), many loving caretakers. Rather, like the rest of his family, all of whom seemed to idealize and fear (and possibly fear for) his mother, Paul behaved much of the time as though there was really *only one* very powerful object in his inner world, and that it was a precariously available and quite dangerous one. Safety, when it arrived, was also precarious and short-lived, and never durable enough to see him through separations, or even through a period of exploratory play. There was no sign of the relaxed, playful reflectiveness we shall see in Angela.

It is also true that on the more microcosmic level of brief, second-by-second encounters, his mother did not wait for Paul to complete an engagement with her or with a toy; nor, however, did she wait and watch with interest when his interest shifted to something or someone else. She took the latter as an opportunity to escape. Paul seemed to be developing with an impaired belief in the durability of his object's existence and in his own ability to prolong its stay or to bring it back when it was absent. In the limited and careful quality of his play, there were many signs that, in addition to the obvious effect on his confidence and emotional life, there was impairment in his cognitive capacities. His anxieties seemed to make all activities, except the most cautious ones, short-lived and lacking in potential for development. (See Murray (1991) on the effect of maternal post-natal depression on infant and child cognition.)

Observation of Angela

Angela was born to parents who told the observer that they worked in a factory. Much later, she learned that they were engineers. In the hospital, when Angela was three days old, mother told the observer that she had noticed that Angela alternated smiles with frowns: 'She goes from beautiful thoughts to horrible ones in the space of a second.' At home, father commented on the baby being nervous, and mused about the idea that their house must be very different from the hospital for her. He hoped 'she would get the hang of it'. Note that the baby is already seen as having thoughts, feelings and acute sensitivities – the very sensitivities and lability to which a very new baby is indeed prone. And the parents seem to have the sense already that *things take time*. This mother, like Paul's, also had anxieties about whether she had sufficient milk, and was for a time quite obsessional about cleanliness and feeding times; but in the second week she said that she had learned that the baby's noises and stretches at night did not indicate dissatisfaction, so she had been able to stop checking on her all the time. Also, she said that she thought the baby followed her more with her eyes now. We can note this mother's capacity to be reassured, her pride in learning something about her baby, and also the sense of respect for the baby's agency and competence, and for her own. There are already at least two figures in the picture, each with some recognizable space and competence of her own.

At 35 days, mother described how Angela did not seem able to grasp the rattle on her own but could hold it if mother helped by putting it into her hand. At one point, she said to Angela, 'You like your friend the pendulum clock, don't you,' and then turned Angela so that she could see it better. At a feed in a later observation, mother showed some irritation and jealousy of the baby's interest in, and seeming preference for, her pendulum 'friend' over finishing the first course of her meal, but she accepted defeat, did not insist the baby finish, and offered some different, possibly more enticing, food instead. A compromise offers a third option to two warring factions. A mother who waits while you express an interest in something else is remaining in reserve in a very significant way, and this is an emotional, but perhaps also a cognitive, experience. We learned that mother could also accept Angela's more active protests. At four and a half months, mother remarked to the observer that Angela had begun to notice that she could pass something from one hand to the other. In fact, Angela became a very advanced baby.

It needs to be added that the sense of resources in reserve was very much present in both sets of Angela's grandparents and in her father, all of whom were patient but not indulgent with the child. At six months, when mother was soon to start working again and maternal grandmother would become the regular childminder, mother offered maternal grandmother the opportunity to feed fruit to the baby. The grandmother replied, 'You give it to her; I'll have lots of time.' At eight months, mother tried to show Angela that her new toy train moved. Then she commented, 'You're not interested in its movement; you've found out it makes a noise. It's your toy, use it how you want.' The observer noted that Angela, who was a thriving and lively baby (little has been said about her personality in order to concentrate on the cognitive/emotional elements), had what psychologists call the 'extension concept' and was able to pull a sheet to get a remote toy which was lying on the sheet. Angela's parents were often together with her, and both of them were tremendously interested in her. For them, it seemed that the world was interesting and that *her* world was interesting. At just under ten months, father told the observer: 'When Angela holds the plastic keys in one hand, she immediately puts them in the other hand, then she shows the empty hand, and keeps the keys!' (He smiled at the last phrase.)

Summary and clinical implications

These three observations have been used to illustrate two possible elements in the sense of agency: the sense of mental agency in relation to one object; and the sense of mental agency in relation to two objects. The latter has been linked with Bruner's (1968) concept of the sense of a reserve. The material from the first baby, Alice, illustrates the capacity of the parents to provide opportunities for both foreground mindfulness (1) and background mindfulness (2a); it also illustrates the existence of related developments in the capacity for two-tracked thinking in Alice herself. Paul's experience and development seem to have been impaired in both respects. The material from Angela, the third baby, was rich in (1) (mindfulness in her objects and in herself) and in (2b) (the sense of an object which can wait for your return).

The sense of a reserve has been linked with the sense of agency, and this chapter has suggested some emotional elements, which may be significant for this apparent cognitive development. Emotional and cognitive impoverishment in one baby has been contrasted with a sense of multiplicity, plenitude and the apparent development of complex 'thinking in parentheses' in two others. Perhaps a sense of emotional agency and intelligence are linked, and perhaps both are linked with an intelligible, interested caregiver who feels that both the infant and his interests are intelligible, interesting and worth attending to, respecting and, sometimes, sitting out.

On the clinical level, I would emphasize that for patients with Paul's difficulties, the important work would involve work at the more active vitalizing level, when the patient was too lost and hopeless, and at the descriptive and amplifying level, when he was emotionally present but confused and fragmented. However, a helpful paper by Rhode (2001) on the sense of abundance and technique implies some interesting distinctions within the descriptive level. That is, what is being described or amplified need not be just what the child or his object is feeling or experiencing; it may be what a third object, a toy or mirror image is doing. Rhode describes her finding that Anthony, a boy with autism, was helped not by intimate, face-to-face contact but by the therapist's introduction of a series of third objects to which both of them could relate, at first only in a parallel fashion. Rhode felt that this series of objects demonstrated to Anthony that room would be made in the therapy for what mattered to him. This was without overwhelming him too much with her intensive attention to him personally. She points out that eventually these objects – a favourite toy, songs and the playroom mirror – became used no longer only in a parallel way but for joint attention and even turn-taking and some symbolic activity. The mirror became big enough to hold both of them, as it were.

It is interesting to speculate on the nature of and development and variety among these various triangular relationships. The ordinary child's experience of his parents as the Oedipal couple is only one permutation. The parents described above in the observation of Angela were, I am certain, at times engaged in conversations which excluded the baby, but here we see them conversing together about her and to her. At such moments, of course, this was not an Oedipal triangle, but Abello and Perez-Sanchez (1981) have suggested that the sense of the parents seen as a couple *for the infant* may be a necessary precursor (or, we might say, accompaniment) to the Oedipal couple who are engaging with each other without him. Rhode's mirror might have seemed to represent something like a father who can be interested in and care for (in both senses) both mother and baby: as she said, there was eventually room in it for both of them at the same time.

Chapter 3

Obstructions to and developments toward sequential thinking

Some connections between phantasy, thinking and walking

Introduction

In the previous chapter I tried to show how at first people, then thoughts, can be felt to wait in the background, as it were, of our minds. In this chapter I shall try to show something about the conditions under which thoughts can wait their turn to be thought about – or attended to – not in the background but in the foreground, just beyond the horizon of our attention, and how this can enable even multiple tracks of thinking. I want to describe some interesting parallels between three children's manner of thinking, conversing and walking. The concept of internal phantasies concerning the self's relation to internal objects offers a means of understanding this. Two of the children had difficulty – and met obstructions – with the natural turn-taking involved in conversational dialogues and inner sequential thinking. It turned out that they also had a problem with the dynamic flow involved in the swinging, alternating movements required for ordinary walking. I gradually learned that, unlike babies Alice and Angela, described in Chapter 2, their internal objects were definitely not felt to be waiting patiently in reserve. These observations were based on psychoanalytic clinical noting of the children's transferences to me, my often bewildered or frustrated countertransferences to them, and the way these relationships seemed similar to the way their feet and legs interacted – or rather failed to interact – smoothly with the ground.

I shall suggest that certain developments in psychoanalytic theory, such as Bion's (1967) theory of thinking, imply a move from a sometimes over-spatial model of the mind to a more temporal model of the nature of such interactions: perhaps, with certain patients, it is useful to think less about unconscious phantasy and a bit more about the activity of unconscious phantasying – that is, its form rather than content. I shall turn in the final discussion to some relevant developmental and neuroscience findings. By quoting these, I shall not be implying that these children's actual parents failed them in infancy (these were not deprived children), but only that development might have gone slightly awry quite early on for a number of possible reasons, including the child's own make-up. What I do want to emphasize, however, is the way inner phantasied emotional relationships may colour our relationship to the world at large, including our body's relation to it.

I learned that the children needed changes to the form and patterning of their thinking, rather than changes to the content of their phantasy or their thoughts. Their phantasied relation to internal objects seemed to colour their feelings about how their feet could relate to the earth beneath them, their posture to the sky above, and their forward movement to the space ahead. At times, all this affected their methods of thinking their thoughts and of following trains of thought, and their freedom to amplify their thoughts.

Developments in Psycho-analysis, edited by Joan Riviere and published in 1952, was based primarily on the four Kleinian papers read in the series of controversial discussions arranged in 1943 by the British Psychoanalytic Society. One of the four papers was Susan Isaacs' great 'The Nature and Function of Phantasy'. In her general introduction to the book, Riviere (1952, p. 16) declared:

> The mind is a whole, the higher functions do not act independently; the unconscious is not a vestigial or rudimentary part of the mind. It is the active organ in which mental processes function; no mental activity can take place without its operation. The original primary mental activity, which usually remains unconscious, we call unconscious 'phantasy'. There is, therefore, an unconscious phantasy behind every thought and every act (except possibly a bodily reflex).

She was including even reality thinking and behaviour as accompanied by these phantasies. Note the term 'behind', however. I think one of the implications of Bion's theory of thinking is that we may now need to broaden out Riviere's statement. It may be more useful to put it thus: there is another thought, or another series of interrelating thoughts, behind and below, *but also beside, above and surrounding* every thought and every act. (I shall not discuss here the possible differences between a 'phantasy' and a 'thought'.) Furthermore – as, of course, Freud and others (Sandler and Sandler, 1994b) have said – many of these phantasies (or thoughts) are not unconscious, only just out of focus, just a little off-centre in a vast web of associations and meanings. Rather than pre-conscious, they may be 'para'-conscious. The somewhat narrow two-storey house with excellent cellarage of the topographical theory has been enlarged by subsequent psycho-analytic theory-building to resemble something resembling a spreading country house or Palladian villa where breadth, lateral thinking and help from unconscious internal objects above may offer as much to mental growth as that which lies below or behind.

In fact, even architectural metaphors are inadequate to capture the full mental-ness of mind, because they are too spatial. We need an image for the notion of the mind's capacity to sense manifold meanings in a single word, a single thought, a single experience, and to describe the way these are always moving on. Perhaps quasi-musical concepts are better: notions such as pulse, echo, resonance, harmony and discord capture the ongoingness of trains of thought, the constant dynamic interchange, and the mobility of thought processes, their demandingness, their aliveness. The brain findings are relevant here: Siegel (1999, p. 13) points out, 'Because of the spider-web-like interconnections, activation of one neuron can influence an average of ten thousand neurons at the receiving ends!'

It is worth stressing the fact that, although the Kleinians were using the phrase 'unconscious' phantasy, they were not setting this type of phantasy in opposition to the conscious apprehension of reality; indeed, they were maintaining that it always accompanied the experiencing of reality. Bucci's conception of the sub-symbolic mode of processing, particularly of emotional information processing, is similar – but carefully supported by cognitive research. She writes that it

> is experientially . . . familiar to us in the actions . . . of everyday life – from aiming a piece of paper at a wastebasket or entering a line of moving traffic, . . . and responding to facial expressions . . . Sub-symbolic processing accounts for highly developed skills in athletics and the arts and sciences and is central to knowledge of one's body and to emotional experience.
>
> (Bucci, 2001, p. 48)

She writes that it cannot be expressed fully in words (except, she says, in poetry; p. 52), but nevertheless it is not intrinsically archaic or primitive. Al Alvarez (2005, p. 59) quotes the Australian poet Les Murray, who writes, 'Poetry is as much dreamed as it is thought and it is as much danced in the body as it is written. It's done in your lungs. It's done in every part of your muscles – you can feel it in your muscles.'

A word about definition: phantasies and thoughts or phantasying/thinking?

To continue with my attempt to broaden Riviere's proposal that 'There is an unconscious phantasy behind every thought and every act (except possibly a bodily reflex)' to the proposal that there are thoughts *beside* and *surrounding* thoughts, brain researchers and cognitive scientists nowadays talk of charac-teristics such as parallel processing and multi-modularity of memory systems (Bucci, 2001). A verb may be more appropriate than a noun (Schafer, 1976). Isaacs and Riviere themselves at times use the term 'unconscious phantasy*ing*', and in fact sometimes use it interchangeably with 'mental activity'. Symington (1993) prefers the term 'emotional activity', but we might add, following Bion (1962b), 'mental/emotional activity'. Urwin (1987) has criticized the cognitive researchers for seeing emotion as slowing down or speeding up cognition, whereas she suggests, like Bion, that it enters into the structure of cognition itself.

As Gerhardt (2004, p. 50) points out, 'each new mode of communication is added to the previous one, but yet none are lost'. The emotional communications through early infantile looks and touches are soon enriched by vocalizations, eventually by words, and gradually by thought-out and thought-through words. One little two-year-old watching his seven-week-old baby brother make mouthing movements as the baby responded to his grandmother nodding her head and talking to him said slowly, 'He's trying to talk.' His mother agreed, and then, the next time it happened, added, also slowly, 'He's listening with his mouth.' (This is an interesting addition to the developmental finding that newborn babies are capable of imitation (Hobson, 2002).) The mother was talking about something more than imitation: she was describing some sort of deep introjective and internalizing process that was occurring. Both mother and son were thinking as they spoke; and, in a way, perhaps, the baby was too.

The term 'phantasy' has tended to carry with it intimations of visual forms and shapes (e.g. the mouth-like slipper seen by the child in Isaacs' (1948) paper), or of drama-like interchanges between self and internal object. Isaacs did not wish to narrow the term only to the visual or dramatic, but, nevertheless, we may need to remind ourselves of the importance of internal experiences of smellable objects, sound objects (Maiello, 1995), textured objects, physical pressures, objects with more or less physical elasticity, more or less rhythm, melodic line, musical form. All of these, like the more visualizable phantasies, have emotive connotations and may be – more or less – thought *about* and dwelt upon. We may wonder whether, for example, a person's internal physical universe allows him space to move freely, or whether he feels strong enough in his mental muscles to follow a train of thought. The visual dimension is clearly a powerful container of phantasy, but an emphasis on visual shapes and forms is in danger of ignoring the temporal dimension. We may ask, for example, 'Does the patient feel he has enough space for thinking his thoughts?' but also, 'Does he feel his internal object will give him enough *time* to think his thoughts?' or time and breadth to follow two parallel – or even diverging – trains at once? Or, at least, to follow the one in a sufficiently meandering fashion so that surrounding landscapes are dwelt upon and taken in, rather than ignored and dashed past?

I would suggest that Bion's (1962b) theory of alpha function (see Chapter 1) implies that reality-thinking need not wait for the developments of the depressive position, but that it begins with the first thought-about thought, and this thought may concern a present object, not always or necessarily an absent object: thinking thoughtfully about a present object may lay the groundwork for later thinking about an absent object; it may also eventually leave room for one thought to be accompanied by another. If attention is too rushed, too fleeting, many thoughts and experiences retain a shredded, patchy quality, and the unconscious phantasy life or activity may remain impoverished. Worse, it may atrophy, as it does in certain empty autistic children or severely deprived children, where, as I suggested in Chapter 1, a technique of reclamation and then description may have to precede more complicated explanation.

However, to return to Riviere's stress on the bicameral nature of mind – of the parallel processing of conscious reality-thinking and unconscious mentation, of two trains of thought occurring in parallel – if I understand Riviere's point correctly, these two need not necessarily be playing in disharmony. They may be functioning in harmony, like the members of a string quartet, or the poets who have dreamed their poems, or the scientists who have made their discoveries in their dreams (Al Alvarez, 1995). The unconscious is not always our enemy; sometimes it is our silent witness or our supporter, echo, friend, adviser, encourager and even teacher. Not everyone is in conflict all the time. After all, how does poetry get written, or music composed, except when the artist has relatively good access to a poetic or musical inner world and, for a period, accord is greater than discord? On a more clinical note, what does it mean when a child who has never used his imagination begins to say, 'I know what we can do – I've got an *idea!*' His ideas have apparently agreed to come when called, or even to appear unasked for. He himself may have become more attentive and friendlier to them, but perhaps they too have become more biddable and responsive to him. Why, for example, do great athletes and great dancers make their runs, leaps and glides seem so effortless and beautiful? Is it only a question of muscles and training? Will a one-person psychology do to explain this, or do we need a two-person psychology? Is it also partly because such people seem to experience (and almost to make) the earth beneath them smoother, less resistant, softer and more resilient, and to experience the air, space and heights around them as something inviting, accessible and smoothly scaleable? John Lahr (1995) wrote that the great tap dancer Savion Glover seemed to be 'playing the floor', and Glover agreed that he was 'feeling the stage for sounds'. The patients who are described below unfortunately stood and moved on a much more recalcitrant planet.

A correspondence between motility and thinking, and the need to include the temporal along with the spatial dimension in work with three children

Some years ago, I became interested in how a child's walking often seemed affected by particular unconscious phantasies, which also appeared in their drawings or dreams and in the transference. One boy, Donald, was always falling over because, it seemed, he was in such a hurry that he leaned over beyond his centre of gravity. He was a very impatient little boy, but there was more to it than that. He and I began to notice how tentative he was in his relationships and in the transference, and how difficult he found it to say a clear 'yes' or 'no' – to 'put his foot down' or 'stand his ground', as it were. His image of his mother seemed to be of someone much loved but fragile. One day he had a dream that he was flying above the earth, wanting to land. But he did not dare land because the ground was covered with beautiful white flowers, and he realized that his landing would crush them. This was indeed his internal dilemma; and as, over the years, his phantasied object strengthened, he became more upright and stronger, and the falling ceased. His difficulties were mainly on the conflictual neurotic level, and although his emotional life suffered, his thinking was not affected on a profound level, and he was interested in explanatory interpretations. The content of his phantasy was more important than its form. Danny and Jean, both of whom were more impaired, were different.

Danny was an overweight boy who walked, spoke and thought in an awkwardly wooden way. He was very bad at sports, even finding ordinary school walks a huge effort, and – as a result – was very much the butt of his schoolmates' mockery. Eventually, after a year and a half of treatment, he took up ice hockey. It seemed an unwise thing to do, because he suffered agonies of terror about being knocked over – a common feature of the game. Although he was still very awkward and slow, he loved the *idea* of being able to slide smoothly over the ice, and we finally understood that this seemed to represent ideal phantasies both about himself and his object. He longed to feel safe enough (and, in his sad pomposity, he somewhere knew that he needed to feel ordinary enough) to let go and move forward in his emotions, his thoughts and his life. The smoothness of the ice seemed to stand for a frictionless, lubricated object that would, in a sense, let go enough for him to move on, pass it by, grow up, and yet still be available to support him. (This is what every toddler needs as he learns to walk upright.)

After another three years of intensive treatment, Danny loosened up somewhat in his movement and his conversation. He had been a very touchy and also very narcissistic and bullying conversationalist, and our dialogue had never been smooth in the early years. I had to develop a technique that was firm enough to withstand his bullying and allow something from me to be heard, yet tactful enough to be supersensitive to his readiness to feel humiliated and so easily roughed up. For him, the great achievement and source of pride was that he finally became a very able roller-blader, with his skills even appreciated by the other adolescents at school. The phantasy of sliding smoothly had not been, I believe, simply a denying or a defensive and manic one. I think he had had some image (ideal, rather than idealized) of how he would like to be – and also how he *needed* to be – moving smoothly over a leavable-behind, smooth, but also continuously supportive object; but he had no means yet of achieving this sort of relationship. His own internal object was claustrophobia-inducing, intrusive and extremely obstructive. One day he talked about how, in the past, he dared not lift one foot off the ground while pushing off with the ball of the other foot, because he felt he would fall if he did so. He had had little concept that the forward momentum allowed the forward foot to come down as the other left the security of the ground. Only a sense of flow could give him that. Eventually, it began to develop.

How do some children learn to welcome novelty and a change of subject (or ground) and others to fear it? Alfred Brendel (2001, p. 325) has written that the conductor Furtwangler's greatest strength was that he was 'the great connector, the grand master of transition'. He asks,

> What makes Furtwangler's transitions so memorable? They are moulded with the greatest care, yet one cannot isolate them. They are not patchwork, inserted to link two ideas of a different nature. They grow out of something and lead into something. They are areas of transformation. If we observe them minutely, we notice that, at first almost imperceptibly, they start to affect the

tempo, usually a great deal earlier than is the case with other conductors, until their impact finally makes itself felt.

(Brendel, 2001, p. 325)

Brendel goes on to emphasize the importance of 'preparation' for a transition. I assume something like this happens in the brain/unconscious mind/body when we move from heel to toe, foot to foot, and there is a smooth flow.

I now want to mention Jean, a girl of ten who was referred because of her clumsiness, depression and underachievement at school. She had an odd, flat-footed, Chaplinesque gait, although it was years before she gave me (or I felt I could take) an opportunity to discuss it with her. We did, however, discuss her clumsiness, which entered into the sessions fairly early, and disappeared entirely within about a year. Jean was a very polite, gentle girl – so polite, in fact, that much of her clumsiness seemed not to be due to embarrassment on her own behalf but on other people's. If someone else said or did something stupid, *she* would trip up! There was also a kind of passive projective identification process going on in the clumsiness, where she was silently, and apparently totally innocently, provoking irritation as she tripped, bumped into things and stepped on my feet. However, as I have said, this physical clumsiness disappeared fairly early on. Her mental chaos and learning difficulties continued much longer. Sometimes, when she tried to tell me something, the sequence of events was so entangled that at times she appeared almost to suffer from thought disorder. It took some years for us to understand together the many factors in her personality that led to her odd thinking, odd language and odd gait.

As I said, listening to Jean talk was extremely confusing, and it was a long time before we could understand what things were making it so confusing. Indeed, in the early years, she talked fairly little, and preferred to draw endlessly repetitive pictures of bleak, narrow houses, often with blank windows and blocked doors. They were usually unpeopled, and nothing much happened in them anyway. Sometimes she drew railway stations but no one ever arrived or left, and it was often raining. Even when things began to move slightly, it was up to me to ask, to push, to pull, which unfortunately confirmed what we gradually saw was Jean's belief that other people were somehow inordinately dependent upon her for her contributions. Adults were seen as kind but fragile and silly, and never magnetic enough, interesting enough, or (as with Danny) safe enough to invite her forward into life.

By the third year of treatment, Jean began to use much more space in the treatment room and to be somewhat more at ease. She became less exaggeratedly polite. She continued with her house drawings, but the entrances were wider and gardens began to surround the buildings. I had spent a lot of time worrying about technique: how not to ask questions about a drawing too quickly, which seemed to produce claustrophobic panic, and yet not to leave her too long, for she sank into depression, darkness and genuine misery if I did. The earlier drawings were full of miserable, drizzling rain. When the roofs in her drawings kept being shown as collapsing, and I tried to link this with an anxiety about a break or some pending external event, like an exam, she would agree politely; yet I never felt these or other explanatory interpretations really reached her. I came to think that, until she could learn to think one thought at a time in any depth, my attempts to make connections between *two* were largely a waste of time. She could not think about how her unconscious thoughts lay behind her conscious ones until she could learn to think her conscious ones more fully and deeply – to explore, as it were, her para-conscious, and to stick by it and own it.

But three years on there was more light and space in the houses, and a sense that movement and life might be possible. I noted, however, that at whatever moment I started to speak, she so easily felt intruded on and crowded that she immediately got stuck and could not move forward. She would simply cut off and only pretend to listen, so there was no dialogue at all. One day, however, she did a drawing of some amazing shoes that could get electrical power from the floor underneath. There was an electrical magnet in the floor: your feet would not need to touch the floor; the shoes would just get the electricity without touching. I pointed out that perhaps she felt that that would be a lovely way to have a conversation: if only my talking did not produce this terrible friction and slow her down; if only it could just give her a 'charge' and let her go on. She really seemed to understand this. I felt that, up to a point, she was right: she needed such an object. She needed to find an object that, unlike her impatient and obstructive internal objects, would not obstruct her passage, a passage which was sometimes highly tentative, at other times unbelievably rapid and spear-like. Jean herself was madly impatient and in some ways quite intrusive.

We came to understand that the confusing, almost thought-disordered talk was due, in part, to her own impatience. But I must stress that it was also due to what she saw as a terrible impatience on the part of her internal listening object. She would start to recount some story involving four points, beginning with the first, but her mind would jump ahead to the third or fourth, because she feared it would not wait and would disappear if she did not get to it quickly. It was therefore demanding her attention. At other times, she would jump to the third or fourth point because she thought it was the thought *I* was thinking and therefore expecting and wanting her to think. Needless to say, this premature jump ahead interfered with getting through thoughts one and two sequentially, on the way to three and four. The result was conversational chaos.

About a year later, I began to observe how she often left it to me to finish sentences for her. For example, she would say, 'Sun in the . . .' and, because of the pause, I would find myself saying, 'sky'. I began to wonder whether this linked with the impatient listening and interrupting object that she suffered from, but which she seemed to invite and even force me to be. It became clear that, in this way, she did not have to experience her own impatience, her own desire to get to the end of the sentence and make herself understood. She also mentioned, extremely casually and complacently, that French was her 'worst thing' at school – the teacher always had to correct her. The session had begun with an account of people in a car stuck in a traffic jam, and I tried to show her how it was always up to me, and apparently her teachers, to get the traffic moving. I added that, when she did suddenly move ahead, my words were like the other cars that she sped past, because she certainly did not listen to them. She did, however, listen with real alertness to *this*. She was a gentle girl, so it had been easy to miss the force with which she was projecting her own vitality and activity into others.

A few months later, there was more material about the kind of listener she felt she was addressing. She spoke about how low ceilings help people who do not have loud voices to be heard, because the voices bounce back. With higher ceilings, they might not be heard at all. I think the real Jean did speak very faintly and did need a very careful, attentive, yet firm listener who could slow her down but still let her go forward, one thought, carefully, at a time. It seemed that she had suffered from a belief that her listener would not wait for her to finish a thought: the listener had either always rushed to meet her and somehow blocked her or else was felt to be too remote.

She finally began to slow down as beautiful lakes began to appear in her drawings, and her inner world seemed to be broadening out. She remembered that on family walks she had always walked rapidly with her head down, simply to get to the end of the walk, and had never looked to the right or left at the plants and trees on either side of the path. She saw that her tunnel vision had been affecting her mind and her learning in a variety of ways. Her conversation became slower and steadier, but, paradoxically, faster and freer. She was no longer depressed, and also much less rigid and more flexible. Finally, one day, she began to talk about her flat-footed walk. She said that she had realized she was afraid to lift her heel and push off: she could do it when she ran, but not when she walked. She seemed to be saying that she felt the need to cling to the earth, just as she had always clung mentally to other people's thoughts instead of pursuing and completing her own first. There was a longing by now, however, for a more coordinated and regulated forward motion. In fact, she began to enjoy dancing and sports, and to improve academically to a marked degree.

Technical implications

In Chapter 1 I suggested that clinical priorities, especially with patients in a borderline or psychotic state of mind, may require us to beware of premature explanatory interpretations that may not reach the patient where he is. Donald was able to work with explanatory interpretations much of the time, whereas, although Danny and Jean were not borderline or psychotic, and *appeared* able to understand explanatory interpretations, I had to learn to pay far more attention to how they were hearing – or failing to hear – my comments than with other children. And it is interesting – after much work on their relation to a listening–talking conversational partner, and as our conversational interactions became more comfortable – that they were able to talk about their difficulties with walking. (Now I would seek collaboration with an occupational therapist or movement therapist in order to work from both ends, as it were.) In Michelangelo Antonioni's film *Beyond the Clouds* (1995), there is a story about a group of Mexican porters who would not be hurried up a mountain in case they left their souls behind. The para- and pre-conscious thoughts – that is, the thoughts that may lie alongside and very close to other thoughts – may have to be explored before those which lie underneath, in the unconscious. Sometimes this involves something as simple as giving the patient time to identify the adjective that he feels belongs with the noun. The lovely smoothness of Danny's ice and the frictionless glide of Jean's electric shoes taught us more about their difficulties and their hopes than complicated explanations of the unconscious symbolic meanings of ice and shoes might have done at that stage. Both patients needed to find a way to get a move on, and this was a start. Once they made that start, and some sort of turn-taking was established in our conversations, with enough room for each thought, it was much easier to begin to make links between one feeling and another, one thought and another, and one experience and another. But this development really did have to wait until each was given its own place and time. Schore (2003, p. 245) points out, 'In order for conflict or competition to occur between the two hemispheric processors, the late-acting verbal left must have access to the emotional appraisals and outputs of the nonverbal early-right processor, which it can then inhibit.' Where there is deficit in the emotion-processing right brain, he points out, it must be repaired before the issues of conflict (and, we might add, the complexities of two-tracked thinking) can be addressed. As these children began to be able to bear to listen and to accept and enjoy turn-taking, so they were able to pay more attention and respect to the thoughts that were waiting in the wings of their own minds, and thus to manage better sequentiality.

Discussion and conclusion: the development of walking and of language

I have suggested that the newer ideas imply that the movement of thoughts is as important as their content: the qualities of internal objects are important, but so are their location and their position. Sometimes our objects need to await their turn in the background – or, for that matter, even beyond the foreground – as it were, of our minds. It is interesting that Knoblauch (2000) describes a way of listening to the patient, and to himself talking to the patient, that takes account of the volume, tone, rhythm, tempo of the contouring of the patient's and the therapist's communications. He points out that certain fundamental changes in the patients began with the changes in the patterning of their responses long before this could be verbalized.

One caveat: it is clear that the parallels between walking and thinking in the three patients I have described in this chapter are not always present. Many geniuses are poor athletes and many athletes are relatively uninterested in abstract thought. Yet the parallels were there in these three children, and it seemed to me that, to some extent, major areas of their development had gone somewhat awry in very similar ways.

Perhaps, here, it is necessary to say a word about the development of walking. First, although it is clear that all – or almost all – ordinary, able children learn to walk, a fascinating book by Thelen and Smith (1995) argues that this is in no way due to a simple, innate neurological unfolding. Nor is it due to simple environmental influences. The complex web of causality which these authors offer instead is a dynamic systems model which analyses the sub-components in the precursors to the capacity to walk (stepping, parallel kicking, single kicking, alternate kicking, quad rocking, standing with support, cruising, walking with support) *and* the way in which each of these interacts with both the state of the infant's mind, body, posture and position, and the environment at any moment in time. Thelen and Smith (1995, p. 16) write,

> The point here is that *there is no essence* of leg movements during the first year. Leg co-ordination patterns are entirely situation-dependent – whether the infant be calm or excited; upright, supine, or prone; deliberately using the legs for exploration or locomotion; on a treadmill (a research tool); submerged in water (also a research tool); or standing alone.

We might want to enlarge this list by asking, 'Excited about what or whom? Drawn toward what or whom to explore?' And what about the feeling of power gained from pushing one's feet down on the floor, or, earlier in life, against a parent's hand, and the pleasure and sense of agency that such pushing contact may give, and the awareness of playful aggressiveness in the caregiver's pushing back? What about the tenderness evoked when the parent responds to the baby's greeting by holding his welcoming feet? Where did Savion Glover get his feeling for playing the floor for sounds? It is important to remember that babies smile not only with their mouths and eyes; they greet us with their hands and feet, too. And the relationship between our feet and the world starts long before we try out the ground. Our sense of rhythm and beat does not wait for the one–two, one–two of walking; it begins with the rests and pauses during sucking, the rests and pauses in looking, or, as Bruner (1968) said, in the alternation between the two. Why do children love to jump up and forward as well as down? Does that space above or ahead beckon or forbid?

A similar dynamic complexity applies to the development of the capacity that underlies the later capacity for the use of language in conversation: namely, the capacity for proto-conversational communication via looks and vocalizations (Trevarthen and Hubley, 1978). Beebe, who has studied these vocalization dialogues between infants and their caregivers, shows how each partner is influenced both by the trajectory and flow of his own states and by those of the other. *And* he influences the other (Beebe and Lachmann, 2002). Gerhardt (2004, p. 31) quotes Beebe: 'you change the way I unfold and I change the way you unfold. The question is what gets internalized from these dialogues and what does the self of the child come to expect from its co-communicator?'

It is important to remember that the right brain, the substrate of the emotional brain (and of non-verbal communication through looks and touch), has a growth spurt in the first year and a half of post-natal life, which then ends; at which point the left brain begins its growth spurt (Schore, 2003, p. 244). This leads to the beginning of language. Siegel (1999, p. 179) points out that there are fast-acting, parallel (simultaneously active), holistic processes in the right hemisphere. There is also some language, in terms of understanding metaphor, paradox and humour. Whereas, in the left hemisphere, there are more slowly acting, linear, sequentially active, temporal processes. Verbal meanings of words are primary. These processes help us determine the sequence of events in a story – not just the emotional power of it. However, as Gerhardt (2004, p. 50) points out, 'each new mode of communication is added to the previous one, but yet none are lost'. Thus, if there are difficulties with sequentiality, we can ask whether this is due primarily to a cognitive problem on the left side of the brain. Or could there be difficulties stemming from emotional relations on the right side? I do not know the answer, but I suggest that the one–two beat of walking is preceded by many earlier one–twos, such as sucking/swallowing, looking/looking away, looking/blinking, uttering/pausing, uttering/listening and so on. Malloch and Trevarthen's (2009, p. 8) *Communicative Musicality* asks how our 'swift ethereal thoughts' manage to move our 'heavy intricately mobile bodies', and also how we read mindfulness in an other simply via external sounds, touch and movements. Their answer is that 'humans move under the coordinated and integrated control of a time keeping, energy regulating Intrinsic Motive Pulse (IMP)', and that 'we live, think, imagine and remember in movement' (p. 9).

Chapter 4

Making links and making time

Steps toward the de-compression of thoughts and the establishment of links between thoughts

Introduction

In the previous chapter I described the way in which Jean's thoughts refused to wait their turn in the queue in her mind, crowding forward and causing confusion in herself and her listener. Here, I want to examine a similar but more extreme phenomenon – a kind of squashing of thoughts similar to that described by one of Bion's (1955, p. 237) schizophrenic patients as 'thoughts getting on top of each other'. The patients described in this chapter could also think multiple thoughts, but they were exceedingly compressed. I also want to look at some of the conditions under which these thoughts could become less crowded, somewhat more loosely linked, and the way in which this development could act as a possible prelude to genuine sequential thinking.

In an episode of *The Muppet Show*, Kermit the Frog forgot about a date he had promised with Miss Piggy. When she demanded he keep his promise, he began to protest that he did not have *time* to go out that evening. Miss Piggy thundered menacingly, 'Kermit! MAKE time!' This is about learning how to make time.

I first want to discuss some contradictions in Bion's theories of thinking, particularly regarding the problem of links between thoughts set us by him in his great paper 'Attacks on linking' (1959). It is interesting that Bion takes what seem to be two rather contradictory positions regarding failures in links, as I shall try to show. One refers to the effect of destructive attacks on the patient's own ego and thinking; the other takes account of something more like a deficit in linking (or what he might later have called an 'unrealized preconception of a link'). The first seems to assume some prior development in the personality of a capacity to conceive of links, or to make links, followed by a destruction of this capacity. The second position describes the patient's inability or incapacity to think or to store thoughts. At such moments, Bion seems to be describing a deficit in self, object or both. Can this distinction inform our interpretive response to our patients' problems of thought disorder and thinking deficit? Clearly, the two positions need not be mutually contradictory: they can coexist at the same moment.

Where there is a real difficulty or deficit in making links, rather than an attack on a previously established link, the therapist may need to attend to certain temporal and dynamic features of the link that can enable sequentiality, ordinality and twoness to be bearable and pleasurable. I will discuss some clinical material from an autistic patient and a psychotic patient with thinking difficulties, and, by looking at technique, suggest some parallels between play and syntax.

The temporal shaping of reality: a modulating presence

Freud's (1920) grandson's reel game and the peekaboo game (Bruner and Sherwood, 1976) have been models for psychoanalytic theory about the absent object and about ways in which the infant comes to terms with reality: usually a reality of frustration, loss and separation. I wish to think, in addition, about an equally primary reality: that is, the reality of the present object, but the present object realized in its dynamic shapes in time, its temporal forms (Robarts, 2009; Stern, 1985). There are, for example, as well as rhythmic comings and goings, rhythmic rockings, ebbs and flows. The present breast is sucked in bursts and pauses, in a basic rhythm of life, which gradually gets regulated, and can become as easy as breathing. Bruner and Sherwood (1976) have pointed out that the peekaboo game is preceded by something even earlier: a looming game, where mother plays with the distance between her face and her infant's face. Modulation and regulation of presence is a task for the infant, which is probably prior to the one of maintaining object constancy throughout absence. Bartram (1999, p. 140) has pointed out, for instance, that it was crazy for her to wait for her two-year-old autistic patient to say good-bye to his mother at the moment when he was having such an obviously difficult time processing the sudden arrival of his therapist. A good-bye implies some degree of prior internalization of a constant object, whereas many children with autism have great difficulty in taking in experience in the first place. Introjection is difficult enough for them, and surely introjection of experience has to precede a more durable internalization and representation. Stern's concept of vitality affects (1985), and vitality forms (2010) – the shared attunements and contourings in which experience is cast – is probably central to this process of introjection. So is Bower's (1974) work on visual tracking behaviour and babies' capacities to anticipate and interpolate trajectories of moving objects – which may bear some relation to the way we learn to follow a thought.

I am offering the looming game and something musicians call the anacrusis – the suspenseful upbeat before the downbeat – as paradigms to be added to the reel game and the peekaboo game. I have, I should say, found myself driven to attend to these microscopic or micro-analytic levels through my difficulties in finding a way of lending meaning to the extremely fragmented and frenzied behaviour of Samuel, a four-year-old boy with severe autism whom I shall describe later. Samuel eventually began to try to conceive of twoness, but it nearly drove him mad. He and I had to learn that thinking two thoughts *takes time*, and time was something Samuel did not appear to have.

Bion on the relationships between thoughts

We owe to Bion the fact that we now have a psychoanalytic theory of the mind which corresponds to our subjective impressions: as well as a whole inner world full of living objects, memories, facts and images, there are thoughts lit up by meaning, powered by their own energy, and constantly interacting with one another. In 'Language and the schizophrenic' (1955) Bion states that he agrees with Freud that the psychotic patient is hostile to reality, and that he also attacks his sense organs and his consciousness. Bion adds that the psychotic patient attacks his capacity for verbal thought and that this involves a very cruel and sadistic type of splitting. However, in addition to sadism, he mentions greed (p. 223):

> I shall also hope to show that the splitting mechanism is brought into action to minister to the patient's greed, and is therefore not simply an unfortunate catastrophe of the kind that occurs when the patient's ego is split in pieces as an accompaniment of his determination to split his objects; it is the outcome of a determination which can be expressed verbally as an intention to be as many people as possible, so as to be in as many places as possible, so as to get as much as possible, for as long as possible – in fact, timelessly.

(Bion continues, throughout subsequent papers, to alternate between descriptions of thought disorder that he ascribes to sadistic attacks and others that he attributes to something more like ego deficit – rather than a refusal to think, at times he describes an inability to think.) He gives a dramatic example of active splitting, with a patient using language as a mode of action for the splitting of his object (Bion, 1967, p. 226): 'The patient comes into the room, shakes me warmly by the hand, and looking piercingly into my eyes says, "I think the sessions are not for a long while but stop me ever going out."' Bion (1967, p. 25) treats this material as the result of a piece of active splitting. He acknowledges that the patient has a grievance that the sessions are too few but interfere with his free time. He takes it as an intentional split of the analyst to make him give two interpretations at once. His evidence is that the patient goes on to say: 'How does the lift know what to do when I press two buttons at once?' (Bion, 1955, p. 226).

Thanks to the later Bion (in *Learning from Experience*, 1962b), where – as Grotstein (1981b) has pointed out – he does have a concept of deficit in the containing object, I think we could try an alternative way of looking at the material: we could see this as a patient who perhaps did not have enough ego or a sufficiently elastic mental container that allowed him to separate those two thoughts. The splitting need not necessarily be seen as the result of an intentional attack. It may have been an urgent expression of two desperately pressing thoughts that arrived simultaneously. The patient may have felt he needed both to be understood at once, by a container that could simultaneously take in both and gradually separate them out *for him* – which, in fact, is what Bion did.

Bion takes up the deficit issue on the next page: he refers to the patient's difficulty in dreaming and in having phantasies. He interprets to the patient that he has no way of thinking about his problem without dreams, and later (p. 236) says, 'Since you feel you lack words, you also feel you lack the means to store ideas in your mind.' The patient said he could not remember what Bion had just said, and Bion replied, 'This feeling is so strong it makes you think you have forgotten things.' After this interpretation of the deficit – which, one can see, gave the patient his mind back – the patient was able to remember.

In the last example, Bion is addressing a general difficulty in thinking or dreaming: that is, in thinking any thought. In 'Attacks on linking' (1959), however, he goes further and examines failures to make, or to allow, *links* between thoughts. He ascribes these failures as due to a destructive attack on the link between the creative couple, but the notion of a deficient capacity still comes in his inter-pretations to the patient. I think we owe to infant observation and to infant development research the knowledge that there are times when the patient can really afford to think only one thought at a time. However, in spite of what I regard as Bion's overemphasis on attacked links, it is important to remember that his attention to the *emotional* significance of disturbances in links, to the emo-tionality running through thinking, was absolutely revolutionary and, of course, is completely lacking in the cognitivists' descriptions of thinking. Parthenope Bion pointed out (personal communication, 1996) that in *Cogitations* (Bion, 1992, p. 216) her father said that a patient's attack on the analyst's thinking may not have been motivated by sadism, but by a projection of his own lack of alpha function. The implication is one of desperate need – that is, of deficit – rather than of destructiveness.

In 1962, 'A theory of thinking' (Bion, 1962a) introduced the idea of 'alpha function': that thinking has to be called into existence to cope with thoughts. 'Thinking' is a noun that derives from a verb: it involves doing something to something, a process that takes something else – time – to carry it out. This paper was followed by *Learning from Experience* (Bion, 1962b), with its theory of the importance of the containing object. Here also was the suggestion that the object could sometimes provide inadequate containment: finally, there is room for a theory of deficit.

Britton (1989) introduced the concept of the 'third position' for thinking by suggesting that where parental intercourse is felt to be too intrusive, the link between child and mother may be annihilated. He stressed the importance of the Oedipal triangular space for thinking. In the cases described below, I shall be referring to deficits, not necessarily in space, but in an inner sense of ordinal time, of sequentiality: that is, in a temporal container. The patients described in this chapter, for a variety of possible reasons, did not feel they had time to think. My own patient, Samuel, suffered from acute impatience, hatred and greed within his own self, but this seemed to be accompanied by an impossibly transient and fleeting sense of an internal object that he experienced as never giving him time to find out about it, the links within it, and those between it and other objects.

Daniel and the conjunctive link

Daniel was a 19-year-old boy referred to a male psychotherapist for panic attacks and a total incapacity to write at school. He later told his therapist that every time he got to the end of a sentence, he felt it was dead and he could not go on. He was very withdrawn, but until now had been able to manage at school. There was some reason to think that he was hallucinating, and he was very obsessional. By the time of the session quoted below, he had been in once-weekly treatment for some months and was no longer hallucinating. He had started to be able to write again, but with enormous difficulty.

This was the first session after the winter Christmas holiday, and I quote from the therapist's notes:

> He comes 5 minutes late and gives an almost incoherent explanation. He then goes on to speak very fast about not being able to study. It is numbing, circular and full of peculiar rationalizations. Daniel refers repetitively to knowledge getting lost and 'falling in a hole', and mentions briefly, before it gets lost in the circular talk, a wish to die.

The therapist talks to him about a feeling of losing what he knows and that it feels like dying. The therapist also says, 'when I go away it is like leaving him with a hole inside him where he loses, forgets the work we did in the past'. Daniel expresses some ambivalence, but does slow down. Then the speed and circularity build up again, and the therapist, with great sensitivity, seems to enable him to slow down again. 'The patient says that he cannot write the word "and", he cannot write the word "the" and he cannot write "or". He uses hyphens instead. He says it is because he is aware his essays are very long, so he cut those words and used the hyphens so as not to lose the meaning.' The therapist says that he seems to feel that, for meaning to exist, there shouldn't be any link. (Daniel is similar to Bion's patient, but Daniel is at least able to insert a hyphen.) 'Daniel agrees and speeds up again, circling in search of meaning as though trying to get inside the text itself.'

What is an 'and'? It is a very special kind of link: it seems to contain a promise of more to come, not a death or a dead end. It ministers to our greed and appetite but also to our hope, expectation, anticipation, and perhaps also to our fear and dread. In music, the suspenseful anacrusis – the upbeat before the stressed downbeat – also contains a promise. It builds up to the stressed beat, or the key word in the song, 'Ta ra ra *boom* de ay'. Unlike my little autistic patient, Samuel, Daniel was not completely out of touch with reality. He at least felt he had to offer some recognition – in the form of the hyphen – to the fact that nouns need link words to join them with other nouns, and maybe somewhere to his need and desire for abbreviated waiting periods. He seems to feel the links take too long, are endless. He wishes to shorten them, as, perhaps, he would like to have shortened the winter break from his therapy and the distance he feels himself from his therapist even when he is present. He apparently wants a tighter, closer link. His difficulty with 'the' may be because 'the' may testify to the particularity and individuality of an internal mother or therapist. Perhaps specificity is a luxury when need is felt to be very urgent and anyone will do.

Daniel was in an acute panic about exams. How should we talk to such patients? What can they understand of our interpretations? Working with autistic children who have no language, one is always concerned to find the word, tone or phrase that will most bestir mental activity and language, the word that will meet and match experience, but expand it a little, too. Sometimes a simple 'Slow down, calm down, it's OK, there's enough time' or 'It's OK, we are back together, the break is over' seems to help.

The 'and' link in play: an ordinal link

In the beginning, Samuel showed interest only in the flowing of water, the spinning of wheels, his own clenched hand, his reflection in any shiny surface he could find, and occasional wild glances at me. After a lot of careful approaching on my part, he became interested in my face, and we often played the looming game, where we put our faces close together and then apart. He began to emerge from his frenzied states and as he was also showing more interest in objects in the room, I introduced toys that I thought might be suitable for whatever extremely early developmental level might be being revealed in his non-autistic moments in the sessions. Children such as Samuel may give up autism, but tremendous developmental delay is usually revealed even in their newly normal moments.

At one point, I provided a ring toy, a series of ever-larger brightly coloured plastic rings on a tapering pillar. Samuel loved it, but hated the fact that the perfect shape could be achieved only by placing the rings on it in exactly the right sequence. He could just about tolerate a pile or a tower of the rings, but he loathed – or couldn't wait for – order, and ordinal relations between things. His solution to the problem was to hurl the pillar away contemptuously, and build a tower of the rings in any order he chose, without using the pillar. He would, however, sometimes decide to build it properly, if I handed the rings to him in the right order, holding my breath and making suspenseful 'And . . . the purple one, and . . . the blue one' before each ring went on. I suppose I was trying to fill the previously intolerable gap with something, which, instead of threatening emptiness to this wildly impatient but also desperate little boy, contained a promise but also a certain sort of teasing torment that was just bearable. This seemed to catch and harmonize with his own tortured inability to wait and to tolerate sequencing, but perhaps it also modified it and made it into a game – the beginning of anacrusis.

Bion says the infant has to learn to modify reality, not to evade it, but perhaps reality also sometimes has to be modifiable and even to modify itself. Animate, living objects are constantly both self-modifying and being modified by the infant. The normal baby has experiences of reality as both un-modifiable and modifiable. This chapter is not the place for a discussion of psychotherapeutic technique with children with severe autism, but it is important to mention that Samuel's autism was apparently present in early infancy. His difficulties with attention span and eye contact, and his impatience with the otherness of the world, had, I suspect, left him closed to – and increasingly deprived of – the ordinary modulating and regulating life experiences that enable cognitive and emotional development to go forward. Extreme earliness of onset can set the child on an ever more divergent path of development (Acquarone, 2007). Work with such severely autistic children thus needs to be developmentally (as well as psychoanalytically) informed: at times, a more intensified technique may be necessary where very early infantile deficits need addressing (Alvarez, 1996).

After four years of intensive psychotherapy, Samuel began to show real interest in three-person relationships, and real jealousy. He not only showed interest in slight changes in the room, or other people in the corridor of the clinic, but began to let me see his interest, and sometimes even his outrage. I think, however (and shall illustrate in later chapters), that his earlier difficulties with links went deeper than an Oedipal problem: microcosmic links, involved in the capacity to look and take in a human face, or to listen to a lullaby, may need to be established before larger Oedipal links can be built.

Discussion: play and syntax

Is there a connection between syntactical link words, such as 'the', 'and' and 'or', and very early play? Does the pre-language of play prepare infants for real speech and for the structure of real sentences? The teasing 'and' is a link – a human one that is free and playful. It may also be similar to what Bion (1959) would call an 'articulated link'. You don't know exactly *when* the ring will come, but you do know that it will come; and, in a way you do know when, because *you can see it coming*. The looming and receding object remains present. The alerting surprise comes in many forms, not always unpleasurable. Brendel (2001) pointed out that Haydn surprised us with the unexpected, Mozart with the expected.

Susan Reid (personal communication, 1994) has referred to the difficulty children with autism have in the 'punctuation' of their experience. This is some-thing Samuel was completely against – like the rests and pauses in music that are as important as the notes. If the patient thinks of pauses as an end of the world, and of his mind, he dare not pause. Sorenson (2000) has written of the importance of maternal transition-facilitating behaviour for the development of secure attach-ment and mindfulness. Samuel eventually became able to look at bricks – two or even more – and also to pour the bricks from a large container to a smaller one. He began to enjoy the suspense about whether they would fall. Normal children love 'Ready . . . steady . . . go!' games. Perhaps suspense is essential to language and is part of what we call prose style. Syntactical speech – structured sentences – unlike the telegraphic speech of the psychotic, involves some necessary capacity to tolerate suspense. Samuel began to use suspense less sadistically: he looked at me as he placed something on the absolute edge of the table, then hesitated, grinning teasingly about whether to let it fall. It became a shared joke instead of a cruel tease.

One could speculate that experiences of bearable suspense – but, more important, *games of suspense* that give symbolic meaning to such experiences – might have some connection with the origin of the subjunctive: what is the balance – between confidence in a secure world and fear of its untrustworthiness – which is necessary for doubt and hope to develop out of fear and manic denials? Instead of insisting on intrusive physical contact with me whenever he felt fond of me or in need of emotional contact, Samuel began to accept using a little chair beside me, and indeed began to start every session by pulling it toward me in expectation of a (proto-)conversation or some playful interaction. The taking and placing of the chair seemed to signal a belief in preparation and preludes, and, more important, in the concept of a place and time for preparation and preludes. Instead of the need for desperate grabs at life, Samuel seemed to be developing some idea of a waiting area and a waiting time that he confidently expected to be followed by something worth preparing and waiting for.

The present object and the absent object – or, for that matter, the foreground object and the background object – are linked by the preparations for an entrance, the preparations for an exit. In musical terms, both the anacrusis – the moment of suspense that nevertheless contains a promise – and the cadence – which ends the phrase or musical piece – are necessary to the form. What gets internalized in normal development is not just an object, or rather two objects, with spatial form; it is an object, or two objects, with a dynamic form – a shape in time. The link words – 'the', 'and' and 'or' – and Samuel's growing acceptance of (and even pleasure in) the rests and pauses in play may suggest something about the way in which the real human world gets internalized. Brazelton *et al.* (1974) point out that the rhythm of looking at inanimate objects in babies is jerky and peaked; at animate objects it is contoured, builds up gradually and decreases – the graph is curvolinear. (See also Malloch and Trevarthen, 2009.)

Stern (1974, p. 192) refers to the slowness of tempo and grossness of exaggerations of mothers' behaviour toward their infants. He says this probably 'closely matches the range of infant preferences and tolerances of rate and degree of stimulus change', thus enabling 'the infant to maintain the identity of the mother's face across its various physical transformations and thus facilitate the acquisition of a stable face schema'. (Presumably to take in two faces at once, a mother's and a father's – even where one is more in the foreground and the other in the background – would require even more time and even more careful study and scanning in the early days of life.)

Gradually, the caregiver helps her baby to learn to shape his curves of attention, and Brazelton *et al.* (1974) have described in fascinating detail how, when mothers wish to engage their babies in a period of interaction, they begin by setting the stage. (Does this help babies later to listen to 'Once upon a time . . .' or 'Well, then, what shall we do?') Then she creates an expectancy for interaction (is this similar to 'There was a . . .'?) and only then does she proceed to intensify his attention by amplifying (the long-awaited noun, the subject of the narrative) or by alternating alerting with soothing movements, sounds and sights in order to capture *and hold* his attention. What she is doing is giving the baby's experience a dynamic form, a shape in time. A 'the' not only underlines the particularity of something, it warns us, and prepares us for the fact that something is coming. Articles, prepositions and verbs are link words, but, like all links, they contain a promise. Without that promise, links are inconceivable and waiting is a nightmare. Alpha function may at times operate in thinking about a present object, which is sometimes close and sometimes distant yet visible (and, of course, audible).

Conclusion

In this chapter, as in the previous two, I have aimed to extend the discussion of features of a single present object to the Oedipal situation, where the child is presented with two objects in a tripartite relation that includes him and leaves room for all three. (See Abello and Perez-Sanchez (1981) on the harmonious triangle that precedes the Oedipal triangle.) I suggest that some links between two objects are made when the link between the two parents is seen as *for* the child, including the child, not excluding him, and their appearance together is timed or spaced sensitively. I have also tried to make a more micro-analytic point about possible preconditions for micro-links, deriving from some clinical and technical examples.

Finally, I should say that I am not suggesting an alternative to previous ideas about how learning of reality takes place. I am arguing that we may need to add to them. Oral frustration, the absence of the object, separation, boundaries, separateness, Oedipal frustration are all alerting experiences. But where disturbance is too great, thoughts may become unthinkable. What I wish to stress is the additional importance of the temporal form in which reality presents itself, and the temporal forms or dynamic shapes in time, by which presence and absence are linked, *and by which two presences are linked*. Two objects get linked in time by being present together in time. Mother and father are linked at times by being *together for and with* the infant.

The research on triangular situations in early infancy by Fivaz-Depeursinge and Corboz-Warnery (1999) shows how babies learn to manage triangular situations depending on whether the parents are experienced as two-for-one or two-against-one. The truly Oedipal link – the one which excludes the child – is surely not the only way in which the 'and' link gathers significance. The movement within or about all living objects is an essential feature of their aliveness: the setting of the stage, the preparations for entrances and exits play a central part in human civilized exchange. Links between different versions of a present object have to be built alongside other different ones concerning absent objects – and our psychoanalytic technique can take account of this. The reel game and the peekaboo game have provided models for the absent object. The looming games, the suspenseful sequencing games and, of course, lullabies and proto-conversations may provide models for the modulating object that has a changing dynamic form in time but is not yet truly absent, just sometimes more and sometimes less within reach.

Part II

Descriptive level conditions

Chapter 5

The equal role of delight and frustration in the development of a sense of reality

Introduction

In Chapter 1 I argued for the need, with certain patients, to stay with the whatness of experience rather than the whyness. This chapter adds a further dimension to the question: namely, the issue of the *content* of such descriptive interpretations. I suggest that interpretations that draw attention to, or amplify, positive experiences or phantasies may be as central to analytic work as is attention to the negative. It therefore *adds to*, but in no way attempts to replace, the usual psychoanalytic assumption (Bion, 1959; Freud, 1911) of the relationship between learning and frustration.

I shall identify four features of the link between frustration and learning:

1   Frustration promotes thinking only when it is not over the limits of the tolerable and thinkable; otherwise, trauma and despair may produce dissociation and cognitive disorder.
2   Apparent 'defences' against frustration and anxiety may in fact be attempts to protect against, overcome or regulate otherwise intolerable frustration or anxiety and to arrive at states of safety and trust.
3   The introjection and internalization of positive experiences are essential elements in the development of emotional life.
4   Mental life and learning.

Good surprises are as alerting cognitively as bad ones, especially where frustration and despair have been the norm. I shall discuss a few technical implications of the difference between interpretations that address frustration and separateness and those that address relief and surprise at discovering a sense of connection.

In a chapter titled 'The necessary angel' (in Alvarez, 1992), I gave an example of a boy getting a bit excited as he was just beginning to conceive of his object (his therapist in the transference) as full of resources and feeling for him. His therapist took this new idea as a denial of a sadder truth. She (like me in Chapter 6, below) made a two-tracked interpretation, which assumed that the apparently idealized experience was somehow false, and that the truth lay behind or beneath these defensive denials. Both of our patients completely deflated after this. I argued in 1992 that if she had managed simply to describe and underline what the child was attempting to communicate to us, he might have been allowed to amplify and consolidate his newfound feeling of hope and trust in her as an ideal rather than an idealized object. I tried to show (pp. 119–120) that Klein's (1952) statement that idealization is sometimes a development had often been forgotten, and idealization was too often seen only as a defence.

This chapter starts by looking at some additional, even more general psychoanalytic concepts that can stand in the way of the slow art of staying at a more simple descriptive level. It argues that descriptive or amplifying interpretations can be respectful not only of negative ideas but of positive – or proto-positive – ideas, and that the latter can lead to emotional and cognitive growth (Music, 2009, 2011; Schore, 2003). It seems that the growing body of brain research suggests that certain forms of pleasure are both essential and good for brain development.

Psychoanalytic theories of frustration

Psychoanalytic theory has grown and expanded as clinical experience with each new type of patient has led to the stretching and partial breaking of moulds. Klein's additions to theory, for example, arose from her experience with very young children and with psychotic phenomena. It is reasonable to suggest that, at this present period in the history of psychoanalysis, child and adolescent psychotherapists may have some contribution to make to questions of theory. Their training in the study of early development and the observation of early parent–infant interaction, and their experience in recent decades (with patients whose level of disturbance, damage and, particularly, trauma and neglect goes far beyond that of those treated 50 years ago), afford much opportunity for the testing of theory against clinical evidence. Work with such patients, I believe, puts the emphasis in some psychoanalytic theories on frustration as the major impetus for learning to a severe test.

Psychoanalytic theorists from Freud onwards have asserted that it is the experiences of unpleasure that educate us and introduce us to 'reality'. In many of his writings – though by no means all (see Balint, 1968) – Freud (1911) pictured the baby as beginning life in a state of primary narcissism, pleasure and gratification, and only gradually learning the truth that he is lord and master of neither his mother nor the universe. Freud at first identified the heartbreak of Oedipal sexual disappointment as providing the first major encounter with truth (1905b), but later (1917) he added the pain and loss associated with weaning as an even earlier wake-up call. Winnicott (1960) – for all his passionate interest in the importance of play and the use of the imagination in developing creativity and, by implication, the mind – is nevertheless close to Freud's position in describing the earliest state of the baby as one of illusion, with necessary disillusionments as the source of awakening. Although neither Freud nor Winnicott explicitly linked this level of gratification or illusion with low levels of cognitive or intellectual functioning, the implication of the word 'illusion' seemed to be that the state is not a particularly mindful one. Melanie Klein (1952), on the other hand, insisted on the early presence of ego function in infancy. The explicit link of emotion with cognitive functioning, which began with Klein (1930) and Segal (1957), was developed much more boldly by Bion (1962b). Bion was the theorist who made the strongest link between frustration and something much more than the simple emotional facing of painful emotional realities – the process of learning and thinking itself. He made two crucial points: first, that a preconception had to meet with a realization for a conception to be born; and, second, that a conception had to meet with frustration for a thought to be born. (Interestingly, he wrote much more about the second stage than the first. It is also worth noting that his concept of the preconception *meeting with* a realization has some hints of the element of perfect fit implied in the theories of narcissism, symbiosis and illusion mentioned above.) In any case, Bion (1962b, p. 29) thought that real learning depended on the choice between techniques for evasion and techniques for modification of frustration. He links tolerance of frustration with the sense of reality. In this book, I argue that we also need to understand that some patients with impermeable or irreparable internal objects need a reality, which can be experienced as being modifi*able*. (And see Mitrani (1998) on the related issue of the object's role in containing aesthetic experience.)

Note, however, that Bion's second statement is much more than a refinement of Freud's view. It seems close to Freud's *Formulations of the Two Principles of Mental Functioning* (1911). Here, Freud suggested that it was the pressure of internal needs, followed by disappointment of their satisfaction, followed by the inadequacy of hallucinatory wish-fulfilling dreams to gratify those needs in any long-term way, that eventually drove the mental apparatus to *form a conception of* the real circumstances in the external world and to endeavour to make a real alteration in them. 'A new principle of mental functioning was thus introduced; what was presented in the mind was no longer what was agreeable but what was real, even if it happened to be disagreeable. This setting up of the reality principle proved to be a momentous step' (Freud, 1911, p. 219). Freud, however, was stressing the importance of emotionality in this development. Bion, in addition, concentrated on the nature of the processes involved in the mental apparatus's 'forming of conceptions'. He was asking: 'But what does this setting up of the reality principle involve?' He was talking not only about a change of emotional content but about something much more radical – the acquisition of thinking itself. Thus came the great intrinsic link between emotion and thought, then the theory of mindful emotional containment, and the theory of alpha function – the process by which thoughts become thinkable (Bion, 1962b).

It is impossible to overestimate the significance of this theory of thinking and its effect on clinical work and technique. Melanie Klein, of course, was the pioneer in this field, with her early paper on the development of symbol functioning in a young autistic child (1930). She and Isaacs (1948) emphasized the way all thoughts were filled with and fed by unconscious phantasy, and Segal's (1957) great work on the development of symbol functioning led to another huge step forward. However, their theories said little about whether there was thinking at the paranoid position (the implication of Segal's theory of symbolic equations, I think, is that it is a substitute for thinking). Bion, though, seems to have left room for the theory of thinking to be extended to even the illest or earliest of paranoid-schizoid levels. Alpha function could be considered to operate, that is, on only one thought (or beta-element) at a time at the simplest and least integrated of levels (Bion, 1962b, p. 35).

I have left a fuller discussion of Klein's theories to this point because I feel there is a central aspect of her theory that has been neglected by Bion in some of his emphasis on the importance of frustration for learning, and that in some of his statements (but not others: see Chapter 4) he took something of a backward step. Both Klein (1952, p. 76) and Segal (1964, p. 54) were careful to say that it was the *strength* of the ideal object and of the individual libidinal impulses that enabled the integration of persecutory object relations and thus the move from the paranoid-schizoid position to the depressive. This is a two-part, two-element, bi-polar theory. (See Appendix, Figure A2.) In a way, so too was Bion's: he had stated that, before conceptions met with frustration to produce thought, the preconceptions met with realizations to form conceptions (but for some reason this first stage of the process has received much less attention than the second). Child and adolescent psychotherapists see many deprived children and also some autistic children, in whom the conception of a good or interesting object barely exists. We therefore find ourselves working at the more basic level of preconceptions, and learning to be alert to very faint signals of hope or interest in the possibility of a good or interesting object, which may appear in the midst of the usual, indifferent, despairing, suspicious or cynical mood.

Klein (1932b) was famous for arguing – in her controversies with Anna Freud – for the *technical* importance of analysing the patients' deepest anxieties. Yet her actual theory of how people progressed from the paranoid-schizoid to the depressive position emphasized the struggle *between* love and hate and its outcome's dependence on the 'extent to which [the person] has been able *to take in and establish his good object which forms the core of his ego*' (Klein, 1957, p. 76; my italics). With some of our illest patients, it is that very taking in and establishment that is at issue and must be addressed in the treatment. Possibly it was the brilliance of Klein's recommendations on technique, together with her work on envy (1957) and on manic defences against depression (1935), which led to Bion's emphasis not only on the negative forces within the patient's self (1959), but on the importance for learning of the negative forces that the self faced. Spillius (1983, p. 324) has pointed out that in the 1950s and 1960s the Kleinian member-ship papers for admission to the British Psycho-analytical Society were inclined to 'emphasize the patient's destructiveness in a way that might have felt persecut-ing to the patient', but that destructiveness gradually began to be interpreted in a more balanced way. A similar balance is necessary, however, in the interpretation of the patient's sense of the badness or goodness in his object, and whether, when the material allows a choice (which it often does), we emphasize separations and separateness or reliable returns and a sense of connectedness. (The latter need not be described in symbiotic terms. See below on the alerting function of pleasurable experiences.)

When frustration is too great: the problem of 'terrible surprises'

I shall not give examples of the way in which frustration promotes learning, because this has been extremely well described and argued in the psychoanalytic literature and needs no further elucidation from me (Freud, 1920; O'Shaughnessy, 1964). I shall concentrate, instead, on situations where it reaches intolerable levels – where thinking is no longer possible. In a talk entitled 'The terrible surprise: the effect of trauma on a child's development', Helen Hand (1997) described how the death of a little boy's father in a car accident produced effects not only on his emotional life and his behaviour but on his thinking. His reactions to the trauma now had a life of their own, long after the event. The child could never finish a story; nor could he understand cause and effect. Despite the continuing loss, this was not a deprived child, but the sequelae were long term.

Many borderline traumatized children have suffered severe neglect (Music, 2009) as well as trauma, and the sense of good objects may be as weak as the sense of bad or abusive objects is strong. The strength of the good or ideal (Klein and Segal often use these terms interchangeably) object is exactly what cannot be taken for granted in the work. Dean, a severely neglected child of alcoholic parents who had spent the early months of his life in hospital with a succession of different carers, saw his mother fall dead in front of him when he was four. At the age of six he was a frantic, frenzied, violent child who seemed to be steadying a little as the early months of intensive treatment progressed. But when his therapist returned from the first long break, Dean said there were no cars in his box. She showed him that the cars he usually played with were still there. He replied, 'Oh, no, those are from a long time ago with another lady.' Separation and loss occurring in the context of an internal object with practically no constancy or substantiality can throw such children terribly. The damage is cognitive as well as emotional.

Perry *et al.* (1995) have shown the effects on the infant brain of early *psychological* trauma, and the subsequent preponderance of attention deficits and dissociative disorders in childhood and adolescence. And Van der Kolk (2009) is calling for a new diagnosis of 'Developmental Trauma Disorder' to be added to the fifth edition of the *Diagnostic and Statistical Manual of Mental Health Disorders*. Disturbance and disorder may be accompanied by delay and deficit in any or all aspects of the personality: in ego function, in the self and its sense of identity, and in the sense of the constancy of objects. When the disturbance is too great, thoughts about separation may become unthinkable until thoughts about reliable returns can grow. We have much to learn about the conditions under which our patients can begin to think these new thoughts. Patients returning after a holiday may not be in a well enough or integrated enough state to be struggling with feelings of missing or loss, as yet. They may have lost contact with any sense of a good or familiar object real enough to be missed. They may need help to find their good object again.

I happened to hear of several deprived, traumatized children who seemed to be confused and disorientated in their first session after the Christmas break. Reminders of the break and the separation seemed to make the situation worse, but alertness to the difficulty in feeling at home or finding something familiar in the room, or in the therapist, or in the child himself, seemed to help. Over-emphasis on interpretations about loss and separateness can sometimes serve to retraumatize such children. Alertness to tiny beginnings of feeling at ease, or comfortable, or safe – or difficulties in doing so – can help the child to get back in touch. Then, if the child is well enough, feelings of missing, loss or anger may begin to emerge. For other children, this second stage may take months to come.

One severely abused child, Joel, returned from the break very disorientated and closed off at the start of the session. A little while later, he became desperate to 'fit some pieces back together' in his play material. After much work on his difficulty in believing that he and his therapist, Judith Edwards, were really back together, and then some expression of his vicious fury, he calmed down a little and seemed somewhat more focused. He drew something, which he said looked like a fossilized feather. Edwards commented that it was interesting: you could see its softness but you could not feel it. (Note how slowly and delicately she approached his petrified softer feelings.) He then added, with a note of wonder in his voice, 'It must have been very protected for three hundred million years in Loch Ness!' Edwards then commented on its survival and theirs. A little later, Joel looked out the window and said delightedly, 'I can see a bluetit!' Here, one can see that the therapist's attention to Klein's 'deepest anxiety' emphasized at first the attention to the anxiety about *finding* an object. Only when Joel began to express his fury did she address the anxiety and anger about losing it. And, in the end, it seems that through both sets of interpretations Joel was helped to find and then secure the object that he had almost forgotten existed (Judith Edwards, personal communication, 2006).

Can some apparent 'defences' against frustration be seen rather as attempts to overcome or regulate frustration and disturbance?

Klein herself (1935) introduced the fundamental meta-theoretical differentiation between defences and overcomings in relation to reparative processes in the depressive position. She insisted that true reparation, unlike manic reparation, was not a reaction formation to guilt, but an *overcoming* of guilt. I have argued before (Alvarez, 1992, 1997) that we may also need this meta-concept of 'overcoming' for developments *within the paranoid-schizoid position*. What is at issue in the paranoid-schizoid position is the overcoming of outrage, fear and despair rather than of hatred, guilt and grief. If love has to be stronger than hate for hatred to be overcome in the depressive position, what, then, has to be stronger than fear to overcome, as opposed to defend against, persecutory anxieties? What enables outrage, fear or despair to be reduced so that good feelings can begin to emerge? Relief from overwhelming pressure of anxiety or frustration can initiate these healing processes, and notions such as Klein's good or ideal object that loves and protects the self (1957, p. 188). Sandler's (1960) 'background of safety', Bowlby's (1988) 'secure base', Winnicott's (1960) 'holding object' and many others suggest a way in which such relief from unbearable pressure may be obtained. (Note that these latter concepts of a 'safe' object are different from that of a 'good' object. In relatively secure children the sense of safety may be taken for granted to some extent and remain in the background, as it were, whereas the good object seems to live more in the foreground. Yet, when abused children begin to conceive of the notion of trustworthiness, they often seem to think hard about it. I think their developmental trajectories are very different from those of more protected children.) Trust in safety or goodness is not a defence; although, of course, it can be used defensively.

What I am suggesting is not new. Klein (1935) stated that idealization and splitting could be used in the service of development, and Bion's concept of projective identification as a needed communication makes the same point (1962b). The use of such apparently 'defensive' processes can therefore be seen to enable new introjections to take place under conditions that should be described as protective rather than defensive. A surge of hope or pride, or a sudden feeling of relief, is different from a manic state used as a defence. A recovery is not a denial, though it may be accompanied by denial.

In Chapter 6 I will give several clinical examples illustrating the way apparent defensive activities may contain *within* them – not simply *behind* them or *underneath* them – deep, underlying needs and healthy, developmental strivings, but a single one will have to suffice here. A profoundly fragmented little boy called Adam, filled with bitter self-loathing, had very little capacity to play. He had had a difficult birth to an extremely depressed mother. Eventually, after two years of treatment, he began to play a game in which he was a friendly but placating little puppy scrambling about at his therapist's feet on the floor. A little while before the Christmas break he directed the therapist to open her travel suitcase, where she was to find a wonderful surprise – a puppy! When she suggested it might imply that he felt he was to be like a new baby for her, Adam could not let it be a baby. He insisted – with some horror – that it was just a puppy, and it seemed clear that he was not ready to surface as *homo erectus*. The therapist learned simply to describe her joy and delight at being given the puppy. By the next Christmas break, the suitcase contained a baby. In the meantime, there had been much work on Adam's feelings of shame and his inability to believe he could *bring* pleasure as a human infant, as well as on his own rather miserly and stubborn unwillingness to give pleasure, which was also marked. It seemed that he was finally able to rewrite internally his birth history and instruct the therapist to welcome him with surprise and delight. At this period, Adam was not denying his birth history; he was rewriting it symbolically (Segal, 1957). That is, the birth phantasy did not seem to be being used as a manic defence against frustrating and cruel truths. Instead, it involved, I think, the beginnings of the construction and establishment of the positive relationship between mother and baby on which all sanity, hope and ego strength depend. I do not think Adam was 'wishing' that his therapist would not or did not leave him at Christmas; I think he was beginning to develop a phantasy of an object that would want him back *after* Christmas. Such phantasies may succeed in giving form and structure to the meeting of a rightful need, not the denial of disappointment in the form of a defensive or denying wish.

Pleasure, safety and delight as necessary to emotional health

Klein (1940, p. 388) writes,

> the shaken belief in good objects disturbs most painfully the process of idealization which is an essential intermediate step in mental development. With the young child, the idealized mother is the safeguard against a retaliating or a dead mother and against all bad objects and therefore represents security and life itself.

Klein is describing how hatred can shake such belief, but we know now that abuse can, too. Chronic doses of terror, pain and despair in young children almost always interfere with normal psychological development and may produce developmental arrest and deficit in the capacity to love, enjoy and feel self-respect; and in the quality of the superego and internal objects. That is, the positive side of the patient's personality may be just as *under*developed as the persecutory side is *over*developed. (See Appendix, Figure A2.) What is at issue is not simply marked splitting between ideal and persecutory or between good and bad (with the implication that both sides of the personality and the world of internal objects are well developed) but *lack of development of the good self and the good objects.* When Klein (1957, p. 188) wrote that a good object that loves and protects the self and is loved and protected by the self is the basis for trust in one's own goodness, she was stressing the infant's libidinal investment in its first external object, and the way in which envy could interfere with this. When we are working with seriously deprived children whose external objects have been unable to receive these loving projections, we often get a sense that the children have given up and we have to work, as it were, from both ends: that is, from the problem of the inhibition in the child's love or failure of his trust, and from that of the internal object's incapacity to like or care for the child. 'You can hardly believe that we are back together' or '. . . that I have returned when I said I would'; 'It is hard for you to believe that I intend to return on 4 January' or '. . . that 4 January will ever come'; 'You are beginning to like coming here' can be accompanied by 'You felt

I liked you when you did that' or '. . . when that happened'; 'You are beginning to feel that I care what happens to you': all of these are ways of addressing what the child does or does not invest in his object, but also what he feels his object does or does not invest in him. For such patients, the process of the introjection of the ideal object and the building up of a sense of the loving or lovable self is long and slow, yet it is vital to mental health. The therapist may address issues of the positive transference and the child's beginning hope of or belief in a positive countertransference without indulging in sentimentality, collusion or seduction. Strong countertransferences of a maternal or paternal nature need delicate handling but need not lead to implied false promises. Fear of implying that we will really adopt the child can sometimes lead to denial and inhibition on the part of the therapist and contribute to further despair where the child experiences the inhibition as rejection. Acknowledgement that someone *should* be adopting him, or that we *should* not be leaving him for a holiday at this moment, need not be done collusively. Yet such acknowledgement can be very different from interpreting to a despairing child that he 'wishes' we would not leave him. The interpretation of rightful need can strengthen the ego of a despairing child. An interpretation of a vain wish can weaken the ego and increase despair.

Pleasurable states as active, accompanied by thought and provoking of thought

Pleasurable states of mind have too often been described in psychoanalysis as passive, using images of adaptation, gratification, fit and symbiosis, which imply a somewhat sleepy, mindless state (Mahler, 1968; Winnicott, 1960). When the child is used to a daily diet of negative states, new experiences of a therapist's return, constancy, reliability and durability can be actively alerting, interesting and thought-provoking. These experiences take place *in the presence of* an object. When these states can be digested, they may promote *mental* development and learning. Klein wrote of the importance of building up a good object for emotional life, but it is clear, I think, that combining this idea with Bion's somewhat neglected concept of 'realization' leads to the conclusion that positive experiences are as essential for mental as for emotional life. Klein herself (1952) said that the baby took in understanding along with the milk. I would go further than Bion and say that positive experiences of a live object are not purely 'realizing' in the gratifying or symbiotic sense. I am sure, however, that they 'feel right' but in a vitalizing, not a sleep-inducing, way. (Because Bion wrote so little about this part of his theory, I am not sure if he really implied mindless gratification and fit, but I think the concept has a flavour of a 'perfect fit', with reality and thought coming in only when frustration and absence make their appearance.) Yet positive factors can be alerting because they are *interesting*: Bion (1962b) posited 'K', the desire to get to know someone, as additional to 'L', the need to love, and 'H', hatred. But maybe K should be seen as *a part of* L, not only of H. In normal development, pleasing surprises are just as alerting as nasty surprises. It is the element of surprise, of unexpectedness, that may evoke delight, reflection and meta-reflection. And this may take place in the presence of an object that is human and alive.

Infant observation and infant research (and Klein's theory, by the way) teach us that there are very few perfect fits, even when objects are present and gratifying. Because the object is alive and mobile, its presence is just as demanding and alerting as its departure and absence. Arrivals and returns are alerting, but so is the simple experience of looking at the mother's or father's face during a proto-conversation. The mobile and expressive features, the widening, brightening, narrowing and dulling eyes, the changing tonal qualities and structuring as the parent speaks and responds all demand attention. As Stern (1985), Trevarthen and Hubley (1978) and Beebe and Lachmann (1994) have shown, a live human being, *when present*, offers a complex, varied and *constantly changing presence*, full of dynamic flows and temporal shapes. It may be pleasurable, but in a demanding way. According to Schore (2003, p. 81), face-to-face communication between mother and infant evokes opiates (happy feelings of comfort) but also dopamine, arousal and elation. (Panksepp (1998) suggests that the dopamine system is connected with seeking and curiosity.)

I do not agree, therefore, with Bion and Freud that it is *primarily* through frustration, absence, separation and separateness that reality makes its appearance and thought is born. Modulation and regulation of presence is a task for the infant – a mental as well as an emotional task – that is probably prior to the one of maintaining object constancy throughout absence. Introjection is often hard work, and surely introjection of experience has to precede a more durable internalization and representation. I think the question of introjection of experience is a subject that has not been sufficiently studied in psychoanalysis. Preconceptions need to meet with realizations, but this 'meeting' is a living, dynamic, imperfect 'articu-lated' link (Bion, 1957a) – not a static one. I am suggesting, therefore, that concep-tions are thoughts, too – that making a thought thinkable can occur even around delightful or joyful thoughts. When Leontes, in Shakespeare's *The Winter's Tale*, discovers that his supposedly dead wife is not a statue but a living being, he gasps, 'Oh, she's warm!' (Act V, Scene 3). Although this is a story about a man in the winter of his life emerging from deepest despair, I think such experiences happen regularly to tiny infants, too. They are processing what Stern (1983) calls the 'slow momentous discovery' of connectedness.

Babies, that is, *think about* present objects when they study their caregiver's smiling face, for example, or savour the taste of the milk or how the breast feels to their hand. It is a fascinating moment when babies begin to explore with their eyes, and then with their hand, the very breast they had previously known mostly by mouth. One ten-year-old adopted girl who had been raised in an orphanage in a third world country, said, musingly, to her therapist (to whom she was becoming very attached), 'Why are you called Jane?' A little later, she briefly stroked the fuzzy shoulder of the therapist's cardigan and asked, softly, 'Why is it so fuzzy?' The language she was using and the question – 'why?' – were those of a ten-year-old, but in reality I think she was doing what a baby does when he explores his mother's or father's face with his eyes or hands, getting to know, reflectively and cognitively, as well as emotionally, not the whyness of his parents, but the what-ness, the isness.

There are many different versions of the present object, and that fact in itself is extremely demanding. Wolff (1965) found that babies showed intellectual curiosity not when they were hungry or tired, but when they were well fed, rested and comfortable. Their curiosity was not driven by frustration; it was freed by satisfaction and good internalizations. Alpha function, I maintain, operates on present and pleasurable objects. Introjection of good objects precedes the inter-nalization of which the great Polish dissident poet Zbigniew Herbert (1999) wrote that good memory heals the scar after departure. I am arguing that where there are no good memories and where thinking and memory are impaired, there is no healing.

Conclusion

As I said, I am not suggesting an alternative to previous ideas about how learn-ing of reality takes place. I am arguing only for a fuller picture, for an addition. Oedipal frustration, oral frustration, the absence of the object, separation, bound-aries and separateness are all alerting experiences. Links between different versions of a present object, however, have to be built alongside those concerning absent objects. That the object can reappear slightly before you expected it to do so – or, indeed, that it can appear *at all* – and that it changes its form from micro-moment to micro-moment are intrinsic parts of its aliveness and need just as much processing as its capacity to leave whenever it wishes. In some patients, the texture, feel, sound and look of a kind or good object may be being introjected for what amounts to the first time. Such moments need delicate handling in our tech-nique, and this need not lead to sentimentalization, collusion or the encouragement of manic defences. They are the stuff of what Freud and Klein called libidinal – and what they and we would also call a loving – life.

Chapter 6

Moral imperatives and rectifications in work with tormented and despairing children

Wishes or needs?

Introduction

In Chapter 1 I described the disabled girl in the wheelchair who needed to try on the identity of a healthy person while seeing someone else experience despair and bitterness on her behalf. She seemed to feel her fate was unfair – it ought to be someone else's. This chapter elaborates this issue by distinguishing between the grammar of wishes in neurotic states of mind and the grammar of imperative needs in borderline paranoid states of mind. It presents material from work with a borderline psychotic ten-year-old boy, Richard, who was in intensive treatment with me in the late 1960s. I began reading over his material one summer in the late 1980s and was very distressed by what I read and how I had worked two decades earlier.

In the interim, the impact of Bion's (1962b) extension of Klein's (1946) concept of projective identification, and the consequent implications for technique explored by Rosenfeld (1987), Joseph (in Spillius and Feldman, 1989) and others, had begun to make a tremendous difference to the work with these patients. I had used a technique with Richard that was uninformed by these developments, full of explanatory uncovering interpretations, and more appropriate to work with neurotic patients. For a period, I believe, it was positively harmful to him. The technique had elements of an unmasking quality designed to reveal the depression and loss that underlay what I thought of then as his manic, omnipotent and paranoid defences. Now I think that these so-called 'defences' were actually desperate attempts to *overcome* and *recover from* states of despair and terror. They carried, that is, elements of basic developmental needs: for protection, preservation, a sense of agency and potency, and even revenge and justice. Richard was full of violence, bitterness and persecution. However, unlike patients who have a more psychopathic accompaniment to their borderline problems, he was filled with violence rather than dedicated to it or excited by it. (With certain traumatized patients who have witnessed or been exposed to violence, and who erupt blindly, I would not nowadays necessarily want to say, 'You did it,' or 'You want to do it.' It might be better to say, 'It is *in you* to do it,' to take account of the depersonalization that may accompany internalization of trauma.) Also, unlike neurotic patients, Richard had little ego functioning. His 'defences' were inadequate to manage his overpowering feelings. He needed, for example, to be able to project, to split and certainly to repress and forget. I shall consider the difference between a desire in the neurotic patient that things *could* be, or *could have* been, otherwise, and a desperate need in certain borderlines that things *should* be, or *should have* been, otherwise.

Developments in psychoanalytic theory

The major theoretical change to which I am referring concerns ideas about the purpose of, and motives for, projective identification processes. (It has some areas of overlap with the reformulations of Sandler and Anna Freud (1985), Kohut (1985) and Stolorow and Lachmann (1980) on the difference between ordinary defences and early structurings, protective manoeuvres, or pre-stages of defence.) Racker (1952, cited by himself in 1968) had emphasized that countertransference was the expression of the analyst's identification with not only the id and ego of the patient but also his internal objects, and should be used as such. Bion (1962b) also made the connection between countertransference and projective identification when he pointed out that the psychoanalyst may play the part of the patient's lost self not only in the patient's mind but in his own mind. That is, the patient may project so powerfully that he may not only feel his analyst is frightened or depressed – he may *make him become* frightened or depressed. But in the 1950s, and even into the early 1960s, Bion (1957b) and others were still describing the projective identification as arising from destructive or defensive and pathological motives. Bion (1962b) then went further: his concept of the analyst as receptacle or container of these projections began to carry the implication that the receptacle could be inadequate, sometimes making the patient project even harder. (Grotstein (1981b) has pointed out that this introduced the concept of deficit in the object long before Kohut (1977).) Bion (1962b) suggested that some projective identifications expressed a *need to communicate something to someone* on a very profound level: he compared the analyst's 'containment' and 'transformation' (1965) of the patient's feelings and thoughts to the primitive but powerful pre-verbal communications that take place between mothers and tiny infants. This, he suggested, is how feelings become bearable and thoughts become thinkable. This, in a way, more democratic, two-person psychology leaves room for either term in the equation to affect the interactions. There is more room in such a model for the object, *ex*ternal or *in*ternal, to have an impact on the system. (For a full discussion of developments in psychoanalytic thinking about children with borderline psychotic problems, see Lubbe (2000).)

Technical implications of developments in psychoanalytic theory

The technical implications of this increased attention to inadequacies of the object have been profound. Rosenfeld (1987) emphasized the dangers of interpretations to borderlines that over-valued the analyst's contribution. He stressed the importance of the healthy forces that could lie in resistances, and of not breaking down idealization too quickly. Money-Kyrle (1947) thought the issue of distinguishing a desperate projective identification from a destructive one a matter of great technical urgency. Joseph has spent a lifetime working on this problem (see Spillius and Feldman, 1989, *passim*). She has expanded the notion of the communicative use of projective identification both technically and theoretically, and has drawn attention to how very pressuring projections may include a need to communicate something that may require lengthy containment and exploration in the analyst, and should not be returned too prematurely to the patient. It is often better for the analyst to hold and explore the experience in himself – for example, 'You feel I am stupid' (without adding that it is the patient's projection of his own feeling of stupidity). Joseph (1978) points out that the patient may need to feel that you are willing to carry the projections long enough to experience the missing part of the patient or else, she adds, to experience his previously unexamined internal object. A disappointing or fragile parental object, say, whose weakness has always been denied, may need gradual uncovering, not explaining away – a move one could describe as from a grammar of explanation to a grammar of description. Steiner (1993) raises the issue at length in his discussion of analyst-centred versus patient-centred interpretations.

Bion (1962b) stressed the normalcy of the need for a container of such communications as a very early infantile human need to be in the company of a mindful mind. An implication is that these emotions communicated are not necessarily emotions the patient wants rid of – they may be emotions that he needs his object to have on his behalf. They may be emotions he needs to explore in the therapist and only gradually to own himself. Furthermore, I am stressing in this book that these need not be negative emotions. Positive states of mind can be conveyed, however confusedly and crazily, through this process of unconscious communication just as powerfully as can Bion's earlier examples of fear and murderousness. Bion said that the psychotic has pain but does not suffer it; one might add that the psychotic also has pleasure but does not enjoy it. As I argued in the previous chapter, preconceptions need turning into conceptions in both areas for normal development to proceed.

The grammar of projective identification: technique with wishes versus needs

I now wish to explore the idea that such unconscious projective communications may, like more ordinary verbal communications, have a grammar. This grammar's variations may bear some correspondence to where the patient is on the neurotic/psychotic continuum – that is, to his level of ego development, and also to the level of urgency and desperation of his needs. Both the neurotic and borderline child may boast in a manic or grandiose manner, or protest and complain of injustice. We may be pressured to admire or sympathize. The countertransference may be similar in both cases, but the motivation of the child may be vastly different in the two situations. In fact, we may be driven to be even more unmasking with the borderline child whose immaturity may make his boasts sound ridiculous and silly. Yet our interpretive response needs to be carefully structured in grammatical terms, which take account of the difference between a desire for omnipotence and a need for potency (Alvarez, 1992). The normal or neurotic child may wish or even demand that things be otherwise, but he can just about bear to acknowledge the way things really are in external reality and in his own heart. He can usually juggle and compare two realities (Stern, 1985), manage a dual perspective (Susan Reid, personal communication, 1988) or binocular vision (Bion, 1950), and two-tracked 'thinking in parentheses' (Bruner, 1968). He can hold a thought in reserve, consider the thought within the thought, and the thought beyond the thought. He can manage meta-cognitive processes (Main, 1991) and self-reflective functions (Fonagy *et al.*, 1991) and some degree of symbolic functioning (Segal, 1957). Borderline patients, on the other hand (in their psychotic moments, that is), are concrete, one-tracked, overwhelmed by the singularity of their state of mind, in danger of symbolic equations and massive splitting and projection. Are *we* in danger of producing premature integrations when we refuse to stay with their urgent imperative single-minded states? Could it even be that there is, at certain very early stages of emotional development, a need for something like a symbolic equation, the nearly perfect fit? It is important to add that these moments need not be seen as mindless – the balance between pleasurable opioids and elating dopamines in the brain may vary from moment to moment, but neither need involve sleepy, mindless states.

There has been much work by developmentalists on how the baby's mind grows, how intersubjectivity becomes internalized as intrasubjectivity (Stern, 1985; Trevarthen and Hubley, 1978). It is a fascinating moment when autistic or other mindless children begin to discover that they like doing something, then that they *like liking* doing it (First, 2001). (When they go further and finally get a dual perspective – for example, that there are two different ways of looking at the same toy – language and pretend play can begin.) Mothers follow their babies' direction of gaze long before babies begin to follow their mothers' (Collis, 1977). Infant observation shows us time and again the way in which mothers light up as they see what has caught a baby's glance – 'Oh, it's the movement of the tree!' Both developmentalists and psychoanalytic observers seem to agree that if a mind is to grow, it requires a meeting of minds and not too many 'missteps in the dance' (Stern, 1977) between infant and caregiver. But also not too few – mismatch, disillusion and separateness are fundamental to learning about reality (Beebe and Lachmann, 2002; Hopkins, 1996; Tronick, 2007). Yet the balance between match and mismatch in our interpretive work needs to be carefully tuned to the developmental level at which – and the emotional state in which – the child patient is functioning at any given moment. Easier said than done!

This brings me back to grammar and the question of levels of interpretation. I am suggesting that interpretations that stress separateness and difference from ideal objects or ideal self – that is, those that make use of the language of wishes and wants – may be appropriate for patients with some ego development, some sense of trust in their objects and some sense of worth in themselves. However great their anxieties, angers and depressions, such patients have sufficient ego equipment with which to examine the gaps in the fabric of the universe. In Latin a verb containing doubt (you wish, you fear, you think, you hope and so on) would be followed by the subjunctive or conditional. 'I may go' is weaker than 'I am going' or 'I will go'. The language of 'You wish but we both know that you cannot [or did not, or will not]' is tolerable where the real alternative is just bearable. I found that if I said, 'You are afraid that you will die without me on the weekend,' the neurotic patient could hear the implications and the alternative possibilities implied in such statements (i.e. that he probably would not die). From his dual perspective and capacity for two-tracked thinking, he can think about both more or less at once.

I learned to my cost that the borderline patient often cannot do this. His panics, and even his manic denials, may express a need for us to understand that he should have – that is, he has a rightful need of – assurance, safety, protection and even justice. He may need to hear something along the lines of 'It's hard for you to imagine that you might make it through till Monday' or 'You feel I should not be leaving you at this time.' This need not involve collusion or seduction or false promises. (See Kut Rosenfeld and Sprince (1965), of what is now the Anna Freud Centre, on the ease with which interpretation of anxiety can escalate anxiety in borderlines.) The child's rightful need for assurance needs understanding, and, except under the most dire of emergency conditions, reassurance should not be necessary. Interpretations of anxiety or loss to an already despairing child can weaken him. Other grammars, the grammar of imperatives, may enable his ego to grow stronger.

The patient and my unmasking interpretations

Richard was referred to me in spring 1967 when he was ten years old. The referring psychiatrist found him a very mad boy with a suspicious, strained appearance and bizarre hand gestures, as though warding off blows to the head. Richard's mother had been diagnosed with manic-depressive psychosis, and had beaten him often when he was a baby. She left abruptly when Richard was 18 months old and his younger brother was four months. She had visited very seldom since then. When Richard came to me he was not learning much in a special school. After his mother left, he had lived with his paternal grandmother for a few months, then with his father and a nanny to whom he was very attached. When the nanny left, Richard's paternal grandmother moved up to the father's house to take care of the children. Father and grandmother were very kind and intelligent people, but very genteel, and I suspect they would have found it difficult to take the grief, horror and outrage that was in Richard, had it ever displayed itself when he was an infant. His aunt, a warm and sensible woman, also had a hand in the children's care. I started seeing Richard twice a week; then, because of his high level of damage and disturbance, we soon increased to four times per week.

I will go through the early sessions in some detail. It may seem a rather masochistic and pedantic exercise – because I was pretty green at the time and the work is not good for many reasons – but I want to look at the grammar and the theoretical and technical implications behind the grammar, so I hope the reader will forgive the piecemeal approach.

There were painters in my house when we started. In the first session, Richard went on past the playroom door, encountering one of the workmen, who kindly showed him the way. Richard was a blond, blue-eyed, slightly plump boy with a very robotic walk. Every step was placed extremely cautiously, as though he were walking blindfolded. He looked terrified but, after a few comments from me and explanations about the therapy, he looked at the wall and said, 'I know what that is; that's paint.' A little later, he said, 'That's a wall!' Later, when he seemed frightened by a noise from the workmen upstairs, he asked, 'Why are they here? Is the house all in bits?'

After a while, he seemed a little less frightened and began to paint in big, sweeping strokes – rather like the painters upstairs. I said that he was now painting like the workmen, and perhaps he was showing me how he would like to be able to paint like those grown-ups. I added that perhaps he often wanted to do what Daddy could do. He said (with it all pouring out in a jumble, the words and thoughts tumbling over each other), 'Yes I do, I do want to, but I *do* work, this is what I *do*, you see!'

I invite you to note my interpretation: 'You *would like to be able* to paint . . .' Also note his desperate correction. I took it as an omnipotent defensive identification, a desire, but could he actually have been communicating a desperate need to be seen by me as being capable of being, or at least of becoming like, a potent and reparative father? I think he may have experienced my interpretation, and many subsequent similar ones, as a crushing reminder of lifelong impotence and maybe lifelong humiliation. He had, after all, been abandoned by two caregivers and beaten by one. Supposing I had said, 'Well, I think I should notice that you can paint too, not so differently from those fellows upstairs'?

Later, when he had calmed down a little, he gave a slightly nervous start after some more noises. I interpreted that he was still frightened, and he said, 'No, I'm not scared. David [his brother] gets scared.' I took it that he was using David to be the scared one in order not to be the scared one himself. I added that, after all, this was a strange place and I was a new person to him. But there had been a general calming down, which I could have underlined by seeing the fear split off into David not as a projection and split, which should be returned and reintegrated, but as something that needed acknowledging and respecting. That is, I could have said something like 'Now you are feeling a bit less scared and you can think of someone else as the scared one.' That is, I could have registered the other half of the split – the *non-scared* half. I also could have acknowledged even earlier that he felt, 'At least I recognize something in this madhouse – that's paint and that's a wall.' Splitting and projection have healthy functions, not only pathological ones. The need and the ability to put one's fear at a distance are not only defensive. They may permit the development of a little trust, and therefore preserve and protect a tiny bit of ego growth. (See Appendix, Figure A3.)

Anyway, Richard went on to explain that it was his conscience that made him scared and then, out of the blue, reassured us both that he hadn't broken Granny's alarm clock. I linked the clock with the feeling of my house being all in bits, and thought that maybe there was a feeling inside him that something was all in bits, but he didn't know what it was. (I was finally not rushing to over-explain!) At last, he began to relax. He took out the glue, looking through his box. Then he said, disappointed, 'But there's nothing to mend!' I wonder now if he was talking there about his tragic situation where there was not a reparable container: the mad, violent mother was not only in bits; she was gone. Also, I had all those painters upstairs and probably wasn't felt to be sufficiently here *for him*. Here, I think one is faced with deficit in the internal object, which needs addressing just as much as the conflicts and defences toward more highly developed objects. This means letting the transference rewrite history for the patient and not rushing to remind him of irreparable painful reality. Perhaps I needed to let him feel he could be like – or could become like – the painters upstairs.

In the second session Richard feared it would be shorter, and he was delighted when I told him it would be just as long, and that maybe he hadn't liked the wait between sessions. He agreed eagerly and said he liked things with no end, for ever and ever. I – I am sorry to say – then began to talk about his mother. I said I knew his mother didn't live with them now and asked if he saw her. He said, in a panicky voice, 'Yes, for ever.' I said I wondered if he wanted to feel it was for ever because he felt it was too sad if it was not. He felt he must have a forever mummy, just as he felt he should have a forever Mrs Alvarez, not just a two-times-a-week Mrs Alvarez. There, although probably under pressure from my countertransference feeling of terrible pain for him, I did convey some understanding of his needs, but I think I was still using an unmasking model. I treated the insistence on foreverness as a defence against sadness, instead of seeing it as a rightful need for continuity. Second, by introducing painful and irreparable external reality at the point when Richard arrived with some hope of a new internal reality via the transference, I pushed him back down into panicky despair and rejected him. At the beginning of the exchange, I could have said something like 'You like the feeling that this treatment is going to go on for a long time – a nice forever feeling.' The infant part of the personality needs a sense of the duration and durability of good experience before it can learn to tolerate interruptions and endings. Grotstein (1983) points out you have to be bonded before you can be weaned.

In the seventh session, Richard told me about a hallucination of a terrible cogwheel spinning round and drilling into his head, and seeing the clock with all its inner workings falling out. I again linked this with his mother and me, and in later sessions began to take up his fear that he had bunged up his mother's works and mine. In fact, I became pregnant twice in the course of his treatment and he showed more and more of a powerfully intrusive sexuality and got more and more into the idea of enjoying destroying my 'works'; and, over the years, of murdering babies. I and others saw this clock in bits, or the drilling cogwheel, as a destroyed object that he felt he had created as a result of his attacks. He conveyed that his other nightmare or delusion was that 'Mother Goose died of grief because she produced a rotten egg.' This was the late 1960s and early 1970s, when the full impact of Bion's ideas about containment had not yet been explored. It was easy to see Richard's increasing sadism as having been freed to come more into the open. In part, this was true, but I did not understand the degree to which it was driven by desperation about an irreparable object, and how my interpretations escalated this by seeming to accuse him of being totally responsible for this state of affairs. I think there was an idea around, which was a parody of Klein, that people got the bad objects they deserved: that is, that an internal bad, violent object became so due to the projections of violent phantasies emanating from the self of the patient. Richard did become less frightened and less psychotic (his hallucinations disappeared), but he also became violent and full of sadistic phantasies. I think I could have helped him to develop restraint far sooner if I had conveyed that I understood his object to have some responsibility for being in bits. (I do not think this would have helped if the apparent psychopathic element had been genuine.) If I had helped him to explore his mad, irreparable and violent internal object, I might have reduced his guilt, rather than increased it. Had I explored the object in whom there was nothing to mend, I might have allowed his preconception of a reparable object (which was clearly there in his reference to its lack) to grow, and also his capacity to identify with a repairing father.

There were periods when his desperation and hatred knew no bounds, such as when he sang bitterly, 'Gotta get a message to you,' and then took faeces from his bottom and shoved it up his nose. Another time, he said, 'I've just got to make you shed tears and then I'll stop.' I did not see this as a rightful need to project and communicate his horrors – I continued to take it as sadism – but at times I was overwhelmed with pity and despair, and so perhaps I shared and contained something. He did begin to learn at school, but became obsessed with phantasies of murdering small animals; indeed, he did kill one or two. I interpreted sadism and jealousy, instead of revenge and a sense of terrible betrayal. After all, I had two babies in the first four years of his treatment, and his real mother had really betrayed his trust.

He complained that I did not know what it was like to be near a light bulb that is about to explode. He was right – I was not getting the message. But I did begin to observe that some of my interpretations seemed to make him even more disturbed. Eventually, after four years' interrupted treatment, I took his material for supervision to Sydney Klein, who was very influenced by Bion. Dr Klein said that I was persecuting Richard with my interpretations about his sadism. Richard's sadism to babies began to reduce. Within three months, he was able to talk about the coming break in a very different way. He sang 'Jesus Loves Me' very sweetly (not in a syrupy way), and spoke about a man on a rope crossing Niagara Falls to

Canada. (He knew I was Canadian.) There is not space to go into his goody-goody voice – which in the beginning I saw as denying his hatred but which I finally came to understand also masked real love. In the last two years of his six years' (interrupted) treatment, he became far more collected, together and civilized. However, it is still painful for me to read the earlier notes.

Discussion: four considerations

I shall discuss four considerations that I now think may be important in the treatment of certain paranoid borderline patients in whom the psychopathic element is not marked. These are only considerations, because the complexity of the human mind, even the child psychotic mind, ensures that there can be no manual: the patient can move back and forth between neurotic and psychotic levels of functioning – or from a three-day-old infant to a six-month-old infant to a ten-year-old child – in the course of a few seconds, and the level of work needs to change accordingly. So, although I shall speak about a certain type of paranoid borderline as forming a group, it is clear that this is an over-simplification. Also, the stress on grammar is a way of thinking about (structuring my own understanding of) such patients – there is, of course, no magic in the words themselves. If we get the emotional understanding right, our patients forgive us the grammar.

Developmental delay

The first point is that psychotic illness in children – however temporary or however much only a threat from beyond the border – almost always interferes with normal psychological development and produces developmental arrest and deficit. Disturbance and disorder may be accompanied by delay and deficit in any or all aspects of the personality: in ego function; in the self and its sense of identity, its capacity to love, to enjoy and to feel self-respect; and in the superego and internal objects. The positive side of the patient's personality may be just as *under*-developed as the persecutory side is *over*developed. (See Appendix, Figure A3.) There have always been clear developmental implications in the assertion by Klein (1952) and Segal (1964) that it was the *strength* of the ideal object and of the individual libidinal impulses that enabled the integration of persecutory object relations and thus the move from the paranoid-schizoid position to the depressive. In many borderline children, however, this strength is exactly what cannot be taken for granted. The process of the introjection of the ideal object and the building up of a sense of the loving or lovable self is long and slow, yet it is vital to mental health. Splitting and projective identification can be seen to be in the service of development rather than as a defence, because they may enable new introjections to take place under conditions that should be described as protective rather than defensive.

I am sorry to say that I believe that, for many years, my work with Richard may have interfered with this introjective process. As I have shown, I often interpreted tiny increments in the belief in an ideal self (him as painter) or an ideal object (a forever mummy), or attempts to split or project badness off into someone else (David, who was scared, or the me who should cry), as defences against persecution and despair. I now believe they could be seen as tiny developmental moves: that is, as attempts to overcome, rather than defend against, persecution and despair. A surge of hope or pride, or a sudden feeling of relief, is different from a manic state used as a defence. A recovery is not a denial, though, of course, it may be accompanied by denial. In certain profoundly depressed children, apparently grandiose, omnipotent boasts, which seem like manic assertions, in fact communicate *a highly tentative question* about whether or not the object could see them as potent. Not all ill-fitting shoes are stolen: some are simply new and need wearing in. But it is unfortunately evident that in the late 1960s – prior to the technical impact of Bion's work, and prior to Sydney Klein's help – I was suffering from an either–or mentality, where the shoes are either yours or mine.

The distinction between defences and overcomings in the paranoid position

Melanie Klein (1935) introduced the fundamental meta-theoretical differentiation between defences and overcomings in relation to reparative processes in the depressive position. As I have said previously, she insisted that true reparation, unlike manic reparation, was not a reaction formation to guilt, but an overcoming of guilt. I would add that we may also need this meta-concept of 'overcoming' for developments *within the paranoid-schizoid position.* At issue in this position is the overcoming of fear and despair, rather than of guilt and grief. If love has to be stronger than hate for hatred to be overcome in the depressive position, what has to be stronger than fear to overcome, rather than to defend against, persecutory anxieties? What enables fear or despair to be reduced so that good feelings can begin to emerge? Relief from overwhelming pressure of anxiety can initiate such healing processes, and notions such as Bion's (1962b) concept of the containing functions of the maternal object, Sandler's (1960) 'background of safety', Bowlby's (1988) 'secure base' and many others outline a major way in which such relief from unbearable pressure may be obtained.

Rectification: imperative phantasies of vengeance

This idea involves an elaboration of Joseph's (1978) point about holding and exploring projective identifications in ourselves rather than returning them prematurely. In this instance I am referring to the moments when the patient may be projecting – or rather externalizing – not a part of the self but an internal object of an extremely bad kind. A psychotic adolescent boy wanted to strangle a seductive but patronizing woman relative. Interpretations of his hatred and anger seemed to escalate them. Interpretations of the fact that he felt *she deserved death for the way she treated him*, however, seemed to calm him rather than turn him into a homicidal maniac. This involves important and often dangerous questions of whether we push it all on to the patient with a 'you' interpretation or let it be contained elsewhere in us or even in some other object. The relieving, calming effect seems to have to do with an understanding that badness needs *to stay out there*. Otherwise, humiliation, despair, shame and revenge can lead to explosive and dangerous eruptions in patients who may have been very heavily projected into.

Kundera, in his novel *The Joke* (1982, p. 229), pointed out that there are two kinds of rectification – forgiveness and vengeance. He describes how a person's whole inner balance may be disturbed when a lifelong object of deserved hatred innocently avoids your plan for revenge and decides to make friends with you and cease to be hateful. (He was referring to a friend who betrayed him and had him sent to a labour camp for *fifteen* years.) He asks, 'How would I explain I couldn't make peace with him? . . . How would I explain I used my hatred to balance out the weight of the evil I bore as a youth? . . . How would I explain I *needed* to hate him?' This kind of desperate, embittered hatred has to be carefully distinguished from the aggression of the more casually brutal, or more coldly murderous, psychopath who, of course, could experience such interpretations as collusion. (See Chapter 7 on this issue.) Understanding desperate hatred and desire for revenge certainly should not imply colluding with acting upon such phantasies, but it can show understanding of the rightful need to have them.

Further rectifications: justice and other moral imperatives

I have suggested that the different kinds of pressure patients put us under carry different underlying grammatical forms and require a different grammar of interpretation. Phantasies may not only be about wishes and imperative demands, but about that which may be, that which could be, or can be (hope and possibility), that which will be (confidence and conviction, not necessarily omniscience) and that which should be (justice). (See the important paper by Anna Fitzgerald (2009).) The sense of justice involves a different kind of imperative from the psychopathic bullying imperative, but it is, nevertheless, an imperative. Where there is little ego to start with and perhaps a cruel, depriving superego, the interpretive grammar of wishes may carry all-too-cruel implications; rather than help the child to think about deprivation, it succeeds in depriving him further. Rather than allowing him to begin to identify with ideal objects, we may be perpetuating the 'disidentifications' (Sandler, 1988).

We may therefore need a different grammar, a grammar of rightful need, one that allows a good object and a good self to grow. I heard one wild, demented borderline child from a very dangerously violent family finally insist, after a period when he was becoming slightly calmer, that of course the therapist would not be cross if he took some food into the session. Then he corrected himself, and said, 'Well, she *should* not!' He had moved from manic denial of his fear to a moral imperative.

The sense of how things should be is connected, I think, to a deep sense of order, justice, rightness, and when the abused or deprived child indicates a longing for us to adopt or rescue him, an interpretation along the lines of 'You wish but we both know that you can't' may increase despair and weaken the ego. 'You feel I should rescue you,' or 'You feel somebody should rescue you,' or 'You feel your mother should not have abandoned you' may strengthen the child so long as it is not said as though containing a promise of actual rescue. Zbigniew Herbert (1977, p. 79) wrote that it was not in our power to forgive on behalf of those who were betrayed.

Conclusion

The argument of this chapter is that the paranoid position has its own logic, its own grammar and its own sanities, and it is at some cost to our egoless patients if we try to hasten their journey to more 'mature' levels.

Chapter 7

Motiveless malignity

Problems in the psychotherapy of patients with psychopathic features

Introduction

This chapter explores the difficult issue of how to understand – and meet – the very particular nature of the destructiveness of the psychopathic child. I draw attention to the difference between the state of mind and inner world of the neurotic, border-line and psychopathic patient, with reference to different types of destructiveness: anger in the neurotic patient; desperate, vengeful hatred in the borderline paranoid; and a cold addiction to violence in the psychopath. I will discuss technical issues and the need to meet the psychopathic patient where he really is – in the inner, bleak emotional cemetery he may inhabit. Honest and brave description of what we are seeing, however costly to therapeutic zeal, seems far more effective than attempts to explain (and thus seem to explain away) the destructive behaviour. Needless to say, the patients themselves refuse to stay put in the neat schematic categories I have outlined, but they do seem to appreciate our recognizing the specific quality of these vastly different states of mind.

The film *Assault on Precinct 13* begins with a sequence of shots of a gang of young men riding around the Watts District of Los Angeles in a car, aiming rifles first at an old black woman, then at a white man, then at a black man. Their fun is at least racially undiscriminating. The aiming seems random, idle, almost whimsical. We get to see the quarry lined up in the sights of the rifle each time, but no one pulls the trigger. The members of the gang seem to be having a good time. (Bruce Chatwin (1987) observed that the word for townspeople is 'meat' in the language of many nomadic peoples.) The scene then switches to a little girl buying an ice-cream from a vendor while her father makes a phone call from a call-box. She returns to her father, but suddenly looks at her ice-cream with dismay and turns back to the van. She does not realize that by then the gang has killed the vendor, and the man standing in the van is his killer. She says, 'Excuse me, I asked for chocolate and you've given me strawberry!' The killer turns and, as casually as he might swat a fly, shoots her in her still-open mouth. It is the casualness that is especially horrifying. The killer does not appear to be angry; nor does he give any sign of sadistic relish. At most, he looks mildly irritated.

In another film, *House of Games*, a man tricks his woman psychiatrist out of all her savings. At first she – and we – are led to think he is in love with her. In fact, he is a member of a group of con-men. When she learns of her seduction and betrayal, she asks, outraged, disbelieving and hurt, 'How could you *do* that to me?' He replies calmly, and with a dismissive shrug, 'But this is what I do.'

Psychoanalysts and psychiatrists have described the lack of conscience in psychopaths, the lack of guilt and remorse for their deeds, their indifference to their victims' cries for mercy. The more modern psychiatric classifications have tried to avoid what had in part become the pejorative and wastebasket use of the term 'psychopath'. But the newer terms – 'conduct disorder', 'antisocial personality disorder', even 'sociopath' – have become inadequate because their purely descriptive level of meaning does not distinguish between destructiveness that is motivated by anger, by bitter hatred, by outrage, by sadism or by casual brutality.

This has been even more true in the field of child psychiatry: this is beginning to change, however, at least in child psychiatric research. Viding (2004) has suggested that psychopathy should be seen as a developmental disorder, and Frick and White (2008) have reviewed the research on the importance of callous-emotional personality traits for a particular sub-group of antisocial and aggressive youth. Unlike previous textbooks, the research shows that the youths themselves know it is not a simple question of anger. Indeed, they seem comfortable with their lack of empathy (Frick and White, 2008). The review suggests that making these distinctions is important for treatment, but it is not clear what treatment the reviewers consider might reach such children. Certainly, motivated vengeful paranoid violence is different from addictive habitual violence. Addictive violence may have begun as a defence against some horror, then gradually acquired sadistic and exciting overtones, but eventually, under certain conditions of lifelong chronicity, it becomes almost motiveless and certainly casual. The enormity of the act may no longer bear any relation to the amount of feeling left in the perpetrator. An addiction is different from a defence. A temporary defensive hardening of the heart is different from a lifelong arteriosclerosis of the emotions. A big freeze is different from a brief chill.

A child with psychopathic features

My own school of hard knocks began with a little girl called Sarah. She was a destructive and violent child who regularly used to attack me physically. When she threw chairs at me in Friday sessions, I would say, 'You are beating me up today because it's the weekend and we have to say goodbye and you don't like being left.' She would agree, 'Yes,' and then kick me again. I would make a similar interpretation on Monday: 'You are kicking me because I left you on the weekend.' Gradually I began to think, 'But she kicks me on Tuesday, Wednesday and Thursday, too!' She simply *liked* kicking people. She had, I learned belatedly, a strong sado-masochistic element in her personality.

After some years of the physical violence, Sarah moved to mental cruelty. She knew how to interrupt – with impeccable, almost musical timing – at exactly the moment when I was finally about to get something important formulated and clear. She knew how to raise hopes and then dash them. It was high art, and her concentration was dedicated, precise and unremitting. If she tried to fly a paper butterfly and it sank, she would turn at the first second of its failure and sneer, 'You thought it was going to fly, didn't you?' In fact, she too had thought (for a moment) that it would fly, but the hope was projected so instantaneously, and was then destroyed equally instantaneously, that it required not simply careful monitoring on my part on a minute-by-minute basis, but *second-by-second* monitoring. I often complained to any colleague who would listen that no one who had not spent a lifetime's *practice*, as my patient had, in defeating herself and others could possibly keep up with such a person. I felt I did care about monitoring our interactions on a moment-by-moment basis, but I wasn't even sure that I *wanted* to be vigilant in such micro-analytic terms, from second to second.

Betty Joseph's writings (Spillius and Feldman, 1989) were helpful in discouraging the superficial use of explanatory interpretations with borderline patients. Her teachings and writings on addictive processes were indispensable (Joseph, 1982). Also, Herbert Rosenfeld suggested to me that Bion's dictum of shedding memory and desire was not appropriate with such patients (personal communication, 1983). On the contrary, he thought one needed to be very vigilant, and always a step ahead, because otherwise they despised you. (Certainly, they seem to be wonderfully alert to hypocrisy.) I would agree with Rosenfeld, as far as the psychopathic part of the patient is concerned, and shall suggest that, long before goodness is at issue, such patients are measuring us for our courage, strength and inability to be fooled. (Their despairing and persecuted parts may, however, require other tender – rather than tough-minded – sensibilities of us.)

These patients are probably at the schizoid end of what Melanie Klein (1935) called the paranoid/schizoid–depressive continuum; and for the most hardened or grandiose ones becoming paranoid and persecuted is actually sometimes something of a development. When, instead of feeling no concern for themselves, they begin to fear retribution, this, strangely enough, can signal a reduction in grandiosity or at least a melting of the emotional ice. The internal object may have begun to take on a little substantiality and life, even if only of a dangerous kind. An object somewhere has become capable of witnessing, and taking seriously, the danger to the self. At least something matters. (Clearly, this is nowhere near the depressive position in terms of concern for others; nevertheless, developments within the paranoid position remain developments and should not be discounted simply because they do not involve depressive position concern or guilt.)

It is interesting that when the psychopathic killer in the film *No Country for Old Men* comes, at the end of the film, to kill the woman who is the wife and daughter of his two previous victims, he seems surprised at her refusal to let him flip a coin that could save her life, if it falls right. She is different from all his previous victims, who fought back pathetically, begged, or tried to bargain for their lives. In contrast, she simply looks at him steadily, waiting for him to kill her. We are spared her murder, but in the next scene he is seen driving down her road, looking in the rear-view mirror as two boys clown about on their bikes behind him. He seems rattled by them and, in the only moment in the film when he loses control, crashes the car and badly injures himself. I think he was rattled by his victim's bleak courage.

Some clinical differentiations between neurotic, borderline and psychopathic states of mind

I would now like to differentiate between anger in a neurotic patient; desperation, outrage and vengeance in two borderline patients; and icy, calculating cruelty in a very young psychopathic patient. I shall then consider four technical issues in the treatment of psychopathic patients. Of course, as I have said previously, live human beings refuse to stay put in these neat schematic categories, and I am using these diagnostic categories only for purposes of discussion. I have also become interested in recent years in the element of psychopathy or personality disorder in some children with autism, an issue that requires more space to discuss (Alvarez, 1999, 2004).

Neurotic patients

In the Introduction, I gave an example of work with a neurotic patient where more ordinary interpretations about anger, due to loss or jealousy, were possible. She was functioning at a relatively well neurotic level, where it can be positively helpful to say something like 'You are cross because . . .' This is in patients where there is some capacity for guilt, some capacity for love, some ego that can process insight into their own aggression, but also some already established self-respect.

Borderline patients

A different situation arose with a little boy called Peter whose therapist was leaving the clinic in a month's time. He came to his session in a very desperate, wild, fragmented state. His mother – who, like him, was upset about the ending and unable to acknowledge it – had taken to bringing him late. He had had a very deprived first year of life, when his (anyway) rather withdrawn mother was profoundly depressed. After a few minutes, he took out a calendar of their sessions, asking when they would be stopping and which one was today. His therapist offered to tick off the days, something they had recently stopped doing. He said, 'No!' and started to tear up the calendar. The therapist said that Peter was cross with her about their meetings stopping (i.e. 'angry because' – an explanatory defence interpretation). Peter got wilder and overturned a chair, the therapist tried to prevent him, and again said that he was angry because they were stopping the meetings. He grew even more excited, banging his head against the wall, something he had done regularly as a baby.

Here, I think it is not enough to interpret anger. There is despair, and the child's desperate impotence and helplessness may be increased and escalated unhelpfully at such moments. He is incapable of hearing the interpretation of his anger, because he is in no fit state to think about and process anger. The necessary ego functioning and the necessary hope are both lacking. Yet, if the therapist is willing to take some of the badness into herself, the child may begin to find things slightly more bearable, and to process the experience. So one might (with some feeling, by the way) say something like: 'It's really *terrible* for you that I'm stopping. You feel you should be able to tear up this whole experience. It *shouldn't* be happening. I *shouldn't* be leaving you.' This would involve acknowledging the child's desperation and amplifying and carrying for him his as yet unnamed, unverbalized, but possibly at least 'pre-conceived' (Bion, 1962b) sense of injustice. (See Chapter 6 for a fuller discussion of the issue of responding to moral imperatives.)

I should also mention the importance of recognizing that some traumatized children act impulsively in states of PTSD and need to be shown that we recognize that it is 'in them to do', which is different from the assumption that they own what they are doing. Violence can erupt as a result of abuse or of witnessing violence, and the child may rightly feel that he did not mean to do it, someone else did it.

In patients who are more paranoid, phantasies (not acts) of others getting deserved punishment – that is, phantasies of justice and revenge – may enable desperate and needed projections to occur and be contained. Joseph (1978) discusses the dangers of premature return of projections with borderline patients. The relieving, calming effect seems to have to do with an understanding that badness needs to *stay out there*. Otherwise, as I tried to show in Chapter 6, humiliation, despair, shame and revenge can lead to explosive and dangerous eruptions in patients who may have been very heavily projected into. This kind of desperate, embittered hatred has to be carefully distinguished from the aggression of the more casually brutal – or more coldly murderous – psychopath, who, of course, could experience the above interpretations as collusion.

Patients with psychopathic features

Williams (1960, 1998) has pointed out that if one worked very carefully with murderers with an adequate theory of splitting, displacement and projection, it was possible to discover that they were not without conscience: they did have a conscience, but only in regard to particular split-off objects. For example, a man who had murdered a woman might not feel guilty about the woman, but he might suddenly feel pity and remorse for an injured pigeon. Symington (1980) makes the similar point that if you look carefully at the internal world of these people, they do have a good object and love for it somewhere, but it is often invisible and hidden. They are not completely conscienceless, not completely loveless. They have an excess of guilt. He cites Heathcliff's symbiotic love for Catherine in Emily Brontë's novel *Wuthering Heights* (1847). I would stress that what also kept Heathcliff going was his belief in her love of him. In some of the colder psychopathic people, however, it would be hard to find even that bit of light in the darkness.

Meloy (1996), a psychologist who has had long and intensive experience with violent inmates in prisons in the San Diego area of California, has made a very helpful distinction between what he calls 'affectively evoked aggression' – aggression evoked by the perception of threat – and 'predatory aggression', which is directed toward the destruction of prey, usually for food-gathering in sub-human species. The latter involves minimal autonomic arousal and vocalization.

> When a household cat is cornered and threatened, the neurochemical set produces a display of affective aggression: hissing, hair standing on end, dilating pupils, active clawing, arching back. When the same cat is stalking a bird in the back-yard, predatory aggression dominates: quiet stalking of the prey, the absence of ritualistic display, and focused attention on the target.
>
> (Meloy, 1996, p. 25)

He states that predatory aggression is the hallmark of the psychopath. (He is careful to distinguish between the severe and mild ends of a continuum of psychopathy, and thinks people from the milder end tend to be treatable.) Meloy (1996, p. 74) suggests that the anecdotal descriptions by workers in forensic treatment and custody settings of certain patients' or inmates' eyes as 'cold, staring, harsh, empty, vacant and absent of feeling', and the consequent feeling of eerie fear, should be taken very seriously. He points out that this experience of chilling fear does not seem to arise with even very dangerous explosive combative patients.

Technical problems with patients with psychopathic features

I now wish to draw attention to a major theme in Symington's (1980) paper: his brilliant delineation of the three responses evoked by the psychopath. He points out that one of the most common responses is collusion. People simply let bullies have what they want. He suggests that this has something to do with gratification of some of our own psychopathic parts. He says that the second common response is disbelief and denial. I think it is possible – but useless or even dangerous – to use psychoanalytic explanation both to the patient and to ourselves in exactly this denying way, in order to evade the disturbing facts of what we are feeling in the countertransference. And these patients know when we are being evasive and cannot stand what they are dishing out. Symington is quite forgiving about the fear such people evoke in their analysts, therapists or jailers, and the naturalness of our cowardly denials. He points out that it is only sane to want safety and peace. The third response is condemnation. These patients do provoke the most powerful feelings of horror, outrage, condemnation and retaliation. Unfortunately, such responses serve only to excite the patient, or make him strengthen his armoury and become even more determined to defeat the therapist.

The hardest thing to do is to look evil in the eye, bravely but not in a retaliatory or condemnatory way. When I finally became aware of how much Sarah relished putting in the knife and twisting it, I was shocked and horrified at first. I would say, 'You really want to break my heart, don't you?' I suspect my use of the word 'really' still carried a note of disbelief, and the vain hope that she would deny it. Instead, she would lean forward intently and whisper – fervently – 'Yes!' I think if you work with these patients for any length of time, you have to grow and change because they change you. One has to get beyond the stage of denial, then beyond the state of outrage, to a state of mind requiring courage and steadfastness, and also, in one sense, respect for the patient's courage in surviving in his empty world.

I want to say something about a book by Docker-Drysdale (1990), a follower of Winnicott who ran a residential unit for extremely disturbed children. She wrote about 'frozen' children who, I think, may be even more ill than Heathcliff and the people Symington discusses. I think we have to leave room in our minds for the fact that some children get frozen so early in life that there is not a lot of love even hidden. Docker-Drysdale makes it clear that she would always be looking for some flicker of feeling in assessing a child for acceptance into school. She writes most interestingly about the difficulty these children have with symbolization and gives an example of a child new to school who may steal from the refrigerator, not because the food has any symbolic meaning, but simply because he's hungry. A couple of years later, by which time the child is very attached to his primary careworker, he may steal from the refrigerator because he is upset by the fact that she is going on holiday: the theft may be full of symbolic meaning. Docker-Drysdale thinks it is important not to confuse the two. Segal's (1957) distinction between the symbolic equation and the true symbol is relevant here, as is Winnicott's (1953) concept of the transitional phase. It is fascinating to watch these children move from vicious acting out, to played viciousness, to, say, a cruel verbal joke, and then to a kinder joke – a progressive process that may take months or years but is nevertheless an important development involving some considerable sparing of the object.

Docker-Drysdale thinks that such children are 'unable to make any real object relationships or to feel the need for them'. And, importantly, 'This kind of child cannot symbolize what he has never experienced or realized' (p. 179). In the same way, I suggest that it is important to find a language sufficiently bleak for the psychopath to feel we are at least attempting to meet him where he really is, rather than where we think he ought to be. In a large part of his being, he may inhabit an emotional cemetery. We can neither exhort nor coax him into the depressive position, and to join the rest of the human race. He will only think we are misguided fools if we talk to him about the anger or loss or pain that he may be years away from feeling. Nor should we imagine he is necessarily defending himself against dependency on us, or refusing to see our goodness. He may *really* see us as useless, because he has a useless internal object. His violence may have begun as a defence against pain, but it may have changed into a way of life.

Docker-Drysdale makes an interesting distinction between experience, realization and symbolization: she points out that it is not enough to give these children good experiences; they have to realize they are having them. This is similar to my own views derived from working with very deprived or very abused children. You may need to interpret, for example, 'You feel that I like you today' or 'You like me today', but you also need to show them that they *like* being liked, they *like* having loving feelings: 'You like to please me, and you like it when I like you.' These children are often caught up in a vicious circle in which they do something provocative, the object punishes, they then do something even more provocative, and they may rarely notice the other (probably very fleeting) moments of good contact. (Such interpretations might need to be even cooler and more matter-of-fact with patients in a psychopathic state.)

Docker-Drysdale's concept of realization is similar both to Bion's (1962b) concept of the need to get 'alpha function' around a thought to make it thinkable and developmental theories of how experience acquires meaning. Stern (1985) described a rather more pleasant set of meanings than did Bion, whereas here the experience we are invited – or rather forced – to share or contain is disturbing and often horrifying, and it is easy to miss tiny reductions in the level of cruelty, for example, or fleeting moments of friendliness. But when these moments come, we can learn not to greet them too eagerly, and not to make too fancy symbolic explanatory interpretations. It seems better simply to stay with the patient and think about one moment of his experience at a time. With psychopaths, Strachey's (1934) concept of 'minimal doses' in the transference probably needs reducing to 'minimalistic doses'. These people often hate any comment too heavy with meaning, because it is felt to be therefore too laden with emotion, and a lifetime of dissociation has led to emotion being seen as loathsome, contemptible or irrelevant.

A second example of a child with psychopathic features: Billy

Sarah, whom I mentioned earlier, was only ten years old, and it was originally hard to believe that such a young child could be capable of such dedication to cruelty. Subsequently, I treated a four-year-old boy whom I shall call Billy, who was referred because of his coldness to his mother. (His mother believed Billy had never looked at her since he was born. In fact, the mother was rarely at home, and the child became profoundly attached to his first nanny, who then left and was replaced by a series of other nannies.) At one point, Billy became very withdrawn, but both before and after this period he had hardened up chillingly. He was an attractive child, who could charm strangers with his intelligence and lively, rather driven sense of drama, but he developed an icy glitter and a manipulativeness that worried even his father, who did not feel rejected by him. Billy was extremely jealous of, and cruel to, his younger, more favoured two-year-old sister, and in his sessions he indulged in slow, calculated tortures performed by a 'doctor' (himself) on a toy baby teddy. I was instructed to speak for the teddy and, obviously losing my capacity to bear it, one day made the mistake of asking, in the teddy's voice, why I was receiving such punishment, why the doctor was doing this to me. Billy looked at me as though I was utterly stupid, and replied, '*Why?* Because I like it!' I had seen him a day or two before sticking the pin of his badge into the teddy's eyes, infinitely slowly and with almost loving relish, and I should have known better. Terms such as 'conduct disorder' do not capture the flavour of such moments. Such destructiveness is different in kind from impulsive anger or fury: it feels lifelong, abiding, enduring. Even in a four-year-old 'lifelong' means just that – Billy's life of bitter disappointment had been inordinately long.

I usually did not refer to the teddy as representing Billy's own baby part, or to infantile dependency feelings being spared. At times the teddy was filled with otherness, and represented, I think, his hated little sister. I believe the desire – and, in a way, as Kundera suggests, the *need* – for rectifying revenge phantasies (not actions) may need addressing for a very long period. The clinician has to decide when the patient is able to accept the return of the split-off or projected part. This may be a few seconds or a few years later. The clinician also has to try to sense when violence has become somewhat desultory and is also no longer needed. Billy had genuine borderline paranoid features, but these were beginning to solidify into something more psychopathic.

Billy's parents were never sure, at that stage, that psychotherapy was what they wanted for him, and it became clear that, as he had become more manageable, his treatment would have to end. He was also less withdrawn and that seemed to be enough for them. The Monday after the weekend when they had rung to confirm their decision that he should stop treatment in a month's time, he came into the session in a bullying but blustering and wild state. First he blocked my path on the stairs down to the playroom. I said it seemed to be my turn to be shut out. Then – for him, in a very muddled way (he was usually icily clear and coherent) – he said, 'They say I am not coming – they asked me what I . . . I don't want to come here any more. No . . . they don't want . . . No . . . I don't want.' I said I thought he was muddled, because he was unsure who did not want him to come. He kept on repeating, as he opened his case, 'I don't want to come any more . . . You're a . . . bad witch.' Yet, although at one point he was facing me, and normally he had the boldest of unchildlike gazes, this time he would not look at my face. Instead, he stared down, somewhere around my middle. I said I thought he was having difficulty looking at me and maybe this was because he was unsure what he wanted and whether I really was all bad. He began throwing all of his toys out of his box on to the floor, but when he got to the bottom layer, which contained the farm and wild animals, he first took out the little lamb, placed it carefully inside a glove puppet and placed a white and a brown foal in front, as though to stand guard over it. They had been good figures, guarding the little lamb the week before, and I was surprised at their survival. Billy went on with terrible and final deliberation, throwing all the other animals out on the floor with total contempt, and grinding his feet slowly and thoroughly onto the soft baby rabbit. He seemed too wound up and icy even to get into one of his sadistic 'games' with me, where the animals were to be killed and eaten. His contempt (and, I think, his despair) was too total even to play. I acknowledged this, but I did comment on the lamb's preservation.

I said I thought that he was leaving a little room in his mind for friendly feelings and some good memories of the time he had spent here. I kept it cool and minimalistic, as I believe was right with him. It saved his dignity and in a way acknowledged his courage in the enormity of his task, which involved managing his own enormous hatred and the hatred he felt others had for him. I did not, therefore, refer to a baby part, or to infantile dependency feelings being spared.

A little later, he shouted, 'You'll be sorry!' and I, feeling absolutely terrible by now, said I thought he felt I should be the one to feel the sadness about his departure. And that maybe he knew I *was* very sad, and didn't want to lose him. After a while, I added that he must feel I ought to be sorry about not being strong enough to have persuaded his parents to let him stay. He began to glance at me a little, then to order me, in a very tyrannical manner, to pick up the toys. I felt the situation was mixed because he was a tyrannical child, and the services he got people to perform in this way were invariably done grudgingly, if not with hatred. But I also felt he was getting more and more desperate, and that he needed me to pick up the toys – to show that I was *willing* to do it because I liked him, not *forced* to do it because I feared his tantrums. Also, he was finally engaging me in a joint activity, in however bullying a manner. So I began to pick up the toys, keeping my eyes on him, which was hard to do when he was glaring so unpleasantly and coldly. I think he was certain, as all tyrants are, that his slaves hated him.

There was a noise from upstairs in the house, and he was startled. I said that I thought he was afraid somebody up there did not like him bullying me like this, and that he felt I really did not like him when he ordered me around like this. (My years of incomprehension and denial with Sarah may have taught me something, because I said this with great seriousness, but note the 'really'.) He started to say, 'I don't want to come here,' but it came out, 'You don't want to come here,' and eventually, making myself look at him, realizing that there was truth in it, I said, 'I think you feel I'm glad you're going.' He gave me a very direct look.

Note that I did not say, 'You are afraid that I'm glad you're going,' as the verb containing doubt – 'are afraid that' – can serve to deny what is really happening between the patient's self and his object. It is important to contain the reality of his emotional experience, and the word 'feel' is less denying. (See Winnicott (1949) on hate in the countertransference.) Looking the patient in the eye bravely means also having the courage to look at oneself honestly.

When it was time to go, he shouted from the stairs, 'How would *you* like it if you had to be put in a box?' and I had just enough time to say that I thought he felt really it ought to be me, not him, to whom this was happening. I let him know I thought he was right, because it seemed that this time it was a desperate, not a cruel, projective identification. In fact, on reflection, I think that it was not even a projective identification – more an acknowledgement of his failure to project, his inability to find and keep an object that could receive his projections. He now rarely saw the beloved nanny of the past, and I think he was describing his own fate as the receiver of his mother's powerful projections. But the further element in his question, which I could not address in the month remaining to us before the termination of treatment, was: 'Do you really care to know, in full, what it is like to be me?'

I suspect Billy knew that a part of me did not.

Discussion and conclusion: four technical issues

I would like to conclude by discussing four issues that arise when working with such patients. In order to avoid Symington's trio of collusion, denial and condemnation, it is important, first, to avoid the last: that is, instead of condemnation, it is necessary to look evil straight in the eye. This implies not evading the full bleakness and horror of the patient's impulses, nor the inadequacy and foolishness of their internal objects and of ourselves in the transference. As the doctor–torturer–child replied to me, 'I like it!' It also implies not evading what they know to be our own dislike, distaste and even hatred for their ruthless, cruel and often brutal treatment of us, their objects and themselves. I do not know if I have conveyed the degree to which Billy's play with the baby teddy was not simply ordinary, aggressive, phantasied play, or why I feel that he was the kind of child who might really have caused an accident to his baby sister, so carefully managed that no one would ever know that it was anything other than an accident.

There was, however, also a desperate paranoid element, and it was important that someone receive the projections that no one had been able to hold, and to be honest about what he knew to be his object's hatred and weariness. Hopefully, one could do this without retaliation. Unfortunately, there was the further problem that his cruelty was becoming the possible grounding for a sado-masochistic perversion. He 'trembled' with excitement in some of his scenes. This certainly needed addressing in later intensive work with him, which was eventually carried out with considerable success.

Second, we must struggle not to collude or deny but to find, unsentimentally, the patient's friendly feelings and whatever faint beginnings there may be of trust and faith. We should not appeal for a good self or good object that is not present, but we need to be alert to the tiniest flickerings of faith and hope that *are* there. It is dangerous to elevate or amplify them; it is far better to play them down. The patient may be able to agree that he is somewhat irritated at the recent break's interruption to his routine, but be nowhere near getting in touch with painful feelings of loss about the gap. Also, at times, we may have to acknowledge, unsentimentally, what he may observe to be our hurt, our defeat and our fondness when the patient cannot do so.

Third, it is usually important to avoid symbolic interpretations of either positive or negative feelings. For example, interpretations along the lines of 'You feel abandoned by me, as you did by your mother' may carry too much meaning, and meaning may simply not be available to patients in these hardened, frozen states. We may need to respect the patient's insistence that he 'just likes' what he does, or is 'just irritated', not angry, today, and that it has no meaning. Then, slowly – perhaps – meaning can grow.

Finally, two-part interpretations directed toward searching out and revealing the patient's vulnerability are usually either dangerous or useless. Such patients are not functioning at the level of the depressive position. They are living in a paranoid world where survival, not love, is at issue. Values of intelligence, daring, courage, skill and triumph – the values of the battlefield – are paramount. Premature interpretations regarding hidden vulnerability or dependence, which the patient has not yet owned, may produce dangerous eruptions or, at the very least, earn the patient's appropriate contempt. It is important, instead, to save his dignity and respect his courage in going on in the face of the dead world he inhabits.

Chapter 8

Issues of narcissism, self-worth and the relation to the stupid object: devalued or unvalued?

Introduction

In this chapter I shall use the Kleinian theory of the inner world as made up of a self in relationship with various internal objects in an attempt to identify three sub-types of narcissism and three sub-types of apparent narcissism in children and adolescents. Several of the sub-types make particular reference to different relationships with a stupid object.

Three sub-types of narcissism

1 Narcissism where the stupid object arises from defensive devaluation.
2 Narcissism and the stupid object where devaluation has become addictive and part of character structure.
3 (a) Destructive narcissism, where addictive narcissism combines with addictive destructiveness; (b) Masochistic narcissism and the problem of the envious, intrusive and watchful object.

Three sub-types of apparent narcissism

1 Apparent narcissism as a developmental necessity where the internal object is felt to be unresponsive to the self's agency and potency. The result is despair, or an attempt to overcome (not defend against) shame with pride.
2 Apparent narcissism where the self is relating to, and identified with, an indifferent, uninterested and uninteresting object: a double deficit, indifference to an indifferent object.
3 Apparent narcissism that is not narcissism but a sense of self-worth: the precious self and the precious world.

I shall look at some of the technical implications of these differentiations and suggest that, on most occasions, all but the first sub-type require responses that are more descriptive than explanatory.

Definition of narcissism

In many of his writings (although not all: see Balint, 1968) Freud conceived of infants as born in a state of primary narcissism, where the infant's own ego was taken as the object of libidinal love. He also conceived of secondary narcissism, 'a regression from an object-relationship which has disappointed through either loss of the object, or some kind of slight by the object, back to a narcissistic love of the ego' (Hinshelwood, 1989, p. 350). Klein disagreed that narcissism was a primary stage or phase of development: she thought that babies were born object-related, but that narcissistic states could coexist with object-related ones at any phase or stage of development. Basically, she said that all narcissism was secondary (Klein, 1952), as did Balint.

Much of the subsequent controversy about the nature of narcissism has concerned the issue of deficit versus conflict. The argument has involved the question of whether the narcissism could be seen as used defensively in a manner that was fundamentally anti-developmental, or as an attempt to satisfy a developmental need (Stolorow and Lachmann, 1980). I shall suggest, throughout a discussion of different sub-types of narcissistic states in children and adolescents, that attention to three factors may help to clarify some aspects of this issue. The first factor is the nature, in the narcissistic patient, of the self's relation to the internal object: is the object devalued or unvalued? And is the self overvalued or, for that matter, excessively undervalued? The second factor concerns the degree to which *either* narcissism based on deficit *or* narcissism based on defensiveness has become addictive: that is, I suggest that the question of habit, chronicity and character, even in childhood, has to be addressed. The third factor concerns the level of symbolic functioning present in the self-regard, and the related issue of where the self-regard lies on the paranoid/schizoid–depressive position continuum. It is debatable whether we should use the language of pathology at all at the higher levels.

Many authors have distinguished between sub-types of narcissism (Bateman, 1998; Britton, 1998; Kernberg, 1975; Rosenfeld, 1987). Others emphasize differences in the motivation for, or function of, the narcissism (Broucek, 1991; Stolorow and Lachmann, 1980). Stolorow and Lachmann distinguish between what the narcissism may be defending against, and what it may be trying to achieve. Both may be operative: a defence against envy (Kernberg, 1975; Rosenfeld, 1987; Segal, 1983) or shame (Broucek, 1991) may also have the aim of achieving a feeling of superiority or pride (Broucek, 1991; Lynd, 1958). The issue of motivation or function was especially useful, because it moved the discussion beyond the strict confines of the self to make reference to the relation to the object: a defence against envy is referring precisely to a problem in relation to an object, not only to the effect on the self.

Most of these latter authors make additional references to the nature of the internal object: Kernberg discusses its devaluation, Stolorow and Lachmann describe the disturbing countertransference for the analyst, and Rosenfeld stresses the takeover of the object's previously admired qualities. I shall be discussing a set of differing relationships between the self and the stupid object. First, I shall discuss three sub-types of narcissistic states of mind; next, I shall discuss three other sub-types that may resemble narcissism but are not. In this second section I shall also explore the differences between narcissistic children with devalued internal objects, where the disparagement was (or at least began as) defensive, and those whose internal objects, for a variety of reasons, have never been valued or admired in the first place – never respected, nor acquired sufficient elevation, as it were, to be looked up to.

I began to think about this distinction (in an admittedly rather literal and concrete manner) after seeing several deprived children regularly placing dolls in horizontal positions – lying about on couches, on the floor of the dolls' house – or rarely even watching television, which in itself is a fairly passive activity. (The parents in these cases tended to be alcoholic, drug addicted or severely depressed.) The dolls were usually said to be 'asleep', but they were certainly never doing anything, and, worse, never even standing up. Adolescents with similar pathology tended to regard their encounters with adults – parents, teachers or therapists – with indifference (not, however, with active contempt). The therapists' counter-transference was often similar to that with patients with defensive narcissism: they felt ignored, useless, not listened to, not seen as able to help. In particular, they were not seen as *intelligent*. Indeed, in some cases, there was no such concept as that of intelligence or of an interested and interesting mind. Adults were seen as stupid, but not necessarily bad. Some abused children, for example, would see adult men as dangerous but at least powerful and of interest, even if only under persecuting and hyper-vigilant conditions, whereas female adult figures, although perhaps seen as kind and certainly loved, were felt to be weak, useless, unpro-tective, unprotected and therefore fundamentally *uninteresting*. I have heard of many children, suddenly realizing that the therapist could understand their feelings, asking, 'How did you know that? Are you a mind-reader?'

Some background history of the move to an internal two-person psychology regarding narcissism

In a seminal paper on the psychopathology of narcissism, Rosenfeld (1964) suggests that the majority of analysts who had been treating narcissistic patients had disagreed with Freud's view that there was no transference. He points out that minute observation of the behaviour of the narcissist in the analytic transference did reveal a transference, but one of a highly primitive nature in which there were serious difficulties in distinguishing between subject and object. Rosenfeld reminds us that Freud himself regarded the oceanic feeling as the longing for God or the universe as a primary narcissistic experience, and Balint (1968) points out that Freud in fact held two contradictory views throughout his life: one a belief in primary narcissism; the other a belief that we were primarily object-seeking. Balint notes that even in the 'Three essays on the theory of sexuality', which is quite early (1905b), Freud said that all object-discovery is in fact a re-discovery. Balint also points out that in the *Introductory Lectures* (1916–1917), Freud said that certain components in states of sexuality – such as sadism, scopophilia and curiosity – have an object right from the start. So, Balint asks, why is it that the other version of primary narcissism became the official version?

Rosenfeld crucially points out that what looked – from a one-person psychology perspective – like self-love was in fact based on identification with an object that was previously admired and whose identity was taken over. In her paper 'On identification', Klein (1955) described this type of takeover as projective identification. (This process should be distinguished from the evacuative type described in 'Notes on some schizoid mechanisms' (Klein, 1946) but the two processes may occur together. In the less extreme (1946) type, the whole self is not changed; the good parts are retained.) Rosenfeld adds that the self in narcissism becomes so identified with the incorporated object that all separate identity or any boundary between self and object is denied. Lack of separateness, he insists, does not nevertheless constitute a lack of an object-relation.

One has, however, to address the problem of some considerable degree of lack in the type of children with stupid internal objects where there has been un-valuation rather than defensive devaluation. The lack is not in an object-relation; it is in the kind of object-relation. The lack may be not of an object or couple but of a lively, interesting object or parental couple. In these cases, the object may seem impossibly remote, rather than, as with Rosenfeld's examples, too close. Managing alone may seem the only option. There may be a link here with the avoidant children of attachment research.

Hamilton (1982) has pointed out that the myth of Narcissus itself is relational. The myth tells the story of the relationship between a 16-year-old youth, Narcissus, and his lover-admirer, Echo. Hamilton (1982, pp. 4–5) writes,

> This adolescent relationship is grounded in the early relationship between the infant Narcissus 'in his cradle' and his mother, Leiriope. In Graves' words, 'everyone was in love with Narcissus even in his cradle'. The term narcissism would then describe a 'love-*relationship*'. In the light of this interpretation, the later relationship between Narcissus and Echo might serve to illustrate some of the pathologies which result when an early, unconditionally admiring, relationship is perpetuated. Echo is a young woman who 'always answers back' and Narcissus a young man who spurns the admirers who pursue him.

The self is superior and the object inferior, but the latter does exist.

The question of narcissistic psychopathology in children

Beren (1998, pp. xv–xvi) points out that in children, although we do not usually find an 'established personality disturbance', we can and do find what she calls narcissistic 'concerns' at all psychosexual and developmental levels. Beren also notes that the literature regarding children suggests that the problems are primarily around Oedipal conflict whereas she believes (and I agree) that both deficit and conflict occur (Beren, 1998, p. xvi). More recently, Kernberg *et al.* (2000) have gone further: they have contrasted the pathological self-centredness of what they call 'narcissistic personality-disordered children' with the normal narcissism of children. They point out that the normal child is able to acknowledge nurturing with reciprocity and gratitude, whereas narcissistic children reveal a sense of entitlement (Kernberg *et al.*, 2000, pp. 180–181). I would argue that the habitual nature of a defence – or, for that matter, of an attempt to repair a deficit – may lead to something more than narcissistic concerns: we can and do find an established personality disturbance in childhood. Nevertheless, defensive narcissism, which begins later in childhood, has a very different feel, because development and object-relatedness have been allowed to go forward prior to the blow.

Three sub-types of narcissism

I shall start with clinical examples of the more traditional sub-type. I hope it will be clear that I am talking about sub-types of states of mind, not referring to groups of children. The same child may move from one state of mind, or motivation, or level of vulnerability or hardness, to another at any particular moment. Nevertheless, the distinctions matter for our technical sensitivities.

Narcissism where the stupid object arises mainly from defensive devaluation

Both the patients I consider here had a good start – a close, if idealized, relationship with their mother and an apparently good relation to their father. The first child, Peter, began to become extremely difficult when he was three years old, after the birth of his sibling. A mild physical limitation seemed to have increased his sense of shame and hurt. There were some physical attacks on his sibling, but most of his attacks were verbal, and the older he got, the better he became at barbed and cruel humiliations of his sibling and his parents. His parents were warm and loving, but easily nonplussed and wounded by Peter's rudeness and arrogance. His reaction to their setting boundaries was grandiose outrage, such as: 'Who do they think they are to limit me?' He really seemed to feel his parents' strictures were stupid, and that anyone who limited him was stupid to think he needed watching in this way. However, unlike the deprived children to whom I have referred, there was passion and outrage in his sense of his parents' stupidity. And there was certainly underlying pain and shame. More important, there was astonishment. How could they be so stupid?! He had some idea – definitely his own – of how an intelligent parent should function: he, Peter, should be given his own way! Peter, however, had never lost total hope in the interestingness of adults, so he was able to maintain good relationships with teachers and to listen to them, up to a point. However, his contempt probably contributed to the fact that he was functioning somewhat under par academically.

Another very arrogant patient, Linda, did not suffer her major blow to her narcissism until she was ten, when her father left the family home for a period. She became violent and furious at all limits set at home, and these attitudes began to spread to school. However, she had already developed a very strong sense of the intelligence of her objects, so only some of her teachers were selected for her scathing contempt. She derided these teachers mercilessly, and some of them came to dislike her intensely, even though she continued to attain excellent academic standards.

Here, it is worth mentioning that the Oedipal situation had been somewhat skewed for both of these patients, in the sense that the relationship with the mother had been at one point too close and idealized, and that with the father undervalued. Both fathers were strong and successful breadwinners, but they had taken something of a back seat at home. I think the narcissism of both children at times acted as a defence against pain, humiliation, envy and jealousy. At the earlier stages of treatment, therefore, I had to tread carefully when I pointed out their conviction of superiority: I tried to leave the door open to another version of themselves, but when the defences were up, I had to do so delicately. These children seemed fully capable of two-tracked thinking, yet explanatory interpretations about the shame or fear of humiliation that seemed to lie behind the arrogance were too wounding. I could make comments like, 'It seems very important to you to feel that you know all about that subject' or '. . . better than your teacher/your parents/me about this'. I learned it was often best to take up a third position and address the idealization of omniscience and omnipotence, rather than the omniscience and omnipotence itself (which simply felt as though I was trying to pull them down from their high horse so I could get on it). That is, rather than concentrating on their difficulty in letting others win, it was often better to wonder why winning itself was so important, so idealized. Gradually, as they became less touchy, I could make two-tracked interpretations about why they were so defensively boastful, and what humiliation I or their school might currently be subjecting them to.

At other times, however, their narcissism had a more complacent quality, as though any challenge to it was a major surprise and shock: 'Surely this adult does not think I should really be treated like a child! Doesn't she know who I am?' This more complacent attitude can signal the beginning of a more permanent sense of superiority in the identity. And its addictive quality can build upon whatever characterological deviances may have been there from the cradle onwards, as Hamilton (1982) says. (I doubt if there need be a dichotomy between the theory of grandiosity as a defence against envy (Kernberg, 1975) versus that of grandiosity as defence against shame (Broucek, 1991; Lynd, 1958) in that the two so often go together. Feelings about the self imply complementary feelings toward the object.) However, as I said, regular defensiveness that goes unaddressed may lead to complacency and on to addictive narcissism and deeper characterological difficulties. Thus, to continue . . .

The stupid object where devaluation has become addictive

Here, I want to draw attention to the way in which an activity that begins as defensive may go on to become habitual and embedded in character structure. That is, the narcissistic position is there even when the person is not under the stress of anxiety or humiliation. When we begin to stand up a little to these sorts of patients, their first experience is not rage: it is disbelief, and then later, perhaps, something more like outrage. I am referring to situations where the process has become addictive and deeply involved in the person's sense of identity. This raises new technical problems.

Peter, whose narcissism had started off defensively but by now had become quite habitual, had come to be seen by his family as a selfish, aggressive and demanding bully. It was difficult for him to change, partly because a vicious circle was set up whereby he tended to look for and expect a fight or an argument, and then, all too often, get one. He had a very legalistic turn of mind, and in the early years I was often caught up in arguing with him, or defending what I had just said. The speed with which he could make this happen was breathtaking.

It is important to stand firm without being retaliatory or mocking when the temptation is to cut the arrogant child down to size. Holding steady is easier where parents such as Peter's are also working to be less placating, say, with their child. (Other parents, with narcissistic features of their own, may take the child out of treatment as soon as there is improvement in the child's external behaviour.)

After three years of treatment, Peter's fighting had less of a grip on him, he was much easier at home, and even at times grudgingly able to acknowledge that he liked coming to see me. (This was after years of insisting that he came only because his parents forced him to.) However, he often still felt he had to hide behind his old stance, I think because his whole identity was involved. The barbs and insults to me returned with full force on a day when he announced that he had been invited to a friend's birthday party six weeks hence. This involved travelling by mini-coach to another part of London for a show, which he would miss because he was convinced that his parents and I would not allow him to miss a session. Over the weeks I interpreted continuously that he was assuming he knew I would force him, that he had not thought to ask if I might change the session to another day. I interpreted that he really liked a fight and preferred that to a negotiation. (I also knew that in the past he had indeed often been forced to come by his parents, so on this occasion I could not be sure if that aspect was a projection on his part or not.) Just a few days before the party, he mentioned that he would be going to it late and that the bus was going to wait for him, with the implication being that he would come to see me first. He would miss the best food, but . . . I suddenly thought to ask who had arranged this helpful compromise (I hadn't heard a word from his parents about it) and it turned out that Peter himself had sorted it out with his friend. I asked if he thought it was odd that he had pretended to go on fighting, to insist that he did not care about attending his sessions, and yet that he had done the responsible and friendly thing with respect to our relationship. He looked as embarrassed as an equivalently neurotic child would if he had been found cheating.

Throughout our work together, I had to approach this boy's more loving feelings with considerable tact. As Britton (1998, p. 46) writes, 'inside every thick-skinned patient is a thin-skinned patient trying not to get out', and he cites Rosenfeld (1987, pp. 274–275) on the danger of traumatizing the sensitive, thin-skinned patient as though he were thick-skinned. I also had interesting experiences with Peter in sessions after he had been particularly abusive. After a few years of this, I realized that he was sometimes a bit ashamed or even genuinely sorry, but he had no idea how to express those feelings; indeed, he hid them. I began to talk to him about the fact that he clearly wanted to make friends again but did not seem to know how to do this. It was very important to get hold of this feeling (of proto-reparation) in him and give it air to breathe.

Destructive narcissism, where addictive narcissism combines with addictive destructiveness

Rosenfeld (1987, ch. 6) identifies destructive narcissism, while Joseph's (1982) paper – although mainly about self-destructive, masochistic processes – is illuminating for its detailed description of the way in which addictive and perverse processes operate in the transference and countertransference. Joseph does not make a sharp distinction between addictive activities and perverse excitements, although I myself think it is possible and useful to do so. Some people get stuck in repetitive, interactive 'vicious circles' without necessarily being excited by them. That is, the narcissist may expect praise and admiration in a more com-placent way, for example, without necessarily being 'turned on' by it. In other people – Linda, for example – the process is driven by a compulsivity that may come to include sexual excitements. In any case, where destructiveness no longer arises simply out of vengeful persecution, but is both addictive and exciting, we have the beginnings of serious personality disorder. There were elements of this in the way Linda described her fights at home. In her tone there was not only persecution and bitterness but fascination, and I pointed out that she seemed to get a charge out of talking about, and having, these fights.

There is, of course, a quite reasonable reluctance to use the term 'personality disorder' in relation to a child, since a child's personality is not yet fully formed. Yet the press nowadays is full of shocked reports of street children who develop a terrible 'anomie' – a soulless attitude to life and to their own and others' fates. And see the film about the casual and brutal violence of Brazilian street children, *City of God* (2002). A plea in the *Journal of Child Psychology and Psychiatry* is relevant here: Shiner and Caspi (2003) stress the need for research on the way child and adolescent personality is related to concurrent personality disorders and to later-appearing personality disorders in adulthood. (See also Chapter 7 on the issue of working psychoanalytically with psychopathic children.)

Masochistic narcissism and the problem of the envious and intrusively watchful object

Interesting work is being done on masochistic narcissism (Broucek, 1991; Waska, 2002, p. 105). Symington (1993) says it does not matter whether the self-observation is positive or negative; it is the self-observation *itself* that is the problem. Anderson (2003) has studied something similar in the risk-taking behaviour in deprived children. They seem to invite attack or accident, because at least it confirms their own interestingness and existence. Anything is better than boredom and invisibility. Some children who regularly get bullied seem to have internal objects that are cruel and envious, but extremely attentive. These envious objects are often intrusive, so the patient feels permanently watched. Gradually it can be understood that underneath the persecution may be not simply the desire for attention but a perverse gratification.

One patient of mine had a compulsion to seek out a bully in whatever class or school she came to attend. And she talked about the bully all the time. It was hard to believe, and even harder to get her to believe, that she really felt she needed that much attention, and the kind of obsessive attention that only a bully could provide. It was truly addictive and perverse, but it offered profound gratification, which was very difficult to shift. To be ordinary, to be temporarily unnoticed, was inconceivable! The first temptation in the technical minefield was to try to help her to stand up to bullies – her masochistic and passive response and refusal to do anything led to one scolding and nagging her, just as the bullies did. But throwing up one's hands and abandoning her was felt to be equally sadistic. Trying not to get over-excited, and even a little bored, while remaining engaged was the best response (albeit very hard to manage) as I tried to show her how much she liked the attention she received.

In another masochistic case, I learned that fragile, over-protective objects seen as stupid can also act to limit the functioning of the patient's own intelligence. I first saw this in a girl with apparent learning difficulties, whom I eventually understood to be 'playing stupid' and helpless, mainly because she thought her maternal object was too fragile and naive to realize that she herself could be intelligent and strong. What can look like destructive contempt, therefore, can sometimes involve an almost protective and loving function. Henri Rey (1988) pointed out that, in borderline patients, the self's internal objects may have to get better before the self can.

The developmental trajectory in narcissism and some further technical issues

In thinking about the developmental trajectory of narcissism in childhood, a word about previous writings on sub-groups may be in order here. Several authors have distinguished between thick- and thin-skinned types of narcissism (Bateman, 1998; Britton, 1998, pp. 46–54; Rosenfeld, 1987, pp. 274–275). Gabbard (1989) refers to a group similar to the thick-skinned as 'oblivious', and Kernberg (1975) refers to the egotist, who is shameless, often with adoring parents, and thus selectively inattentive to criticism. The thin-skinned (fragile and vulnerable) are said to have low self-esteem, but Broucek (1991, pp. 59–62) points out that they are nevertheless still very self-centred. I would add, from the perspectives of child development and the trajectory of child psychopathology, that it may take time to build a thick-skinned narcissist. My impression is that, while Danny (the rather bullying boy I described in Chapter 3) had narcissistic skin that was very thick and probably lifelong, Peter's was only medium-thick: in spite of himself, he had a heart.

However, I do not wish to underestimate the difficulties of working with the thick-skinned type of child. It requires great firmness and strength both with the patient's arrogance and with our own desire to retaliate by cutting them down to size. I find humorous exasperation often manages to save their dignity; it also avoids getting the therapist caught up in counter-productive retaliation yet allows one to give vent to some genuine irritation. At the early stage of my work with Danny, however, even humour would have been of no avail. His narcissism was accompanied by a powerful paranoid overreaction to perceived belittlement, and humour would have been perceived only as mockery and humiliation.

Three sub-types of apparent narcissism and the question of technique

Apparent narcissism and the need for self-respect: an over-valued self as a developmental necessity where the internal object is felt to be unresponsive to the self's agency and potency

I have borrowed the term 'developmental necessity' from Stolorow and Lachmann (1980). Kohut (1977) described this as compensatory. Stolorow and Lachmann insisted that it was important to distinguish between narcissism as a defence in a person with a more developed personality, more ego and more object development, and narcissism as 'a pre-stage of defence'. They thought that narcissism in the two different sub-groups had a similar function – regulating self-esteem (pp. 18–20) – but that narcissism in people with extremely damaged self-esteem was a 'developmental necessity' – not, the implication was, a developmental *impediment*, as in the case of the defensive use.

It is interesting to consider how comfortable we become in using the language of psychopathology to describe normal development. 'Pre-stage of defence' might well be given a name of its own by a student of child development: how about the baby's and child's need to be of interest to the parents, to bring a light to their eye, to make them laugh (Trevarthen and Hubley, 1978). Reddy (2008, p. 136) suggests that showing off occurs early in the first year of life and indicates a tendency to seek 'heightened visibility'. Trevarthen (2001) thinks that a central emotional development in infancy is the balance between shame and pride. Lynd (1958, p. 252) pointed out that the opposite of shame is pride. She distinguished between arrogance and self-respect, hubris and philotimo, which means honour and inviolability (p. 258), and said that only a man with true pride can have true humility. Bion (1957b) also distinguished between pride and arrogance, and we might add that the infant's sense of his capacity to give pleasure is as important as his capacity to receive it.

Previously, I have described Danny, a boy who had a deep sense of shame and unlikeableness (Alvarez, 1992, pp. 181–182; Chapter 3, this volume). He was referred to me at the age of eight for failure to learn at school, aggressive behaviour and a worrying fascination with lighting fires. His parents felt that he had missed a lot as a baby and young child due to illness in the family. Danny presented as a pompous, boastful but also dead and depressed boy who had little idea how to interest his listener, or how to play. He had few friends. After about a year's treatment, he had learned how to restrain his aggressive outbursts, to be a little less boastful, and to make a few friends. He came in one day and told me that he and a group of boys at school were playing at jousting. He had the strongest shoulders in the class, so he was the horse, and he and his friend were the best pair. I commented on his pleasure and pride in being able to show me a friendly, strong side of himself, and he then continued, excitedly, to say that sometimes he galloped his friend all the way to school. I have explained (Alvarez, 1992) why I felt that challenging this (at that moment) would have produced a typical hopeless deflation, and why I think such 'lying' attempts to pressure us into admiration can sometimes be seen not as bullying projective identifications but as something that might be better termed 'anticipatory identifications' – as a sort of hopeful question hidden under the guise of an insistence. That is, 'Could you ever see me as . . .?' This can lead to an overcoming of, rather than a defence against, shame and envy. I did not say, 'You want me to see you as . . .' (with the implication '. . . but we both know that . . .'). Instead, I said that he felt *I was to see him as strong and brave and dashing*. A few days later, when he was in a stronger state, I could talk about the fact that he often exaggerated when he felt low.

Another little boy patient of mine, Toby, had been born nearly blind in one eye. He recovered, was cared for by his very devoted parents, and his trauma from the surgery and limitations during his early life was not as severe as it might have been. However, he was a difficult child, and at times his feeling of being extremely precious to his objects was compounded by an arrogant feeling of being special and in need of special protection. Nevertheless, as he began to feel stronger psychologically (he was already quite recovered physically) his masculine identification started to grow. At six, just before a break, he developed a taste for pop music and performed – with a great stamping of feet and a certain macho thrust to his gait – a very rhythmic song. Then he roared another one, playing an imaginary guitar at me very sexily and aggressively. He seemed to be undergoing something of a recovery from a deep sense of damage and helplessness and was showing me his slightly delayed, Oedipal (and still somewhat narcissistic) potency and sexuality. I think it was important that I enjoyed and was impressed by this and showed it. (I shall discuss my countertransference response in more detail in the next chapter.) I found myself thinking that it could be very difficult for the parents of a baby born in such danger to see him as potent and to allow themselves the safety and confidence to dream of his future as a healthy, strong man, a dream every male child probably needs his parents to have for him. Toby, however, was not a deprived child. It was only one part of his identity that was inhibited. That is, I think he had no doubts about his lovability or his interestingness, only about his strength and potency.

Apparent narcissism where there is a relationship toward – but also identification with – an indifferent object: a double deficit

These are the patients I mentioned in the Introduction whom I began to think of as children for whom adults and the world were deeply uninteresting. For a long time, I had an atypical experience of complete indifference whenever one little boy patient, Jacob, threw away his drawings. It took me some while to realize that really they *did not matter* – neither to him, nor to me – and many of them had been carried out in a very desultory manner: 'I am a child. Children draw. I'll do a drawing to get her off my back for a bit.' This was certainly his attitude to the demands at school – dutiful compliance with no real learning – but, because children draw, I had foolishly looked for meaning in the drawings. He was doing it dutifully for me, but his heart was never in it. The meaning was absent. (See Ferro (1999) for a similar example.) It was important to show this child the lack of hope and faith, and therefore meaning, that lay in every single one of his communications. (This has been written about most evocatively by Ogden (1997, p. 4).) Jacob did not think that what he produced could be of interest, nor did he think his object's reaction would be of interest to him or could possibly lead to more interest. The world seemed empty. (I shall mention Jacob again in Chapter 11.)

In some children – far more deprived than Jacob – the *apparent* narcissism reveals indifference, boredom, contempt and often, initially, astonishment that the object could be interesting or interested. These objects are different from those of Rosenfeld's and Hamilton's patients, which were too close: these objects are impossibly remote, and the only solution is to go it alone. Our countertransference may be similar to that in the more straightforwardly narcissistic case, but a study of the nature of the internal object is illuminating. In the more severe cases, the dire effect on introjection and internalization leads to a situation where not only the world but one's own thoughts are uninteresting. Learning and cognitive functioning are often profoundly impaired. Thoughts may not be felt to be sufficiently interesting to be examined, owned or worth following up or following through. The analytic work has to start at this level – and note that the patient cannot be bothered, because he does not believe it will be worth it. As the object (and the contents of his mind) grow in interest and importance, envy may arise as an important feature, but this is not necessarily evidence that the previous narcissistic indifference arose as a defence against envy; rather, that envy has to be experienced once the object gains in stature, and that the normal process that every baby, toddler and latency-aged child goes through – of envying all those things that grown-ups can do – has to be negotiated all in one go, as it were.

Apparent narcissism that is not narcissism but a sense of self-worth: the precious self and the precious world

I first became interested in this issue after hearing regularly about an infant observation where the mother seemed to be particularly devoted and attentive to her baby. (Since then, I have seen several others with this quality.) The baby thrived physically, emotionally and cognitively, but our seminar wondered whether such perfect mothering, even if it facilitated development on the two-person level, could possibly survive Oedipal tests. Yet the father was an active, equally generous presence, the marriage seemed good, and the mother seemed to feel that the world for and to her baby was as valuable and interesting as he was. It was hard to fault this family. Yet the child himself was strikingly precious to his mother, and we had many debates in the seminar.

After almost two years (we were going to miss some Oedipal challenges, and also the birth of the next sibling), the mother, who had trained as a midwife, told the observer that her own brother had died as a baby when she was eight years old. We were able to understand that her own son had indeed been precious to her – not special in the narcissistically gratifying sense, nor primarily as a means of triumphing over her own mother. An overcoming of bereavement and loss through the process of mourning, as Klein (1937) said, is very different from a manic defence against them, and I think this was probably why the group was so often moved and also delighted by listening to the observations of the mother's love toward, and skills with, her baby, and the baby's 'love affair with the world' (Mahler *et al.*, 1975, pp. 70–71). I think we were seeing the results of depressive position development in the mother. (I am grateful to Luciana Tomassini's criticism of my pejorative use of the word 'special' and for pointing out that loved babies are also 'special' in the sense of being unique to their parents (personal communication, 2004).)

Again, if there is some wonder and un-narcissistic respect for the diversity and fecundity of life on the part of the parents, this also need not lead to a narcissistic outcome for the child. 'Special' need not imply 'superior'. The more confident babies and children seem to have a sufficiently strong sense of self, which enables them to move forward to a *self-forgetful* engagement with the world. Their talents and achievements can be felt to be shared *with* the internal parental objects – and even siblings – rather than won alone or in spite of them. It is a very important moment when a previously despairing child or adolescent manages to share some minor success with us: we need to be able to celebrate such moments without either going along with the invitation to be derogatory about it or going over the top. Of course, this is all relative. I am in no way suggesting that the normal child does not experience huge sibling rivalry or envy toward parents – it is a question of degree and balance.

Conclusion: consequences of recovery and further technical issues

Kernberg (1975, p. 256) has suggested that rage is a common result as the narcissism lessens. Resnik (1995, p. 95) has pointed out that narcissistic depression results when the psychotic recovers from his delusional world. Kernberg has also said that the narcissistic character must undergo severe depression and suicidal phantasies, and if such people do not have sufficient ego strength to tolerate it, their life is in danger. Where the ego is weak, he would offer supportive psychotherapy (Kernberg, 1975, p. 256).

I have seen this problem of depression and suicidal phantasies in the defensive and addictive narcissists (many of the more deprived groups seem invigorated by a change in their object and self toward greater robustness). However, I think there is sometimes a way of dealing psychoanalytically with the problem of the depressive collapse without the need for external support. If we consider that the patient's psychopathology dictates to him that he has only two choices – to be superior or to be desperately inferior – then it may be a mistake to be felt to be confirming this narrow duality. There is, after all, a third option, and the descent can be made easier for the narcissist when he discovers that other pleasures are available, begins to relinquish control a little, and sees how he has been idealizing power, or control, or whatever it takes to be top dog. Otherwise, the crash can indeed be devastating. Asking what is so terrible about being an ordinary member of the human race (implying that we are, too) can sometimes help to begin to deal with the delusion that only one of (the two of) us can be superior. As Waska (2002, p. 106) wrote, much depends on whether the narcissism is nearer to the depressive or paranoid-schizoid position; and, where there is something of the former, rage about a discovery of the maternal object's sexuality, say, may be accompanied by great relief and some enlivening (Alvarez, 2010b).

I should add that, where the narcissism has become addictive, there are certain interesting diagnostic overlaps with dissociative states, Asperger's syndrome and even autism, and here further investigation is needed. Some similar technical problems arise, and some of the consequences of recovery are similar. Of interest here are Joseph's (1981) description of a type of psychic pain that involves coming alive and which is different from depressive pain, and Tremelloni's (2005) book on the 'melting of the ice' in autistic and psychotic adults. For the patients recovering from the syndromes of apparent narcissism, depressive collapse is unlikely. It is my experience that they begin to take more pleasure in life.

Chapter 9

Types of sexual transference and countertransference in work with children and adolescents

Introduction

I became interested in the question of normal sexuality during the supervision of therapists treating severely sexually abused or, in many cases, sexually offending patients (Cottis, 2009; Woods, 2003). I then began to wonder whether I was recognizing it in my own traumatized or corrupted child patients. It is an interesting and delicate moment during the process of recovery when less perverse, more normal sexuality appears mixed with, or sometimes even disguised by, the more habitual perverse phantasies.

I shall have to start with some writings in the adult field first. There is relatively little written about what has been called post-Oedipal sexuality in the child field. A few writers in the field of adult psychoanalytic work have drawn distinctions between perverse, eroticized and normal erotic transferences (Bonasia, 2001; Wrye and Welles, 1989). Some have also distinguished between countertransferences in the analyst of an eroticized versus a normal erotic nature (Davies, 1998; Gerrard, 2010, 2011). I want to think about whether these issues could have any relevance for our child patients. Freud (1905b) and Klein (1945) have taught us much about the child's sexuality in relation to his interest in and attraction to his parents as sexual beings. But can we also detect some origins in earlier experiences in infancy of the child's later capacity to feel himself a sexual being, capable of being wanted by an other? How might such a feeling of sexual self-worth differ from narcissism?

A brief history of psychoanalytic ideas on childhood sexuality

Just as Freud widened the term 'mental' to include processes that took place in the unconscious part of the mind, he hugely widened the term 'sexual'. First, he widened it beyond the sphere of the genital, to include various perverse impulses that he found appearing in the phantasies and dreams of patients who did not practise such pursuits in their actual lives. He concluded that sexuality had many manifestations besides simply the genital union of coitus, and that the origin of these non-genital activities and phantasies lay in a pre-genital period in earliest infancy – a period of what he called 'polymorphous perversity'. The source or instinct had an aim, and the aim was release of tension.

At that early period of psychoanalysis, the objects of the aim – that is, other people – were seen as of relatively little importance (Freud, 1905b). Tensions arose, as it were, in their own right in the erogenous zones, where membranes were sensitive, such as the mouth, the anus and the genital area: they were described rather like itches that needed scratching. Yet the later case study of Little Hans, like other Freud case histories, gives a very different, richer, more subtle impression: we read of painful conflicts between jealousy and tender love, for example (Freud, 1909).

Freud (1905b) also identified what he called certain 'component instincts' – such as voyeurism, exhibitionism, sadism and masochism – which, although perverse, became perversions only if they subsequently became fixed and exclusive preoccupations. Ernest Jones (1967, p. 317) says that Lord Tansey asked why Freud had not used a word like 'love' or a phrase like 'desire for union', where he might have avoided the odium that came down on him for suggesting that infants were sexual (even perversely sexual) beings. And, in one way, with the hindsight of later studies and later theories, we too can feel irritated at the apparent pathologizing – or even perversizing (if there is such a word) – of the love life of babies. However, in another way, Freud was doing the exact opposite – attempting to find the normal elemental threads in the pathological. The problem is that the normal in the normal infant was conceptualized in the language of pathology. We still sometimes do it. We could try some alternatives, in response to Tansey. Nowadays, instead of polymorphous perversity, we might want to use a word that conveys the global passionateness of babies – the way, when they greet someone, their excitement and delight shows in every part of their bodies. They greet us, as adults do, with smiling eyes and mouths, but they also welcome us most eloquently with their circling hands and wriggling feet.

Freud thought that integration, when it came, arrived through the Oedipus complex, at around the age of three, whereas we would nowadays understand that it is the sheer otherness of the parents (even at the two-person, pre-Oedipal stage of earliest infancy) that first induces integration. The normal baby is attracted to his objects, and if they give him time to ponder and linger over his experience, this, in itself, is highly integrating. Moreover, the baby is also attractive *to* his parents.

But back to some limitations in Freud's concept of 'component instincts'. Here, written a century ago, is William James's bow to complexity:

> The traditional psychologist talks like one who says a river consists of nothing but pailsful, spoonsful, quartpotsful, barrelsful, and other moulded forms of water. Even were the pails and pots all actually standing in the stream, still between them the free water would flow. It is precisely the free water of consciousness [we could add 'of unconsciousness', too] that psychologists resolutely overlook. Every definite image in the mind is steeped and dyed in

the free water that flows around it. With it goes the sense of its relations, near and remote, the dying echo of when it came to us, the dawning sense of whither it is to lead. The significance, the value of the image, is all in this halo or penumbra that surrounds and escorts it – or rather that is fused into one with it and has become bone of its bone and flesh of its flesh.

(James, 1992, cited in Crapanzano, 2004, p. 18)

James's beautiful, almost biblical prose can be just as good as that of his brother, Henry! Even the brain researchers and geneticists are warning us of the danger of thinking too much in terms of pails. The modern brain models and genetic models are extremely detailed and they are not simple. They describe an awesome complexity (Alhanati, 2002, p. 116; Solms and Turnbull, 2002). Of course, we cannot entirely dispense with pails either, but a word such as 'elements' or 'aspects' of sexual feeling seems better. Or the notion that some feelings and thoughts take place in the forefront of our minds while others remain in the background, not always unconscious, maybe only preconscious, as Sandler and Sandler (1994b) have suggested. Maybe another term could be 'paraconscious' – existing beside but a little in the shadow, as it were.

Freud, of course, also had something to say about normal adult sexuality. Although in the 'Three essays' (Freud, 1905b) he did leave room for two currents in human libidinal life – the sensual-erotic and the affectionate – Likierman (2001, p. 90) points out that he did not regard the affectionate current as a primary, irreducible force. We had to wait for Klein to get that. Fornari (quoted in Lupinacci, 1998, p. 411) has suggested that the discovery of infantile sexuality dazzled Freud so much that it overshadowed his vision of adult sexuality – specifically of the transition, at the moment of sexual and emotional maturation, from the infantile type of sexuality to the real existence of two genitals bound by a relationship of reciprocal symmetry. Lupinacci (p. 411), agreeing with Fornari, writes, 'We have here the idea of a creative and civilized complementary state of structures and functions in the male and female, in which each member of the couple, taken individually, is limited and dependent, needs the other, and has in turn something to give to the other, to the mutual advantage of both.'

Phillips (1993, pp. 102–103) makes a related point about the nature of kissing, particularly in adolescents. He points out that there is more to kissing than the elements of sucking or eating. He suggests there is also the return of the primary sensuous experience of *tasting* another person, and that the kiss is the image of reciprocity, not of domination: 'When we kiss we devour the object by caressing it; we eat it, in a sense, but sustain its presence. Kissing on the mouth can have a mutuality that blurs the distinction between giving and taking.'

Klein, while holding to Freud's theory, in fact replaced the notion of component instincts with the notion of part-*objects*. Klein and her followers were emphasizing that it was the otherness of people that attracted us and affected our development. As is well known, the breast as the primary object of need and desire became the focal point of Kleinian theory, although Klein also said that the baby took in understanding, along with the milk. Later, Bion (1962b) wrote of the existence of a preconception in the newborn baby of a mind, what O'Shaughnessy (2006) calls an object that gives psychological containment, a psychological object. Klein also wrote of the baby's interest in the mother's face and hands, but it is only now that we know that interest in people's faces arrives on the scene as early as the interest in breasts and bottles: that is, immediately after birth, on day one (Hobson, 2002). I love the developmental research and Bion, but we can see that moving up the body from genitals to faces and even minds may take us away from sexuality. In any case, Klein (1945) taught that these early experiences of love and hate toward the primary object coloured and influenced the later developments in the Oedipal phase.

Green (2000), who has questioned whether infant observation and child development research have anything to contribute to psychoanalysis, is equally critical of what he sees as the Kleinian emphasis on infancy and what he thinks is its consequent neglect of sexuality. He is certainly eloquently vituperative on the subject of infant research. For instance, he asks, 'What of the researcher who no longer calls the parent of the infant the love object, but rather "the caregiver"? Do caregivers have sexual desires, do they love, do they hate, do they have phantasies, do they dream – who cares?' (p. 58). And in a paper asking whether sexuality has anything to do with psychoanalysis, he suggests (Green, 1995, p. 871) that 'The contemporary and fashionable focus on object relations, pregenital fixations, borderline pathology and theories and techniques drawn from observation or child development have obscured the meaning and importance of sexuality in psychoanalytic theory and practice.' He also says that even the penis started to be seen as a giving and feeding organ – in other words, as a breast (p. 876). He maintains that the role of a sexual relationship is not to feed and nurture but to reach ecstasy in mutual enjoyment. He thinks that the anal, oral or, in other terminologies, the depressive position and the paranoid-schizoid position being seen as older or deeper means that they are equated with being more important. He says that this reflects 'an anti-sexual attitude which implies that sexuality is superficial' (p. 879). Vituperation aside, he makes a very interesting theoretical point when he says that, as a result of Freud's great paper *Beyond the Pleasure Principle* (1920), 'We have focused on death instincts, but Freud, instead of sexual instincts, speaks of life instinct. Life or love instincts' (p. 877), and Green says we have neglected this. I think he may have a point there, but Judith Edwards (personal communication, 2010) has noted that is not so in Klein's (1958) paper 'On the development of mental functioning'.

I want to take account of Green's criticisms but to argue that he has left out something important from Kleinian theory. As is well known, Segal (1957) is responsible for the distinction in psychoanalytic theory between a symbolic equation and a symbol. The symbol is used not to deny but to overcome loss. It is worth mentioning that the concept of symbolization is different from the Freudian concept of sublimation, because the former does not simply describe a transformation – that is, a change in the form of expression of an impulse or instinct. It involves a more fundamental change – that which results from a process of mourning and growth via internalization. It involves facing the pain of the loss that the little girl can never marry daddy, nor be mummy; the little boy can never marry mummy, nor be daddy. We have all had patients whose lives have been driven and ruined by a difficulty in accepting such relegation. Symbol-formation is costly: it involves relinquishing possession of – or narcissistic identification with – the primary object, *and* – at the Oedipal level – relinquishing the role of being a full intrusive 'member of the wedding' so that (as the American writers I will mention term it) post-Oedipal sexuality can appear in its own right. Even if it is the case that many papers have concentrated on patients whose level of illness involves pre-Oedipal problems, I think Kleinian *theory* – with its concept of the depressive position and its distinction between pathological and healthy types of identification with the sexuality of the parents – leaves plenty of room for sexuality.

One point I wish to make, however, is that Kleinian thinking tends to stress the self's feelings for the object. But what about the self's phantasies of the object's feelings, even sexual feelings, for it? How are we to think about both aspects of the sexuality of our child patients? Can we distinguish between narcissistic self-evaluation and something like a feeling of sexual self-worth (Gerrard, 2011) that is sufficiently comfortable to enable self-forgetfulness, not narcissistic self-preoccupation?

The question of the normal erotic transference and countertransference

In a paper titled 'Sexual excitement and countertransference love in the analyst', Gabbard (1994, p. 1083) noted that the psychoanalytic literature (since Searles in 1959) had been remarkably silent on the subject of erotic countertransference feelings. He made the interesting point that sexualization may defend against feelings of love (p. 1091), which he said are relatively more difficult than lustful feelings for many analysts to acknowledge. He said that the value of consultation with a colleague cannot be overemphasized, but that only by tiptoeing to the edge of that abyss can we fully appreciate the internal world of the patient and its impacts on us.

Davies (1998), a relational analyst, goes into the abyss. She explores the concept of 'post-Oedipal adult sexuality' and suggests that it challenges the fundamental assumption that, whenever erotic feelings enter the psychoanalytic space, the analyst always stands in the role of the Oedipal parent. She says that this can fail to recognize significant developmental changes. Gerrard (2010, 2011), an English adult psychotherapist, takes a line similar to that of Davies, who points out that Oedipal desire is romantic and idealized, whereas post-Oedipal desire tolerates imperfections and can experience disappointment without the death of desire.

Davies (1998, p. 752) is not talking about eroticized and therefore pathological infantile transferences but rather what she calls 'that form of sexual aliveness that most often . . . marks the termination phase of an analysis . . . with the deepening intimacy and potential interpersonal space of successful analytic work'. She agrees with Searles (1959) that this involves a kind of mourning and relinquishment on the part of the analyst, a letting go of the patient to have his own adult sexual life. But she is stressing something more than the letting go: this is the analyst's responsiveness to the patient's possibly new aliveness, in particular in her paper when it first appears in a patient who was previously dead to his sexuality. Something similar may happen in despairing children and adolescents when they experience a new vitality. Davies's patient was an abused and previously pro-foundly depressed man who pointed out one day after he was finally beginning to show signs of recovery that Davies was flirting with him. At that point, she became aware that she had been.

Davies proceeds to discuss the difference between the Oedipal child and the post-Oedipal child (p. 753) who is struggling to experience the self as the object of another's sexual interest *when the other is not the Oedipally idealized parent figure* (p. 759). Davies suggests that the post-Oedipal parent is in a constant state of experiencing, processing and recognizing his or her child's emerging sexuality and that the child is most acutely tuned into the parent's ongoing struggle. She gives a telling example from her own family.

But back to the previously depressed patient who saw Davies was flirting with him. Davies then disclosed to him that she had indeed been flirting. He asked her what those people who wrote the books on the shelf behind her would think of that. She suggested that they should explore this, but he then became nervous and wished to close the door on the subject. However, they returned to it in subsequent sessions.

My view is that I agree with Davies's suggestion regarding the task of the post-Oedipal parent (in life or in the countertransference), but I think there is a way forward for the therapist that need not involve actual disclosure. I think Davies could have said something like: 'You are beginning to feel you are a person that people feel like flirting with.' I agree with her that a simple falling back on 'shoulds' and 'shouldn'ts' does not get us very far with deprived patients, and I would certainly add that explaining the situation away as immature Oedipal phantasies does not either, and that it is important to be receptive. However, I think that it is unhelpful to make the situation too overheated for the patient. I believe disclosure could really overburden any patient. To me, a more descriptively respectful appreciation of the new development seems to be enough.

Nevertheless, I think Davies's and Gerrard's ideas on the role of the post-Oedipal parent in development are very interesting.

One final word about flirting. It need not be seen as a purely seductive act. If it is occurring on the symbolic level, it can involve a type of playing, of acknow-ledging attraction, but under safe conditions where the internal Oedipal triangle of which Britton (2003, p. 55) has spoken is kept intact, respected and acknowledged.

The question is: are any of these papers relevant for psychoanalytic work with children? These are clearly delicate issues especially now that we are so much better informed about the ubiquity of sexual abuse of children. I want to ask some questions, and I shall also offer some speculation about some possible pre-Oedipal origins of sexuality, which may link some developmental research with questions of sexuality. The research can be wonderfully illuminating, but much (not all) of it has neglected babies' bodies, and it has certainly neglected infantile sexuality. But some of the newer work may have some relevance to these questions.

I shall begin with an attempt, through clinical examples from children, to distinguish perverse sexuality from disordered sexuality, and both of these from normal but delayed Oedipal sexuality. I shall follow this with an example, where a budding adolescent sexuality allowed some important pre-Oedipal history to be rewritten *via the post-Oedipal sexuality*. I shall discuss the issue of the developmental implications of the parents' responses to all of these levels for the way in which we transform and use the feelings at each of these levels in the countertransference. At the post-Oedipal stage, I am wondering about psychoanalytic technique in the presence of a child's real sexual feelings and sexual self, as opposed to when the child is sexualizing some other feeling for defensive purposes.

An example of perverse sexuality in a child

Seven-year-old David was diagnosed with pervasive developmental disorder with autistic features, and he was delayed in his language, thinking and symbolic capacities. The therapist gradually learned that he also had a foot fetish. I had noted that several therapists had started wearing sandals during the first warm week of summer, and there had been major reactions from almost all of their patients whom I heard about in supervision. (There are important issues here regarding how we should consider our dress, especially with easily over-stimulated patients.) In any case, some reactions to the sandals were more radical than others. David began looking at his therapist's feet in sandals with a terrible leer. He accused her of having smelly feet, but he was clearly staring at them with a horrible fascination. Also (and we came to think this was very important), although his leer seemed to accuse her of collusion – that is, of liking being dirty and disgusting – it also seemed to invite loathing and disgust for him on her part. Thus, there was something cruel and sadistic but also something quite masochistic in it.

I had seen an almost fetishistic preoccupation with feet in certain deprived children, and although David's therapist and I discussed the possible *origin* of the original preoccupation in the history of babies left too much on the carpet watching feet coming and going but never seeming to stop long enough, and yet never able to be forgotten about because the baby was never sufficiently up on the lap and looking at faces, that was clearly not the whole story. There was obviously *far more to it than a reaction to, or a defence against, pain*. We talked a lot about David's feeling of being loathed by and disgusting to his mother, which had been real, but also about what now seemed to have become the dangerously addictive quality of his preoccupation. This boy's leer evoked disgust. It was a bit similar to the way in which my own autistic patient, Robbie, would look at me – not lustfully, but so lasciviously that although I felt no fear, I did feel a powerful desire to brush him off.

Uriah Heep and Caliban know they are despised. Making yourself ugly and distasteful is better than submitting to seeing that in someone else's eyes, as Sinason (1992, p. 119) has noted with physically disabled children. The child's pleasure in getting the disgust he expected and sought may even, in the worst cases, turn into sexual excitement.

We puzzled a lot about David. We were certain he was not sexually abused, and we wondered not about how he came to feel disgusting, nor about why he might try to project that feeling into others, but about how he might have discovered the final twist upwards into the excitement. (Maybe if there is not enough excitement and fun in the love relationship, especially where the love is limited, you grab it where you can.)

The following material provides no answers, but it does at least give a sense of the steps in the progression of what amounts to a perversion.

David had been considerably improved in recent months, much less interested in feet, and much more interested in normal – although, for his age (six and a half), rather immature – play. This play had given him genuine pleasure and delight, but not perverse excitement. Sometimes there had even been real symbolic play. On this occasion, he greeted his therapist, whom I shall call Cathy, quite normally in the waiting room, with only the briefest of glances at her feet. (The look at her face as he greeted her was more lingering.) The session started with one of these new, immature, but more normal pieces of play. He began by spinning on the office chair in her consulting room. The game involved Cathy stopping the chair intermittently and saying, 'There you are,' at which point David would giggle and spin it again. It was a kind of peekaboo, and Urwin (2002) has suggested the appearance of this game often signals the child's emergence from an autistic state. Cathy wrote, '*At times* his grin seems somewhat fixed and slightly "grimace"-like, although his giggle seems more real.' (It was vital for her to monitor the difference in order not to collude with or escalate the more perverse moments. However, we must also leave room for our receptive response to more ordinary excitements when they finally come, for children who have got into states where they have previously known only the perverse kind. Otherwise we collude with the despairing patient's view that there are only two choices: the thrill of perversion or the emptiness of a too-sober normality.) They continued to play this spinning game for a little while and at one point David spun the chair very fast, thereby bumping his knee quite hard on Cathy's chair. He then squealed in an excited laugh. The therapist knew about David's language delay, and tended to keep her language simple but emotive, so she said simply and sympathetically, 'Ohh, ouch.' But David immediately ordered, 'Cry, Cathy!' She said to him that he bumped his knee and now he wanted her to cry and she wondered why. He said, 'Stu-pid!' and laughed. Cathy then said to him, 'I think David thinks it's stupid to cry but it's not stupid to cry if it hurts.' She had many times before witnessed his cruel mockery of an injured child doll, but he may also have felt she was stupid not to *get* that she was the one who should contain the projective identification – to suffer the hurt and do the crying for him. (Usually, by the way, she did, as did the therapist of the child in the wheelchair in Chapter 1.) In any case, he responded to her insistence that it was not stupid to cry by announcing with a leer that he had 'smelled the guinea pig's feet'.

Here, we can clearly see some of the steps in the progression to a fetish. First David is hurt; then he tries to project the hurt into his therapist; then, when she does not fully contain it in herself, I think he feels overwhelming self-disgust; and then the smelly feet have to belong to someone or something else – the guinea pig. A hurt baby self isn't just despicable; apparently, it is also disgusting. And what do you do with a profound feeling of self-disgust? I guess one way through is to project and control the disgust. We never quite understood how it got to the final stage of perverse erotization in this child's development. Clearly, though, the technical response to a perverse moment needs to be very different from that to a defensive or protective manoeuvre, and certainly from that to more ordinary excitements (Anne Alvarez, 1995; Chapter 7, this volume). A descriptive-level response, probably a fairly cool one, is far better than an attempt to explain it away, as it were, as a defence.

Disordered sexuality

I now want to move on to two examples of disordered, but not precisely perverse, sexuality. An autistic patient of mine, Joseph, had a repetitive preoccupation with making two dolls dance or jump together while seeming to talk to each other in a pseudo-language. The game was far too private and exclusive to be called real pretend play – the jumps always occurred in one spot, and even the dance involved only the tiniest of circles around the dancers. There were never any leaps because, I think, there was felt to be nowhere interesting to go. The problem, I believe, was not anxiety about the unknown but rather extremely deep boredom. There was simply nothing or nowhere interesting enough to pursue. (This may involve the difference between devalued and unvalued or stupid objects: see Chapter 8.)

On one occasion, Joseph arrived in what appeared to be a really quite loving mood toward me, and this time the animals kissed each other very gently on the side of the face, laying their cheeks against each other and murmuring tender-nesses. I did not feel this was perverse at all, nor even overly sensuous. However, it did not stop. It went on and on, and I began to think it had started with what seemed like real love but even Antony and Cleopatra must have got up occa-sionally and gone out for a breath of fresh air and a good long walk! The behaviour was addictive, but not actually perverse, yet this certainly raises important technical issues concerning how to unstick the patient from his habitual ways and help him to move on. I responded somewhere between a descriptive level and a more intensified level by suggesting that I was sure they were a bit tired of kissing and might like to climb the hill (of the couch) to see what was on the other side. Eventually they did so, and Joseph showed me this with pleasure.

The next example is from another of my cases, where I also think the sexuality is disordered but not (as yet) perverse. Like David, this little boy, Michael, was very turned on by my first sandal day: he lunged across the room with the set, closed, grim mouth that I had learned held in a desire to bite. (I suspect this began to occur when he was two months old and refused feeding when his mother went back to work soon after he had recovered – physically, but not mentally – from a series of traumatizing surgical operations.) He had often tried to grab my knees with that look and had attempted to press his penis against me. Now, after a quick glance at my feet, he tried to do the same thing again. I felt he was experiencing a very confused, overwhelming, half-suppressed and hugely *compressed* set of impulses – oral and genital at once but all of it somehow terribly condensed. I tried to clarify this a little, but it was very difficult to slow him down and help him experience feelings one at a time, as it were.

In any case, a few days later, a little calmer, he looked again at my feet very intensely and *asked* if he could bite my toes! There seemed to be no genital excitement this time, so I felt this was a bit of a development: there was only one desire – to bite – and at least he could allow himself to experience it, instead of suppressing it.

Subsequently, returning from a summer break, he heard what he took to be a man's footsteps upstairs. He had always scampered to the other side of the room when he had heard them previously. Michael was a very omnipotent and Oedipal child but his fear of a father was compounded, I think, by the early radical and intrusive surgical interventions. I spoke of his fear of the daddy especially when he was being possessive and bossy with me. Toward the end of the session, he observed that the couch was not really a bed and that I did not go home with him or travel with him on holiday. He also asked what might be upstairs, and I felt that another space/place was opening up. Klein (1945) suggested this referred to the mystery of the inside of the mother's body, while Crapanzano (2004), an anthropologist, referred to the significance of that which lay beyond the horizon – imaginative horizons. (See also Britton (1989) and Edwards (1994) on the sense of space opening up.)

I suggest that the powerful compression of Michael's passions was disordered, but not really perverse. When he could slow down to experience one passion at a time, as it were, he could experience curiosity and think.

The normal sexual self and questions of technique: that is, use of our countertransference responses to these

Lupinacci (1998, p. 418) offers some interesting ideas on the role of the two sets of parents in the Oedipus myth. She points out that the narcissistic, egocentric Theban parents tried to kill their infant, out of fear of his hostility, and that the Corinthian adoptive parents, while kind and loving, are somewhat idealized and sexless. She notes that both need integrating in the patient, or the child, but also in the analyst at work. She describes the need for the analyst to struggle with his own Oedipal impulses and to integrate his or her softer Corinthian aspects with his firmer Theban ones in order to facilitate the patient's integration (p. 418). Lupinacci, like Klein (1945), locates the origins of the Oedipal phantasies of their patients in earlier, pre-Oedipal experiences with the early mother and breast. Her technical recommendations have much in common with Britton's (1989) comments on the parents' response to the child's Oedipal or pre-Oedipal feelings in the course of development. But it is clear that Davies (1998), the analyst with the flirting patient, goes further than attention to a soft, warm, maternal counter-transference response. She is clear that she is speaking of a normal *erotic* countertransference to the post-Oedipal adult sexuality occurring in the patient.

Thus far, I have been talking about developments in sexual feelings in the self toward a sexual object. I now want to look at the question of the development of the self as a sexual being as an object of others' sexuality. I suggest that although this is partly linked to the baby's gradual identification with the parents, it is also likely to be linked with early developments of the baby's feeling of being potent enough to awaken responses, interest and delight in the caregiver. (That is, parents do not only satisfy basic bodily needs for food and holding. Nor do they offer only mental containment.) Laznik (2009) is interesting on the importance of the normal cannibalistic impulses that parents feel toward the edibility of their babies. I realize Green (1995) would say I am privileging early infancy, but I am trying to trace the possible origins in infancy of a feeling of sexual self-worth in adulthood. Clearly, as I just implied, symbol-formation and a resultant capacity for identifications (not pathological over-identifications) with the sexuality of the parents play huge parts, but is there something else, too? Are there some elements that need to be examined in addition to the familiar ones concerning the importance of feelings toward the breast, and the facial and vocal reciprocity we hear so much about from the developmentalists? Is there room for actual infantile sexuality, without reducing sexuality to dependency or infantile needs?

First, I want to mention the sense of agency and potency (not omnipotence) (Alvarez, 1992). Studies have shown that babies enjoy finding that they can be the cause of events, and become considerably withdrawn when they fail and experience a feeling of inefficacy (Papousek and Papousek, 1975). The studies let the babies make bells ring and lights come on, but we know that the main causal effects for the baby take place in his interactions with other human beings. It is fun to make rattles shake and any various other stuff happen, but, in the earliest months, one of several things that matter most is to be able to make someone's eyes light up. The capacity to entertain and give delight is being studied by Trevarthen (2001) and Reddy (2008), and I want to stress that this relationship is different from the need for a feeding or even a containing object in either the Bion (1962b) or Bick (1968) sense: it concerns the need for a responsive interested object capable of being delighted.

Here is an observation of a baby with a certainly good enough mother, who in the first seven months of his life seemed a little too passively accepting of his mother's busyness with other things. Around eight months, as she prepared to return to work, the two seemed to have formed a stronger and more vital bond. He had found more power to attract and keep her attention through smiles, coos and vocalizations, and she seemed to have more desire to be thus captivated. Then, at nine months, they were both just beginning to recover from the flu and quite subdued again. The baby tried two different methods of getting his mother to gaze at him and respond. Both methods failed, but it is the difference in the methods that I wish to discuss. First, he cried a few times but gave up when his mother continued with her weary tidying and did not respond. (His cries had never been long or loud.) Then, at a moment when he saw her standing in front of him, looking vaguely in his direction, he smiled widely and blew a raspberry. A month before, she would have laughed and/or imitated him, but now she simply continued to look beyond him at something in the room. He then turned over to his dummy and went to sleep.

The crying baby asks for comfort; the smiling and performing baby asks for something like delight, to bring a light to someone's eyes. This need not involve a manic defence. He needs comfort but also an accessible and reachable object – impressible, interested, pleased to be entertained (Reddy, 2005; Trevarthen, 2001). (I have previously suggested (Alvarez, 1992) we need a word for a process that may be a foundation for, and a prelude to, reparation – the wish to give something to someone not in order to repair a damaged object but to add to the pleasure of an already intact object.)

Trevarthen (2001) thinks the emotions of shame and pride shown in infancy are central to development. Bion (1957b) distinguished between arrogance and pride, as the Greeks did between hubris and philotomo (Lynd, 1958). A very depressed boy had in the past been very skilled, like David, at getting attention by behaving or speaking in a manner designed to evoke disgust, but he did not know how to use more ordinary methods of getting attention. After a few years of treatment during which he gave up his old ways, one day he said to his therapist, 'I like it when your eyes are wide,' seemingly because this meant he could be sure that she was interested. This involves an early integration between both self and object but also within the self – 'I have the power to make a (positive) impact on you.' It arises as an important development in children recovering from lifelong depression, and it is important to be clear when we are seeing simple manipulative and narcissistic seductiveness, and when we are seeing a desire to show and give pleasure rather than simply to show off to make someone else feel inferior or helplessly ensnared. Attracting need not involve seducing.

Childhood sexuality: the question of the parental object's role

What is the line between an all too seducible parent and one who allows the sexuality without being seduced or seductive? A child (or, for that matter, a baby) can feel himself capable of giving pleasure to an other. How can we respond to showing, without encouraging showing off and narcissism? How can we facilitate self-forgetful showing where the thing or activity being shown is more important than the shower, but the shower is also appreciated?

A clinical example of delayed Oedipal development

In Chapter 8 I described a little boy patient of mine, Toby, who was born nearly blind in one eye, a condition that necessitated several operations. He recovered physically, but seemed to feel himself to be a child who was somewhat over-precious. However, as he began to feel stronger psychologically, his masculine identification started to grow. At six years old, just before a break, he developed a taste for pop music and performed – with a great stamping of feet and a certain macho thrust to his gait – the song 'Don't Stop Thinkin' about the S Club Beat'. He also roared, 'Super star, with your big guitar!' not exactly sexily but with a new sort of stomping vitality. He was really monitoring my expression, and I am sure it showed some pleasure. His behaviour was so much more spontaneous than his usual, very controlling approach in the room. He seemed to be having something of a recovery from a deep sense of damage and helplessness and was showing me his slightly delayed Oedipal (and still quite narcissistic) potency and sexuality.

I said in Chapter 8 that I imagined that it could be very difficult for the parents of a baby born with such physical damage to see him as potent and to allow themselves the safety and confidence to dream of his future as a healthy, strong man. Here, I would like to add his future as a *grown-up, sexy* man. In this situation we need to be interested not in the acorn in the oak tree – the baby self in the adult – but in the oak tree in the acorn. I wonder now if Toby's very devoted parents' capacity to find him attractive as a baby could have been affected by his facial imperfection. Looking at him, you would naturally feel concern, which is not the same as the parents' pleasure and pride in their baby's healthy body and face.

I think this raises the question of the importance of the positive counter-transference. I enjoyed Toby's dancing, although my response, though positive, was not particularly erotic. Another child whom I saw some years ago at the clinic, Nicola, had been extremely deprived and rejected in her infancy and had become chronically depressed but also dissociated and hard in spite of being adopted at 18 months by very loving parents. She spent most sessions getting me to be frightened on either my own behalf or hers, with near-throws of objects close to my face, or dangerous entanglements of her body in the furniture.

After about a year's treatment, when she was 11 years old, she showed me a dance she was doing at school, and some steps from one the older girls were doing. Her dancing gave me a new pleasure – she seemed much softer, more shy and less defended than usual. The dancing was modest, but the lightness, grace and yet sexiness were very attractive, and I am sure my eyes and face – and my words – revealed my pleasure and appreciation of this new Nicola. (I said something like,

'What a lovely dance!') I do not think Nicola was being seductive. And, finally, she was not being provocative. I think she was trying out something new in our relationship and trying to give the kind of pleasure she had not been able to give as an infant to her extremely rejecting other. Puberty was possibly being experienced as a kind of new birth where her painful history could be partially rewritten via a tactful appreciation of her newfound attractiveness and grace. Certainly, more work was necessary to move beyond a situation where sexuality could be the main vehicle for positive experiences. She needed to find other ways of opening up and pleasing her objects.

Conclusion

In conclusion, there is still much work to be done on an exploration of our counter-transferences to our patients' bodies and sexuality at all levels – pre-Oedipal, Oedipal and post-Oedipal. I have speculated on some possible origins of the latter type of object relationship in the baby's ability to give pleasure, to make an impact, to entertain by the use of his body, his facial expressions and vocalizations. I have not had time to discuss his wit and intelligence. When someone makes us laugh or says something intelligent that is not pedantic or exhibitionistic, it gives us pleasure and is certainly attractive, and sometimes even sexy. How we use this sort of countertransference in ways that do not explain the moment away as a purely Oedipal or seductive act – but do remain sensitive to a possibly healthy new development – is a delicate issue. Sometimes the positive transference is harder to take and stay with than the negative; and when it is sexual, too, it demands much courage, honesty and respect from us in our countertransference responses.

Chapter 10

Under-integrations and integrations at the paranoid-schizoid level

Introduction: Bick's controversial views on unintegration

Marianne Moore ends her great poem 'The Pangolin' with the way each dawn steadies man's soul with new hope (Moore, 1968). This chapter contains some reflections on the treatment of unsteady and unsteadied children. In the late 1960s Esther Bick made a very interesting, but controversial, distinction between helpless unintegration and defensive disintegration through splitting processes for defensive purposes (Bick, 1968). A source of some confusion is that at some moments when she referred to helpless unintegration, she referred to it simply as a *state* (she even mentioned 'fluctuations' in this state). At other moments, however, she referred to it as *characteristic of* the primary *phase* of development. In 2004, at a conference for teachers of infant observation, Joan Symington apparently agreed with Bick on the notion of this as the primary *phase (or stage)* of development (Symington, 2004; see also Symington, 2002). There followed considerable debate about this subject (O'Shaughnessy, 2006).

To start with Bick's original paper, 'The experience of the skin in early object-relations', it is a very short and condensed article but quite categorical in tone. She wrote (Bick, 1968, pp. 55–56):

> The thesis is that in its most primitive form the parts of the personality are felt to have no binding force amongst themselves and must therefore be held together in a way that is experienced by them passively, by the skin functioning as a boundary. But this internal function of containing the parts of the self is dependent initially on the introjection of an external object, experienced as capable of fulfilling this function. Later, identification with this function of the object supersedes the unintegrated state and gives rise to the fantasy of internal and external spaces. *Only then the stage is set* [my italics] for the operation of primal splitting and idealization of self and object as described by Melanie Klein. Until the containing functions have been introjected, the concept of a space within the self cannot arise.

She continued (p. 56), 'The fluctuations in this primal state will be illustrated in case material, from infant observation, in order to show the difference between unintegration as a passive experience of total helplessness and disintegration through splitting processes as an active defensive process in the service of development.' She said the former were conducive to catastrophic anxieties and the latter to the more limited and specific persecutory and depressive ones. Furthermore, she went on (p. 56):

> The need for a containing object would seem, in the infantile unintegrated state, to produce a frantic search for an object – a light, a voice, a smell, or other sensual object – which can hold the attention and thereby be experienced, momentarily at least, as holding the parts of the personality together. The optimal object is the nipple in the mouth, together with the holding and talking and familiar smelling mother.

Bick gave examples of babies trembling, of making disorganized movements, and of her patients' feeling that their skins could not hold them together and that they might spill out. Although it can be seen that she listed several different types of 'containing' object, she narrowed it down in the clinical material, and in the title of the paper, to the idea that such an object was concretely experienced as a skin. In my experience, the other types of integrators should be given equal weight.

Several questions arose in discussions of Bick's paper. I shall address them one at a time, adding some thoughts of my own.

Can all apparent unintegrations be seen as the result of disintegrating processes acting upon prior integrations?

The concept of deficit (in the USA) and this somewhat similar concept of helpless unintegration have led to controversy for good reasons. They have seemed to challenge Freud's great insight into the dynamic nature of thought processes – their inherent meaningfulness and purposiveness. This is an old issue. Fairbairn (1952, p. 14) pointed out that, although Freud's concept of repression was the foundation-stone upon which the whole explanatory system represented by psychoanalytic theory was built, this had nevertheless not been an unmixed gain, because it left no room for the idea of ego weakness (which Charcot had ascribed to the hysterics he and later Freud were treating). In child work, we might add, the dynamic model which implies that every state of mind, however pathological, arises from meaningful motivation leaves no room for ego *immaturity* and therefore for the idea of something like helplessness.

Regarding the issue of active motivation (intentionality) influencing states of unintegration (that is, are these patients and infants not so helpless?), it is interesting to read Wittenberg, who seems to have kept an open mind on the issue and whose approach is closer to Bick's than to Klein's and Bion's. In writing of primal depression in her little autistic patient, she referred to Bick's concept of adhesive identification, and said that her (Wittenberg's) arms, her lap, her attention seemed to be the 'string which pulled [her patient] John's mentality together'. She added, 'at the moment of my withdrawal, John's mentality fell apart, or perhaps he let it passively do so rather than suffer utter hopelessness. Where another child might scream in rage or fear, John experienced his object as unreachable and so he gave up in despair' (Wittenberg, 1975, p. 93). Note Wittenberg's subtlety in addressing the whole issue of intentionality in states of despair.

My own view is that psychoanalysis, psychoanalytic treatments and brain researchers still have much to learn about states of despair, which are certainly different from the depression of the depressive position but also different from melancholia and from states of persecution. I suspect that giving up is different from dissociation or splitting. The one may be a response to despair; the others to terror or hatred. There are, of course, different types of giving up, some (not at all) helpless. In Chapter 1, when discussing Robbie's collapses, I mentioned the way in which, as the years progressed, he could use and misuse his passivity in quite active ways. This in no way puts into doubt the helplessness of his original states, but it is a lesson in remaining vigilant in discriminating one motive from the other – especially when they appear together at the same moment! (See Samuel's complicated and mixed motives later in this chapter.)

In the issue of the *Journal of Child Psychotherapy* devoted to this debate, I (Alvarez, 2006b) suggested that one part of the confusion, and even of the controversy, could be avoided if we speak only of a (possibly temporary) 'state' of un- or (as I prefer to call it) *under*-integration, rather than the more enduring 'phase' of development marked by unintegration referred to at times by Bick (1968) and, later, by Symington (2002). The following attempts (partially) to address the question.

Do unintegrated states exist at all? The question of the degree of cohesiveness of the early ego

I would certainly agree with the suggestion that defensive or destructive disintegrating processes exist, but my clinical experience also leads me to maintain that so does the type of helpless falling apart that Bick describes. The brain research may offer support here. Trauma researchers have described dissociation as a protective mechanism that cuts or blocks neuronal connections in the brain – between thinking and feeling, for example, as a reaction to abuse or trauma (Schore, 2003). However, Perry (2002) has also described a very different condition arising from lack of dendritic and synaptic growth in the brain due to neglect. It is possible to imagine that a baby or child with weak brain growth would be less likely to summon necessary defences against stress. The type and sophistication of the 'defences' available to the infant seem to depend on his age and stage of emotional and cognitive development. (See the discussion of Papousek and Papousek's (1975) research in Chapter 2.) Such children or babies seem to lack integrating processes, and, I suggest, not to be attacking them. It is important to note also that the brain researchers see dissociation as an automatic and protective mechanism that can become unproductively habitual, rather than as something defensive and somehow intentional. We may also need to leave room for the possibility that chronic dissociation in infancy and childhood produces such an extreme level of cognitive delay that, in other words, chronic disintegration may lead to unintegration. Chronicity and severity are major factors in all pathology, not only psychopathology. In Chapter 1 I mentioned that I had witnessed such emptiness in some patients, that I came to doubt that such states were indeed sought defensively by them. I concluded that – in some cases, at some moments – they were not: the patient was truly defence*less*. Too long spent in such states – too early – can lead to atrophy of function, if not of structure.

An article about training health professionals in the Neonatal Behavioral Assessment Scale (NBAS) and its use as an intervention was published by Hawthorne (2004). This refers to full-term babies and to the huge differences between them. The scale measures such things as level of functioning of, for example, the autonomic system. 'Babies who show tremors, startles, changes in color, and stress signals are still working to get their autonomic system under control, and may need containment and quiet handling' (p. 3). The scale also measures the state system, which assesses the capacity for habituation: that is, babies' capacity to get used to things. 'Babies who wake easily to certain stimuli and cannot get themselves back to sleep are more likely to have trouble protecting their sleep by themselves, and will need help, such as sleeping in a quiet darkened room' (p. 3).

With pre-term infants, Negri (1994) tells us that, from a prognostic point of view, once homeostasis has been achieved, *the organization of the different states* toward the 42nd week of gestation is a milestone in the pre-term child's mental health. The paediatricians look for real wakefulness and real quiet sleep, not a continuous undifferentiated state. 'The child's states can be defined as organized once he can remain in a well-defined state for significant periods, with *a gradual shift* from one to the other. Sudden changes of state signal the child's vulnerability, as can its motor and postural behaviour' (p. 109).

I believe the gradual shift is crucial: I have seen several patients – and none had been a pre-term baby – where I eventually had to learn that the jump from one state of mind, or thought, to another was not a flight or an evasive technique; the patient simply lacked certain vital links that facilitate transitions. His experience lacked contouring transitions, and it is quite a technical challenge to help to build these up. (See Chapter 4 for a more detailed discussion of making links.) It is my impression that when we attempt to slow down the defensively driven or manically evasive child, we see the anxiety, depression or anger against which the speed was defensive; with the child whose links are defective, we see first bewilderment, then curiosity, but later even delight at the idea that something could fill the gap or be dwelt on at greater length.

Such transitions are not always to do with changes from positive to negative or vice versa: sometimes, it is a question of how to get down from an over-excited state to manageable pleasure. I have often seen playground-type slides, rather than dangerous cliffs, start to appear in the material as the idea of bearable transitions has begun to grow. (See Sorenson (2000) on the importance of maternal transition-facilitating behaviour.)

Is unintegration the primary and earliest phase of development? Do Bick's ideas challenge the views of Klein and the developmentalists?

While I agree with Bick that it is important for technical therapeutic precision to distinguish between *states* of unintegration and states of defensive or aggressive disintegration, I do not think that this need in any way lead to the assumption that such states should be installed as characteristic of the earliest phase of development: that is, as primary. I thought the Kleinians, with support from both infant observation (founded by Bick herself – Magagna *et al.*, 2005; Miller *et al.*, 1989; Reid, 1997; Sternberg, 2005) and infant research on babies' competence and readiness for engagement (Stern, 1985; Trevarthen, 2001), had clearly demonstrated the existence of an early rudimentary ego and some degree of innate object-relatedness. Babies have been found to be hugely more integrated and competent than previously thought, and to be object-expecting, object-seeking and object-using (Stern, 1983). Many researchers have suggested that there probably is a 'virtual other' in the brain whose outlines are filled in with experience (e.g., Braten, 1987, 2007). Mirror neurons are now being studied and are thought to be a possible element in and candidate for such innately given interpersonality (Rizzolatti *et al.*, 2002).

Is integration a necessary precondition for object-relatedness?

A further question is whether an infant in an unintegrated state can be object-related. In states of under-integration – that is, at lost or desperate moments – the object that the baby is seeking (if he is able to seek anything) is not necessarily that which provides nourishment and love, but rather one which is first capable of holding him together. Cohen (2003, p. 70) does a lovely integration of Klein, Bick and Bion when she writes in her study of premature babies: 'I hope to show that the baby seeks integration, and this search needs an answer . . . The baby needs to be held and then is held – thus experiencing both the holding and the notion of someone thinking about what it is needing.' The question of the baby 'seeking' integration may be a difficult one, because seeking does not sound particularly helpless. Bion's preconception helps us here. I think we see something like pre-seeking or proto-seeking. I have seen even autistic children look for something without knowing what they are looking for, but recognizing it when they get it. Thus, I do not agree with Bick when she says: 'in its most primitive form the parts of the personality are felt to have no binding force among themselves'. Nor do I agree that the containing function comes only from the external object. Some babies (probably most babies) are born with a good deal of inner cohesiveness and solidity. But *all* babies have their limits, and surely levels of integration fluctuate throughout the course of even the most solid baby's day.

Sander (1975) was one of the first to point out that a necessary precondition for the baby's relatedness to the caregiver was some ability to have what he called 'organized states': in the more organized babies, their states of being (say sleep *or* wakefulness) are fuller, more clear cut and more lasting. Organization, he said, involves an anticipation of an event, expectancy for recurrence and sequencing. And he showed that this affects brain development and the capacity to relate, and it is aided enormously by having a continuous caregiver, rather than numerous changes of carer.

What else remains of value in the Bick argument? Do some needs take priority over others?

The notion of a hierarchy of preconditions is helpful: it goes along with Bick's idea of necessary preconditions for relationship without requiring that the preconditions involve a total phase of development. And see Brazelton *et al.*'s (1974) findings on the way mothers get their babies comfortably positioned *before* beginning to relate to them. (See also Brazelton and Nugent (1995).) If we assume that some babies are born more (and some less) integrated than others, and that every baby has fluctuations in the course of his day, then we can still understand that there may be a set of priorities of needs – in other words, that there are certain pre-conditions for good introjections and internalizations to take place. (Nowadays, analysts are talking about this in terms of technique. See Joseph (as early as 1978) on the need for containment with patients who are difficult to reach, and Steiner (2004), who states that containment may need to precede the patient taking responsibility for himself.) Many of us have found that there is no point telling a desperately fragmented patient that the reason why he is so upset is because of the break he has just had from analysis until he is sufficiently calm – first to realize we are back; then to listen. The calming down is the first problem. Because the need for oxygen takes physiological priority over the need for nourishment, a baby held too close to the breast cannot suck *unless and until he can breathe*. When a person suffers a haemorrhage, the blood supply to the periphery decreases, but it continues to flow to the vital organs – heart, kidneys and brain. A baby held too far from the nipple and too precariously in his mother's arms will cling to the nipple with all his might, but may not take in much milk, may not explore the nipple and breast much, and certainly will not enjoy himself. A sure grip not only permits but may also be a necessary condition for relaxed, pleasurable intro-jections. Thoughtful introjections depend on secure, even leisurely, background conditions. Wolff (1965) has shown that babies first need to be well fed and comfortable in order to be relaxed enough and alert enough to be interested in the world. A distressed baby's curiosity is very different from that of a satisfied baby: it is narrower and more limited by its urgency.

Thus, where I do agree with Bick and Symington is that *some* degree of integration is a *necessary precondition* for a relationship to a good object, a clear sense of a bad one, and a projection outward into a bad one. We have all had patients too ill to manage these processes, and it is an important moment when they finally get focused enough to manage it. Waddell's (2006) patient made contact with a good object and it settled him. The same sometimes holds true for the integrating capacity of bad objects. I have also occasionally seen autistic and psychotic patients move from a state of fragmentation to hallucinating, say, a terrifying object – but such a progression may be a development because some part of the world is finally *not* inhabited by the bad object. (See Rodrigue (1955) on a similar case.) Badness is focused, contoured and finally locatable within a confined space. In reflecting on how one develops emotional cognition, Blomberg (2005, pp. 35–36) describes how, for her little patient Armando, everything in and around him was full of huge, catastrophic dangers. If something frightened him,

> he collapsed and screamed with anxiety. He was not angry or frightened of something else. He was therefore unable to be scared of anything, an enemy out there. The 'nameless dread' [Bion, 1962a] . . . was so all-embracing it did not have a representation. It could not be seen at a distance. It just was.

The question of integration at the paranoid-schizoid level

The Kleinian thinking regarding the integration achieved between love and hate at the depressive position is well known. Here I want to consider the issue of integration at paranoid-schizoid levels. First, I think we need to remember that the process is not akin to the kind of thing that happens when we blend the meat, vegetables and stock together to make soup. It is probably more like a *pot au feu* or a casserole. Identity of the parts is respected, at least some of the time. 'Coordination' is a useful word. Siegel (1999, p. 321) makes a related point in his book linking brain research with psychotherapy: 'Integration recruits differentiated subcomponent circuits into a larger functional system through a fundamental re-entry process. The co-regulating, mutually influencing state of re-entrant connections is called "resonance".' He stresses (p. 127) the prior importance of differentiation and specialization – that is, in particular, 'the differentiation of primary emotional states into specific classification of emotions'. Integration enables distinct components to be functionally linked. Bion's (1962b) concept of alpha function is interesting here: my own image is that we can lend meanings to individual thoughts, somehow letting them expand in ever-widening circles of meaning, so that two previously quite distant thoughts get linked, a little like sets of ripples when we throw two stones into a stream. But we can and should not force them together prematurely.

It is interesting that Klein herself (1963, p. 300) wrote repeatedly about the fact that early integrations take place in relation to part objects. Likierman (2001,

p. 17) reminds us that Klein noted the paradox in the fact that she had said both that the process of integration was based on the introjections of the good object, primarily a part object, the mother's breast, and that splitting off bad experiences was the basis of relative security in the young infant. Recent studies of brain anatomy in abused children have demonstrated an associated reduction in overall brain size as well as the specific functioning of impairments in the development of the corpus callosum – the bands of neural tissue allowing for the transfer of information between the two halves of the brain. De Bellis *et al.* (1999) point out that disintegration and dissociation of anatomically distinct parts of the brain are profound effects of trauma. (See Schore, 2003, pp. 213–214.)

We still have much to learn, I think, about how to facilitate good and safe introjections and how to respect or facilitate beneficial splits. Below, I offer a list of some identified integrators that have technical implications for our work.

Modes of early pre-depressive and pre-Oedipal integrations and integrators: technical implications

Containment in Bick's terms

In 1968 Bick followed her identification of states of helpless passive unintegration by suggesting a variety of ways in which *the object facilitated integration* – for instance, the nipple in the mouth together with the holding and talking mother with her familiar smells. She also discussed how a light or a voice could hold the attention (and, of course, we know even more now about the importance of the caregiver's face and eyes as a powerful magnet for attracting *and sustaining* attention (they are different); I shall return to this below). But Bick's major emphasis was on the idea of the skin as the container of the unintegrated parts of the personality. We might want to add the importance of the feeling that one's skin – and, for that matter, musculature, hands and feet – can also keep *out* over-stimulation or intrusions. There is also the need to feel held up, as well as firmly down and in. (See Robertson (2005), who writes of the importance of providing a baby at risk of cerebral palsy with a 'nest', rather than leaving it on its back with its arms flailing.) When these various containments fail, adhesive processes may ensue (see the difference below between toddler Harriet's gaze when she felt well held, as opposed to when not).

One of the discussion groups at a February 2005 conference debating this issue asked whether Bick conceived of good unintegrations (Winnicott (1945) did), but we might also wonder about necessary adhesions. The setting in psychoanalysis provides a very powerful holding and, for that matter, structuring and settling experience in its predictability of the meeting space and regularity of the timing of sessions. It is the essential frame for the work.

In an infant observation, a 15-month-old girl, Harriet, who was usually fairly well integrated, had begun to fall apart somewhat. Under the usually containing ambience at home, her gaze on the observer tended to be interested, curious and sometimes slightly mischievous. But in a period of fairly minor stress at home, she had been rushed into her older sibling's brand-new playgroup and left to wander about aimlessly while her mother concentrated on settling her sibling into the new situation. Harriet was not protesting, even though at home she was usually quite able to protest. Here, however, she looked quite lost and vacant. She then noticed the observer, held her gaze on several occasions, and literally seemed steadied on her feet and quietened in her body each time she did so. According to the observer, this holding look was very different from the usual, more animated one. I think the rushing and temporary lack of her usual maternal containment had 'unsteadied her soul' and left her in a more under-integrated state than usual. As I mentioned in Chapter 3, Antonioni's *Beyond the Clouds* recounts a story of Mexicans warning some travellers not to go up a mountain too quickly for fear of leaving their souls behind. A mother in such a moment might gather her toddler into her arms, and the child might thereby re-find himself. In a similar way, therapists sometimes remind a lost-looking child that he is having difficulty remembering this room, rather than interpreting upset or anger about the break. The latter feelings can come when the child has found his therapist and himself.

Containment and transformation in Bion's terms

During this same period in the 1960s, however, Bick's idea was paralleled by the growing recognition of another, *at times very different*, type of containment outlined in Bion's (1962b) description, with its implications for the thinking mind and for sanity. Bick's notion of the appropriate response to a helpless unintegrated state has much to do with holding and sometimes with soothing (Miller, 1984). Bion's idea is of a container receptive to and working upon projections of a powerful and active kind. His idea of containment involves something far more than soothing a distressed baby (or a patient). It involves being filled up with feelings that may be highly disturbing, and the attempt to transform these and communicate them back to the patient in a bearable form are done at considerable cost to the mother (or analyst) – that is, after much work on her own feelings. The technical issue is how and when to return the projection back to the patient. (See Chapter 1's example of the girl in the wheelchair.)

Alpha function, holding through time, and regulation in relation to the fullness and durability of experience

Both Bick's and Bion's concepts, though different, make use of spatial metaphors, such as those involved in the available lap and arms, and the mind's receptivity. Yet, as Winnicott (1954) pointed out, temporal integrations matter, too. He stressed that holding through time facilitates the sense of going-on-being. It might also facilitate the going-on-being of the object. I became interested in the whole question of the length of time given to introjective mechanisms when working with my autistic patient Samuel. How *do* we acquire an inner sense of the durability and sustainability, returnability of our objects, as well as of ordinal time, of ordinality and sequentiality?

A paper by Mendes de Almeida (2002) has interesting things to say about technical issues with severely disturbed children. She writes of the importance of integrating different levels and registers of experience. However, she also describes an earlier stage of identifying experience, which she calls 'relating to a mind to be'. She argues (p. 3),

> With these children we often find ourselves 'thinking aloud' as if 'broadcasting' for us and for them what we are observing, noticing, what is surprising or intriguing to us, as well as what seems, through our observing eyes, to be surprising and intriguing them. We share with them, in the very core of our relationship, the emergence and building up of thoughts, from impulsive discharges of discomfort to possibly more elaborated experiences of containment and transformation of needs and intentions to be communicated
> . . .

> As if talking to an internal listener within ourselves, we demonstrate to the child that there is a space/mind, where mental content – feelings, sensations, perceptions – even if in a fragmented state, may be registered, processed and possibly acquire some shared value of integrated experience. Our investigative 'thinking aloud', similar to the mother's exploratory talk to herself and to her baby about its needs, shows flexibility and fluency of thought: within a mental space, one situation may be seen and explored in its various aspects and possibilities.

This links affect to experience and both of these to thought. I would underline Mendes de Almeida's point concerning the echoing or amplifying of 'impulsive discharges of discomfort', especially with children with very weak or inhibited projective mechanisms. She is also illustrating, I think, how to cope with the further problem of facilitating new introjections and new links in the brain as well as the mind.

Note also Schore's (2003) suggestions, which I outlined in Chapter 1 on the importance of the recognition and identification of unconscious affects that were never developmentally interactively regulated or internally represented. Dissanayake (2009, p. 23) refers to the noteworthy nature of the signals presented by the mother to the infant:

> The visual, vocal and kinesic elements used multimodally in 'packages' by mothers are *simplified, repeated, exaggerated and elaborated versions of adult communicative signals*, which, interestingly, are all similar to, and possibly derived from, affiliative expressions that adults use with each other in normal positive social interchange: open mouth, eyebrow flash, smile, looking at, head bobbing backward, body leaning toward, head nodding, soft high-pitched undulant vocalizations, touches, pats, kisses.

Dissanayake emphasizes, however, that we must not diminish the role the baby plays in eliciting precisely these signals. The work of Fonagy and Target (1998) on mentalization has some connection here, although I feel that they are working at higher levels than the work of the authors cited above would imply. Fonagy and Target hope to develop a 'theory of mind' in their patients, whereas Dissanayake (2009, p. 23) is working at a more primary level – that is, to develop a 'sense of an emotional person relating to another emotional person'.

For example, in Chapter 1, I gave an illustration of alpha function providing something like self-resonance in helping a five-year-old, David, to process some very early dangerous respiratory failures. He got his therapist to cough and choke with him in unison, in exact replays, until, over time, the gagging sounds became part of their playful joint repertoire. I suggested there that patients deep in the paranoid-schizoid position may need much help in getting alpha function around various elements within each side of the split, either the good or the bad, long before they are ready to integrate the two. In David's case, it was a so-far unthinkably terrifying experience.

Some years ago, I was struggling to treat an excessively fragmented and at times frenziedly driven four-year-old, Samuel, with severe autism. He appeared to suffer from both un- and dis-integration. (See his difficulty with the 'and' link in Chapter 4.) Although at times he actively resisted experiences which might have provided some degree of integration, at other moments I had the strong impression that he simply was not able to integrate. Although Samuel's lack of integration was much less floppy than my patient Robbie's, the two situations seemed to have some degree of helplessness in common: both children seemed to lack an internal 'sun' to steady their soul. (I saw many similar cases subsequently, and not all were autistic: some were severely neglected and deprived emotionally, with considerable cognitive delay; some had a diagnosis of pervasive developmental disorder.)

Samuel was always on the move in the room. His gaze also never rested on anything for more than a second or two. Neither people nor toys – indeed, nothing outside his ritualistically clenched hand or the flow of running water or the spinning of a wheel – could catch and hold his attention. Yet he kept moving his body and his eyes as though he might be looking for something that he could never find. This type of fragmentation had a very driven quality, and the speed itself certainly led to something that could be called dis- rather than un-integration. After many months' work, Samuel began to take some brief interest in simple objects in his box, such as a little brick, and to explore them, but always only one at a time.

Finally, after another few months, he began to pick up two of these little blue bricks. First, he would look at them briefly, as though for a fleeting second he was examining and enjoying their sameness, their symmetry and the way he could place the two together. I cannot stress enough how fleeting the moment of looking was, for, at the second moment, he seemed to be overcome by something clearly unbearable, which looked like agitation, confusion *and* excitement. Then, at the third moment, he would suddenly squash them together and hurl them into the air. I felt that the second moment involved some sort of desperate state of unintegration, in that he seemed unable to know how to look at two objects at once. The third moment, the explosion, seemed more like an active disintegrating activity. If it was an enraged attack on twoness, such as in Bion's 'Attacks on linking' (1959), I felt it was partly an attack on the *incomprehensibility of twoness*.

A further six months on, Samuel slowed down a little. (I think such slowing down is crucial to the exercise of alpha function, Bion's (1962b) concept of the function of the mind that makes thoughts thinkable and experience meaningful.) He became able to study the shapes of the bricks closely, to build towers with them and add others, and to post some into appropriate holes in shape-sorter toys. During the earlier period, however, I had the clear impression that Samuel had real difficulty in looking at two things at once: I came to think that he was having difficulty in coping with profound excitement and with incomprehension. How could there be two of something? How could he look at two at once? I think he was having difficulty with the comprehension that twoness could be available to him *in time* – which time would enable him to look at both, not necessarily at once. In fact, from the way he first began to look at my face and to meet my eyes, I got the impression he had never learned how to scan, which is how people look at eyes and faces. Perhaps he did not realize that the first thing would still be there if he looked at the other. His gaze seemed too fixed, and then he would have to tear his eyes away, rather as babies do in the early days of life until they learn to scan. They start scanning around six weeks and it is firmly established by three to four months (Stern, 1983). Samuel needed a 'container' – a less spatial but equally limited term is the developmentalists' 'regulator' – that could help him to find out not only how to make do with one object or thought but how to have two, in *sequence*, one at a time. In fact, as he began to use his eyes more, and meet people's gazes from greater distances, his acute short-sightedness improved, and his glasses' prescription approached the normal. I guessed that he was finally using his eye muscles.

I think this may have been facilitated by my attempts to soothe and calm him as he first examined the bricks, but also by my attempts to maintain his interest in them. I had to get in quickly before the moment was lost, to assure him of something like their durability and continuing interestingness. I also tried to find words and phrases – quietening but affirming ones – to accompany his obvious interest in and fascination with them: 'Yes, look how blue they are. And they fit so neatly together, don't they? And what a nice shape. And they're both the same, aren't they? – much as you might do with a six-month-old who had started to explore the material world. However, even a six-month-old would have a longer attention span, would be able to get more pleasure from looking, and anyway would not necessarily be so frustrated and enraged by the problem of the awkward otherness of things.

The importance of rest and pauses for the digestion of, and recovery from, experience

It is interesting that while Bion (1962b) refers to the importance of digestion of experience, Brazelton *et al.* (1974) go further: they speak of the need both to digest and *to recover from* interpersonal experience. Of what might such recovery consist? It must have something to do with matters such as time to process, think and reflect as well as time to forget and to empty the mind. Developmentalists, such as Stern (1974) and Beebe *et al.* (2000), who study vocal dialogues between mothers and infants, pay as much attention to the pauses, and the type of pause, as they do to the vocalizations themselves. (Anyone who has treated asthmatic patients will have noted their difficulty in taking a breath or, for that matter, a breather.) Dreyer (2002), in her dissertation linking the ideas of Montessori with psychoanalysis, stresses the importance of disengagement, unintegration and pre-symbolic movement – the importance of rests and pauses in time, and emptiness in space, for brain, mind and body to develop coherence. I think this adds an important new dimension to object-relations theory and theories of infant development. The stress of both is on the importance of the 'object', and of engagement with it, whereas here we are pushed to think about the importance of the object's staying *out of the way* of the self's efforts at integration at certain crucial moments.

During infant observation it is not difficult to see the difference between a baby who feels (through either anxiety or concern for the object) that he *must* engage, at whatever cost, and a baby who engages when he is ready and because he wants to. Over-stimulation is costly and some forms of hyperactivity can ensue. Indeed, the Neonatal Behavioral Assessment Scale measures such things as autonomic stress, exhaustion and overloading after a period of engagement: the measure concerned is termed 'The Cost of Attention' (Brazelton and Nugent, 1995). With certain aloof avoidant children with autism, it is important for the therapist to keep her voice quiet, and to time her interventions carefully in order not to bombard the child (Alvarez and Reid, 1999). With another adolescent patient of mind, even my question 'What are you thinking?' could be felt to be so demanding that he had to prepare his thoughts in advance for me. We both had to work hard to get me out of his mind so he could think his own thoughts at his own pace. Then, in his own time, perhaps relate them to me.

Live company: its capacity to attract and then hold the infant's attention

In writing about the object that holds the baby's attention, Bick (1968, p. 56) wrote, 'The optimal object is the nipple in the mouth, together with the holding and talking and familiar smelling mother.' Attention, however, before it can be held, sometimes has to be caught and elicited. When the baby is not seeking or has given up seeking due to dissociation or depression, a more animated response may be required. For alpha function to operate, the object has to be seen to be worth attending to in the first place. We often see certain neglected children who are sluggish mentally, suffering from a kind of lifelong but not a particularly active depression. They seem to be full of unvalued, not devalued, objects. One of the groups in the aforementioned February 2005 conference pointed out that uninte-gration can be used as a defence against trauma. But here I am thinking more of the consequences of neglect, not trauma, and of depression rather than terror.

I think we see some children where apathy is a result of having never quite felt pulled together. O'Shaughnessy (2006) suggests that unintegration is a default condition, a pathological condition, and I would agree, with the proviso that we understand that some babies *start* precisely there and may have needed a stronger tug on the lifeline than they got. Stern (1974) and others have demonstrated that, in infancy, the maternal gaze and the constellation of vocal and facial behaviours that may accompany it exert a strong effect on both eliciting and holding the infant's gaze. Attention, as Meltzer *et al.* (1975) say, has to be 'paid' and, as Klaus and Kennell (1982, p. 77) put it, the face, voice and breast of the mother act as the magnet that lines up the iron filings.

Brazelton was the great pioneer of the research study of the origins of reciprocity. But the reciprocity between mother and baby that he found is not about containment in either the Bick or the Bion sense. Once the baby is settled and contained, we read about the mother's improvisations, alertings, amplifications, deliberate alternations, movement, change, variations on a theme – activities that are, by definition, issuing only from a live psychological object full of otherness. Brazelton *et al.* (1974) describe how the mother often *exchanges* one activity for another, sometimes soothing when alerting has contributed to the child becoming upset, sometimes alerting when his interest is flagging. Later, once such experiences are internalized, the magnet's attraction is represented inwardly, so the normal child is drawn to seek contact with a living object that can produce novelty and that he now expects to find. Our job, with certain empty or under-integrated children, is to offer something like this magnet. I shall offer illustrations of this in Part III – on work at the intensified level.

Conclusion

This chapter has suggested that a concept of under-integrated states might go some way to resolving the controversy between those who take Bick's view and those who take Klein's regarding whether babies are born unintegrated or integrated, and whether signs of unintegration are really the result of defensive or destructive disintegrating processes. I have tried to work my way through these controversies by emphasizing that a state of un- (or, as I prefer, under-)integration need not imply a return to some sort of primary state of unintegration, but that Bick's distinction between unintegrated and disintegrated states may lead us to note that *some degree* of integration is necessary for object-relatedness to work. A starving or unheld baby may be too fragmented and desperate to relate.

I have also tried to identify some types of integrations and integrators that take place prior to the integrations of conflicting feelings at the depressive position. Some of these pre-depressive and pre-Oedipal integrations may involve making negative thoughts thinkable, but they may also involve integrations of positive moments with positive ones – that is, making positive thoughts both thinkable and durable. The final integrator in the list involves the element of 'live company' – the alerting, amplifying or awakening object that is discussed in the final section of this book.

Part III

Intensified vitalizing level

Chapter 11

Play and the imagination

Where pathological play may demand a more intensified response from the therapist

Introduction

In Part II I gave examples of, and arguments for, the therapist's attempts to enlarge meaning without feeling compelled to offer alternative – or 'deeper' – meanings. In this section, I argue for the existence of moments when the therapist needs to provide something more vitalizing and intensified – an insistence on meaning. In Chapter 1 I discussed the processes of reclamation (Alvarez, 1992), generation and demonstration (Reid, 1988) as well as the need for a firm response to addictive or perverse behaviour. Here I wish to discuss the issue of the degree of engagement of the therapist in the child's play.

Psychoanalytic therapists are trained to explain or reflect and describe children's play, yet at some moments many go further and play *with* the child. At times this may involve taking a role, which involves playing *on behalf of* (possibly only on behalf of a part of) the child. Sometimes this is invited or demanded by the child, but in certain cases, with very neglected children, the therapist may *initiate* such dramatization, and this leads to differences among psychoanalytic therapists about how active such contributions from the therapist should be (Joseph, 1998).

My view is that such controversies might be resolved if we take into account the state of mind – and therefore the needs – of the child (and of his internal objects) at any moment in time. This will involve attention to the level of his symbolic functioning as well as to issues of deficit, defence and addiction. The examples of reclamation that I give in Chapters 1 and 12 concern situations where we are calling the child into contact with an object, and also recalling him to himself when there is severe deficit in both the self and the internal object. I called Robbie's name, put my face into his line of vision, and – eventually, when he surfaced – received a very touching response. With certain dissociated children, this direct interpersonal approach is ineffective – or, worse, persecuting – whereas a call enacted via a figure in the child's play may reach him from something like a safer distance. An interpretation to the abused child that the baby doll, say, could protest but is not protesting may not register: we may need to go further and produce an actual realization of something that is only, as yet, a preconception (Bion, 1962b). That is, we may need to dramatize emotionally, via the play situation, that the abandoned baby doll can call or cry for help, and even complain. With most such children, this should not be done prematurely, before the previous situation of helplessness has been fully explored. Nor should it be done where the patient is exploring the idea of being in identification with the abandoner for a time, and is therefore able to project his victim self into someone else. Nevertheless, at a certain point with a lost, vacant child, it can be extremely focusing and enlivening. At other moments (perhaps with the same child in a more hardened mood), such behaviour would involve colluding with sadism, and a cooler response is required. Sometimes we may need to introduce, for the despairing and hopeless child, the idea of a benign figure that might have, or even *should* have, rescued him from abuse. At other times, this would be premature, as he may need much more time to process his many bleak experiences of abandonment to his fate by his so-called carers. The situation can change from moment to moment in a single session.

I shall re-examine the three points on the symbolism continuum – one identified by Winnicott (1953) and two others by Segal (1957) – and suggest two further points at the pathological level: namely, desultory empty meaningless play; and addictive perverse play. I shall also discuss some technical implications of working with these types of pathological play.

The issue of the importance of play and the imagination

A while ago, I heard a Canadian novelist, Ted Chamberlain, arguing on the radio that dreams and the imagination are crucial to our lives. To prove his point, he told a story about a nation of native Canadians in northern British Columbia. During a particularly harsh winter, all 170 of their horses died. Outsiders said that they did not need them on the reservation, now that they had trucks and cars. Anyway, it was clear that they could not afford to replace them. By the next winter they had 120 horses! Why did they need them? John Grady, the hero of the first volume of Cormac McCarthy's *Border Trilogy* (1992, p. 6), gives one answer: 'What he loved in horses was what he loved in men, the blood and the heat of the blood that ran in them. All his reverence and all his fondness and all the leanings of his life were for the ardenthearted and they would always be so and never be otherwise.'

For the native Canadians, and for John Grady, horses charged their imagination. For some native Canadians, this is more than simply an individual personal imagination; it is also to do with their dearly loved cultural heritage and values (Brody, 1982). Such a vision may seem romantic, or even sentimental, and certainly there are major differences between romantics and classicists in their view of the importance of the imaginative life. For example, even Charlotte Brontë, who wrote the highly romantic *Jane Eyre*, was bothered by the seeming immorality of her sister Emily's *Wuthering Heights* (and even, perhaps, destroyed Emily's childhood prose, as she had her own). Charlotte was suspicious of the lure of phantasy and of its addictive and 'idolatrous implications'. She felt that she herself had come to worship creatures of her own imagination, and had allowed them to rival God (Miller, 2001).

There are some echoes of this issue, I think, in the various psychoanalytic attitudes to dreams, the imagination, and to play (Bion, 1962b; Freud, 1920; Klein, 1952; Meltzer, 1983; Winnicott, 1953). When *should* we tell our friends or children to 'stop dreaming', 'stop playing about', and when should we respect someone's wildest dream? When are our dreams deeply creative, even visionary? When are they at the very least healing? When do they obstruct development? And when are they positively perverting of development? When, as clinicians, should we interrupt a child's play (or an adult's conversation) to 'make an interpretation'? And when might that be the equivalent of waking someone in the middle of a dream? When are ideal or even idealized objects purely defensive and when do they involve emotional and even cognitive developmental achievements? Do we sometimes see ideal states as defensive when they are expressing a kind of reality? In his book *Who is the Dreamer who Dreams the Dream?*, Grotstein (2000) urges us to hang on to a sense of the awesomeness and mystery involved in the very fact of dreaming. One could make a similar plea for the imagination. And see Da Rocha Barros's (2002) views on certain dreams as steps toward thinkability and true symbolic functioning.

Early psychoanalytic thinking placed phantasy as a wish-fulfilling exercise opposed to the reality principle. Susan Isaacs and other Kleinians (Klein *et al.*, 1952) challenged this opposition. Isaacs hugely extended the zone in which unconscious phantasy was thought to operate. It was widened to accompany far more activities; it was deepened to the earliest stages of infancy; but the most radical expansion of all was to extend it forward, out of the depths of the selfish self, to meet 'reality'. Isaacs (1991, p. 109) wrote, 'Reality-thinking cannot operate without concurrent and supporting unconscious phantasies.' As I pointed out in Chapter 3, Joan Riviere (1952) made the coupling between reality and the unconscious even closer and gave the unconscious even more equal status.

Later, Hanna Segal's (1957) theory of symbol-formation became, for many, a vital yardstick for assessing how close the coupling between unconscious mentation and reality-thinking might be – the higher the symbolic processing, the closer might be the coupling. True symbol formation was thought to arise out of a process of mourning for the lost primary objects and to be connected with the depressive position, with acknowledgement of loss and separateness.

It is interesting, however, to note that Riviere, unlike Segal, did not seem to stress separateness so much as harmony between the couple. She emphasized the bicameral nature of mind, the parallel processing of conscious reality-thinking and unconscious mentation, of two trains of thought occurring in parallel. These two, as I suggested in Chapter 3, need not necessarily be playing in disharmony; they may be functioning in harmony. In Chapter 5, I also tried to address the question as to whether separateness and loss are really the major elements on the road to symbol formation – or whether some hope and belief in (and possibly 'preparation' for) alternative forms of goodness play their part, too. Both Klein (1952) and Segal (1964) stressed that it was the strength of the good object and good self that enabled the development to the depressive position, but the importance of the

(Handwritten notes at top of page:)
1. Symbolic equation (this is that)
2. transitional object level (this on the way to that)
3. real symbol formation (working through what it means)

sense of goodness can be under-emphasized or taken for granted when we are pressing our patients to face their hatred and feelings of persecution and loss. Babies are weaned from the breast *on to* an alternative form of feeding called cups and solid foods. They are not weaned to a condition of starvation. I agree profoundly with Grotstein (2000) that there have not been sufficient attempts to distinguish between the depressive position and infantile melancholia – or, as I have put it, between the depressive position and despair (Alvarez, 2010b). However negative the content of play and the imagination, the capacity to play at all and to use the imagination to create forms implies some measure of hope.

Psychoanalytic theories of phantasy and play

In the early years of psychoanalytic work with children, play tended to be seen mostly as a source of information about the child's past or current preoccupations – as something like a dramatized projective test. Freud (1920) suggested that when his grandson played his reel game, the boy was compensating himself for his mother's absence by staging the disappearance and return of the objects within reach. Isaacs (1948) added that the child's play 'consoled' him for his mother's absence. Nevertheless, missing from her account was the (then still-recent) Kleinian distinction between processes that are defensive against pain and depression and those that are designed to overcome it and foster growth (Klein, 1940). With the later theories of Segal on symbol formation and Winnicott on the transitional area, we can now see that much would depend on the child's inner state of object relations as he played the reel game. Was he playing it mainly in order to deny his mother's absence and, more important, her significance (playing on the level of a symbolic equation)? Or was he playing it to gain some control and make her absence more bearable (playing at the level of a transitional object)? Or did he have no doubt about either her significance or her absence, but was exploring and trying to learn more about the properties of absentable objects in their own right (playing at the level of real symbol formation)? I shall later add a fourth possibility (concerning meaningless, desultory play) and a fifth (concerning addictive and perverse play).

(Handwritten note in left margin:) meanings of the reel game

Many psychoanalytic theorists – and, for that matter, developmentalists – have subsequently looked at the implications for learning about the reality of loss, pain and frustration (Bower, 1974; Bruner et al., 1976; Murray, 1991) via the study of variations on the peekaboo game. However, to return for a moment to the early, more general formulation of the meaning of play – in a series of papers in the 1920s, Melanie Klein described a way of reaching the unconscious in children by using a method similar to that of free association used by Freud with his adult patients. She analysed the child's talk and conversation, much as Freud did the talk and dreams of his patients, but she also observed and tried to understand the meaning of the child's play. It was clear that Klein considered playing to be a deeply meaningful act, but the important thing for her was the unconscious phantasy that lay behind it: making conscious the significance of the content of the play would bring relief of the child's anxieties. A modern development has arisen from the work of Betty Joseph on ways in which the patient subtly influences the analyst and nudges him into some kind of behavioural enactment. Joseph (1998) points out that this is even more likely in child work. Her view is that, for the child analyst, as for those who work with adults, the crucial element in the setting is the therapist's state of mind. She goes on to suggest that once a piece of play is understood and interpreted, the therapist would probably stop joining in. I would agree with this for the more neurotic-level children who are able to play mostly communicatively. But what of those who cannot play: that is, those with major ego, self and internal object deficits? Or those whose play is pathological in the sense of involving concrete symbolic equations or addictive or perverse play? Some children who have been rarely or never understood do not know what understanding is. The more advanced ones, when they first notice the therapist 'understanding' them, often ask, 'How did you know that? Are you a mind-reader?'

The treatment of borderline and psychotic children and the infant studies of the steps in the development of the capacity to play suggest that content is only half of the story. Its formal qualities and levels matter enormously. There is much more to play than its underlying symbolic meaning, however important that is. Slade (1987) points out that we tend to think of our work as uncovering meaning, but that by helping children to learn to play we are helping them to make meaning.

The significance of play and the imagination for introjection and thinking

The overpowering quality of the play of Ruth, whom I shall describe later, had much in common with the lies told by the deprived and traumatized children I described in the 'Wildest Dreams' chapter in *Live Company* (Alvarez, 1992). In their case, however, I felt that what was paramount was the developmental need to have the object believe in a brighter future than that of which the self could conceive. I agree with Caper (1996) that play involves a probing of (and an experiment on and with) the object, but I am not so sure that it depends on the very clear distinction between internal and external reality that he – and, for that matter, Fonagy (1995) – seems to ascribe to it. Children can bring crazily omnipotent phantasies or lies as a way of trying out a phantasy of a rightful need – of a sense not of how they *wish* things had been but of how they feel things *should have been* or *should be*. To my mind, this is not necessarily denying reality; it may be exploring the idea of a reality of a different kind. (See Chapter 6 for a fuller discussion of the issue of moral imperatives.)

If the probe gets the right answer, this can signal the beginnings of an over-coming, rather than a denial, of persecution injustice and despair. Human beings are born with deep social and biological needs but also, if they are not too damaged, with some sense of a rightful order of things. In those terms, play may reflect a different ordering of reality. I hesitate to call it simply 'internal' reality. Fonagy makes it sound somewhat too weakly real for what I think can happen via such phantasies. How about a *potential* reality or an *anticipated* reality? Better still, a *rightful* reality, based on a sense of what ought to be there (or to have been there) – that is, of the rightness of things. Are demands for, say, justice and compassion in a police state based on denial or on a vision of a better world? Stern (1985) describes a little boy playing with a doll family and two houses during the divorce of his parents. None of the sleeping combinations work, until he finally puts the parents together in their bed, and the little boy back in his own bed. He says, finally, 'There, all better.' In internal reality – or should we call it potential reality? – couples can come together, and internal history can be rewritten in healing ways that are at the symbolic level and not simply wish fulfilments of an omnipotent kind. I believe that this can produce not only emotional but cognitive growth. Trevarthen's (1993) phrase 'playing into reality' is helpful here.

Infant studies: the importance of playing 'with'

Child development research has stressed the importance of play for cognitive development (Bruner *et al.*, 1976; Vygotsky, 1978), and others have carried out studies about what kind of play is helpful to learning. Sylva and Bruner (1974) write that you need a sensitive partner for play to be useful in helping solve problems – to guide but not dominate and also to take pleasure in the activity. In the same book – which explores the role of play in development and evolution – Bruner (1972) cites the common finding that young chimpanzees seem to be able to play most freely when their mother is nearby. (This is also found in research on attachment theory with young children.) Hutt (1972, p. 211) points out, 'play . . . only occurs in a known environment and when the animal or child feels he knows the properties of the object in that environment; this is apparent in the gradual relaxation of mood, evidenced not only by changes in facial expression, but in a greater diversity and variability of activities'.

In play, the emphasis changes from the question 'What does this object do?' to 'What can I do with this object?' Lynne Murray's videos of the babies of postnatally depressed mothers provide a powerful illustration of this when, at 12 months, they are asked to find an object hidden openly under an inverted cup. The baby of the depressed mother can hardly be bothered – hidden objects exert no magic for him. The baby of the normal mother not only finds it immediately but plays with it extremely irreverently for several minutes. She is clearly finding out everything she can do with that object. Her curiosity is alive and well (Murray and Cooper, 1997).

Some neglected children who suddenly start to ask us apparently intrusive questions about whether we live at the clinic, or sleep on that couch, may be beginning to develop a little healthy curiosity. We may be able to fan this without either over-exciting or further depriving an already deprived child – not by answering or refusing the question, but by wondering along with them.

The continuum of levels of symbol formation

I shall stick to the classic Winnicott/Segal three-point continuum for the time being, but, as I said, I shall eventually consider a fourth and a fifth point on the continuum, too. In the meantime, it is important to register that developments in the psychoanalytic theory of symbol formation added a vital new dimension to the theory of play, beyond the question of mere content.

First, Winnicott (1953) suggested that we needed to study the period of growth toward symbolism which he saw as a journey from subjectivity to objectivity, from fantasy to reality, from illusion to disillusion. On this journey, he identified an intermediate area, a transitional zone that lay between the two ways of relating to an object. This transitional zone was an area of experience intermediate between the pure narcissistic illusion that everything belongs to oneself and the mature awareness of separateness and indebtedness, where true symbolic functioning was possible. Thus, if the child uses his teddy as a transitional object, he partly recognizes that the teddy is different from the primary object (breast or mother) and partly does not recognize this – nor, according to Winnicott, should he be made to do so too soon. Winnicott says that this is an area that must go unchallenged and should exist as a resting-place, a paradox, which is necessary and should be respected on the journey toward true symbolic functioning. I think he means that the therapist should not be continually reminding the patient that the teddy is not mummy and is only a defence against loss, separation and dependence. He seems concerned that this would neglect the other half of its meaning – that is, that the transitional object is the child's first major experience of independent possession – and neglecting this could interfere with the child's creativity and development. The teddy, after all, is the child's own.

Subsequently, Segal (1957) went on to emphasize and to elaborate the distinction between true symbol formation and the symbolic equation. She seems not to have mentioned an intermediate area. She notes the difference between the difficulties a neurotic patient might have in playing the violin and those of her schizophrenic patient, who explained that he no longer played the violin because he could not be expected to masturbate in public. In the latter case – that of a symbolic equation – she points out that the substitute's own qualities, its violin-ness, are not recognized or admitted. The symbolic equation was used to deny the absence of the ideal object or to control a persecutory one, and it belonged to the earliest stages of development. Tustin (1980) has added to the understanding of functioning at this level with her concept of the autistic object as being without symbolic meaning. Here I wish to reiterate my position that there are other pathological states in infancy, besides those involving symbolic equations (Alvarez, 1992). There are situations where the object is seen as not fused with oneself but, on the contrary, as impossibly remote and unreachable. Segal (1957, p. 57) writes, 'The symbol proper, on the other hand is felt to represent the object . . . Its own characteristics are recognized, respected and used. It arises when depressive feelings predominate over the paranoid-schizoid ones, when separation from the object, ambivalent guilt and loss can be experienced and tolerated.' She goes on to say of the true symbol that the symbol was used then (at the neurotic or normal level) not to deny but to *overcome* loss.

Unfortunately, I have made many psychoanalytic interpretations that assumed a capacity for such symbolic functioning in the patient – an assumption that was not always justified. I think we still have much to learn about *the steps in the development of symbolic capacities*. We may need to understand that such 'overcoming' of loss, besides facing it, involves some faith that something else still matters, that life still has meaning, and not everything is lost.

To return, for a moment, to the intermediate area – when I first read Winnicott's paper, I read the statement as saying that the transitional object is the child's first *not-me* possession. Much later, I realized that he also intended it to be read as saying that the transitional object is the child's first not-me *possession*. I think that certain despairing children – for whom faces, voices, toys and play objects may never have been lit up by shared experiences with a companionable parent – may arrive at the transitional phase from a place very different from that dominated by symbol equations or illusion. Here is the possibility of the fourth position on the continuum. They may have begun in a place marked neither by illusion nor by symbolic equations but by *symbolic emptiness* and desolation, where objects were too far away, rather than too close. Interpretations may need to understand such a child's newfound delight in possession and ownership of his object, in its capacity to return, to be reliable. With more well, more manic neurotic patients, whose omnipotence is defensive against more ordinary impotence, we may need to remain alert to issues of separateness and weaning. But where apparent 'omnipotence' is actually an expression of a need for potency, one might also need to understand the patient's need to have a different, less clinically depressed view of himself: that is, as someone capable of attracting someone's liking, attention or interest (Alvarez, 1992; Reddy, 2008). Much of this can be addressed by the therapist on the descriptive level of work, but in some instances something more intensified may be needed, as I shall try to show.

It is perhaps worth stressing that I think this expanded Winnicott/Segal continuum or dimension is important with every type of patient, not only with the deprived and severely depressed. A child may crouch in a cupboard a few sessions before his therapy is due to terminate due to the obvious pregnancy of his therapist. The content – that he has a phantasy of being inside his therapist, just as her baby is – may be fairly clear. But is he turning away, on the symbolic equation level, by finding a better place of his own? Or is he communicating that 'at least' this will have to do, because he half knows she is going and he is not the occupant of her cosy place, and he half has to deny it and find and make his own place: that is, is he half acknowledging her significance and the significance of the impending event, and half asserting his independence (at the transitional level)? Or is he fully cognizant of the meaning to himself of what is happening, and exploring thoughtfully what it might feel like to be that baby inside her, while painfully knowing that he is not (symbolic level)? Here the same piece of play might be full of meaning, loss, poignancy and symbolic significance, and fully in touch with external reality (her pregnancy) and internal reality (his loss).

At such a moment, one can make more symbolic explanatory interpretations. These are not easy choices to make technically, but the flavour, mood and atmosphere offer essential clues to help us to avoid mistakes. To imply to a desperate child clinging frantically to a symbolic equation (insisting, for example, that we are not leaving or that he is coming with us) that he 'wishes to be our baby but cannot be' might increase despair and helplessness. The child may really know what he needs – a reliable durable object – and the therapist might instead acknowledge that the child feels she *ought* to stay, and to let him be her baby. He might also need reminding she has found another new therapist for him who will try to help him, as she has.

This is still work at the descriptive level, but in the next example – with a child in a state of chronic hopelessness – the therapist may need to move the work on to another, more fundamental level, where meaning is not simply elaborated but insisted upon by the therapist.

A clinical example of a patient at a fourth position below or beyond a symbolic equation: technical implications for working with meaningless play

I want to consider the question of desultory, empty play. I think this is a fourth position that is not at all the same as the level of symbolic equation. It is about the impossible remoteness of the object, not its over-closeness. Thus far, I have been writing about play having meaning, but we need to be straight with ourselves and the patient when we begin to sense that the play is meaningless. This is now a familiar phenomenon in work with autistic patients. Elsewhere (Alvarez, 1992), I have described my belated discovery that Robbie, an autistic patient, was repeating an originally urgent question – was he 'a bit too early'? – in a completely dead and stale manner, and how it took me too long to realize it meant nothing.

But even less ill patients can get stuck in meaningless acts, as I described in Chapter 8 in relation to a type of *apparent* narcissism. A few years ago, a very persecuted and despairing, but not psychotic, patient of mine (Jacob) – who, by then, was somewhat better, happier and more able to learn – was throwing away a few of his drawings. I wondered why I never minded when he threw away his drawings, whereas, when other patients did something similar, I interpreted it as an attack, a rejection or an act of terrible and profound despair about their own talent. Of course, sometimes it is appropriate: waste needs to be thrown away. Yet, with Jacob, I had for too long and too often felt almost nothing – only a matter-of-fact feeling as though he were throwing away a used tissue. I suddenly realized that the drawings really *did not matter* – neither to him, nor to me – and many of them had been carried out in a very desultory manner: 'I am a child. Children draw. I'll do a drawing to get her off my back for a bit.' This was certainly his attitude to the demands at school – dutiful compliance with no real learning – but, because children draw, I had foolishly looked for meaning in his drawings. He was doing them dutifully for me, but his heart was not in it. The meaning was absent. It was important to show this child the lack of hope and faith, and therefore meaning, that lay in every one of his communications. (This phenomenon has been written about most evocatively by Ferro (1999), and by Ogden (1997, p. 4).)

Addressing this took courage on my part the first time I became aware of it. It requires delicate handling in order not to wound the child or to convey that *he* is uninteresting: the point is to convey that we understand that he feels both he and we, together with the encounter between us, are uninteresting. We may even need to interrupt the (seemingly but falsely playful) playing child or over-chatty adolescent to convey our own demand for, and insistence on, a more real meaning.

Once, when my autistic patient Robbie was a grown man, I asked him what he was thinking. He replied in a dull manner, 'I helped Mom sweep the leaves today.' This was not said in his old autistic, crazily excited way but, though sane, it was nevertheless dutiful and dead. I interrupted and said, 'No, no, tell me what is *really* in your mind. Look around in it a bit!' He thought for a minute, then began singing, most tenderly, a line from the song 'The last waltz with you'. When he looked into my eyes for answers to questions he himself somewhere already knew (for example, the dates of our Christmas break), or tried to read my thoughts to tell me what he thought I wanted to hear, I had regularly interpreted that he was looking in my head, rather than his own. But on this occasion it seemed to be more effective when I made an active suggestion. I think I was addressing a deficit, rather than just a defensive or manipulative misuse of the deficit, but these bad habits of mind certainly also needed addressing at other moments.

A clinical example of apparently transitional play which was in fact at times closer to a symbolic equation, at other times more addictive and frenzied

A seven-year-old girl patient of mine, Ruth, was referred because she was being bullied at school, and also was not learning at anything like the rate her obviously very high intelligence would predict. She had one of the richest and most highly developed imaginations I have seen in the consulting room. Her vocabulary was wide, and always delightfully apt: one day, in our joint play, I had to pretend to be astounded at the fact that she, an escaped prisoner, was riding a flying unicorn and dressed in 'regal finery' (her words). Her stories were dramatic, exciting, full of suspense and variety – surely pretty good candidates for symbol formation or somewhere up there between transitional and symbolic functioning. However, in another way, they were not really so varied. She was always an astonishingly all-powerful, heroic, triumphant figure who invariably produced wonder and awe in her maternal and sibling figures in the play. (There was rarely a father present.) In the beginning her heroine was also often cruel. I was always to be the kind but extremely gullible mother, sleeping peacefully after breastfeeding my baby, made to awaken suddenly to strange scratching sounds, then to terrible cries from the baby. Ruth had unleashed a horde of rats that were eating my baby! I played my part in this for some time for reasons I shall explain later. (Ruth always kept her own name in the stories and I was puzzled by this. I now think that perhaps it was a clue to the relatively low level of symbolic functioning in the play. It was a little too real to her for it to be purely symbolic in nature: it was closer to a symbolic equation.)

After some time, I began to notice that, for all her charm and liveliness, Ruth's eyes were always darting and never really met mine for more than a fraction of a second. She simply did not – and, perhaps as a result of a lifetime's bad habits of mind, almost could not – listen. Any comment of mine on her play that was not within and part of the play itself, however short and simple I made it, evoked a frustrated sigh and a 'Yeah, yeah, OK. Now, can we get on with the game!' I felt as if she had a stopwatch on me. Needless to say, she was not listening at school, playmates were giving up on her, and she was falling behind in English because she could not be bothered to spare the time to see how words were spelled.

It was important to address Ruth's bullying contempt for the stupidity of all mother figures: she had an iron will, and I learned to be quite firm in insisting that I must be heard occasionally. Gradually the stories began to alter in content: Ruth was no longer an anti-hero; she was a hero. There was less cruelty, only amazing Tarzan-like leaps, made to evoke my astonished pride. One day, when she was playing the part of a wild and powerful schoolgirl who rescued all the other girls from dangerous killers, Ruth turned into a peregrine falcon and then a phoenix who came back to visit and bring joy to her fond and sad head teacher once a year. I had begun to feel that a bit of what I said began to get in, but the pace of her play, for all its liveliness, was too frantic, compulsive and closed to be called truly transitional. But, of course, Ruth was not psychotic. She was *able* to come out of the stories and be very coherent and businesslike about changes of time and so forth, and she was able to be very loving and reparative (physically) to her parents and me. However, for a variety of reasons, she was not yet *willing* to come out of them. And the habitual nature of her unwillingness led almost to an incapacity. (The chronicity of conditions can set in very early in life, and, as Perry *et al.* (1995) have shown, states can become enduring traits.)

I also had to attend, however, to the fact that part of Ruth's motivation for this hyperactivity was to bring to life a depressed maternal figure, to produce a reactive interested object. (Her parents had told me that they were both depressed during her infancy, but at that stage I did not know why.) I had anyway learned that it was important for me to react to her projections with some emotion – sometimes positive, sometimes negative. She had generally become somewhat calmer, but one day she began playing in a wild, over-excited way. I felt she was about to go over the top (which often led to her utter exhaustion and collapse, and usually a physical illness, the next day), so I said that I was not going to play my part in the pretend play today. I explained that I thought she was getting too excited for her own good (that is, excited by her own power and cruelty) and that I was not going to go along with that. She slowed down, for a moment looked absolutely desolate, and then tried to sit on my lap with her back to me. This was her usual way of getting in touch and making friends again, and until then I had accepted it. But she was eight years old now, and I thought of her usual inadequate eye contact – the darting glances with which I had been preoccupied lately. So I made a sort of suggestion: I pointed out that it had not occurred to her to try looking at me instead of cuddling up; that looking is also a way of making up and making friends again. Ruth, courageous spirit that she was, sat on the couch and looked across at me for some minutes. I was going to write 'looked steadily', but actually it was rather unsteady, because she clearly was not used to doing it. But I believe she was *practising* looking me in the eye. (Remember, normal babies learn this type of visual convergence and leisurely scanning at three or four months of age (Stern, 1974).) A few moments later, she made a slip of the tongue that confused me until she spoke, very solemnly, of something that explained to me why her parents had been depressed long ago. (I had made no mention of her parents up to that point.)

As I have implied, for some of the time in my response to Ruth, it was enough to stay at the descriptive level by agreeing to play my part as either a pathetic baby part of herself or a not very intelligent mother object. I felt something important about her infancy was being processed. (Her mother was in fact very intelligent and lively now, but to a tiny infant her past depression could have seemed as if someone was simply not getting it.) However, when the play began to get mindlessly frenzied, it was important not to play along with something sado-masochistic and ultimately disturbing for her. But it was also important not simply to abandon her to a state of empty depression. I had to be firm enough both to discourage it and to offer something else in its place. Both the encouragement and the suggestion of an alternative (eye contact or other playful ways of having an exciting time together) involved more active intensified techniques than those at the purely descriptive level. Discouraging perverse excitements has to be accompanied by a confident assertion that there are other ways of feeling alive, and of feeling in touch with an alive object. Otherwise, the patient believes he has only two choices: over-excitement or the abyss.

The problem of perverse play: a fifth position on the symbolism continuum

It may be worth making distinctions between both the concreteness of symbolic equations, and the emptiness described above, and a further step down the symbolic ladder: the development of addictive and perverse relations to objects via play or phantasy. Here we can agree with Charlotte Brontë on the dangers of idolatrous and addictive play. (And see Joseph (1982) on addictive conversational chuntering in a masochistic adult, and Freud (1930, pp. 149–158) on fetishism.) Some apparently symbolic violent 'play' may in fact be more like practice for the real murder. Yet, even with the most perverse and bizarre behaviours or pre-occupations, the quality may begin to change during treatment. *Any* physical object, or behaviour, may move up or down the continuum, *without any change in content*. For example, it is fascinating to see the sometimes quite frenzied and perverse rituals of autistic children begin to become less addictive, even desultory and empty, but then move to being provocatively designed to frustrate and annoy the therapist. Even though the ritual may appear to be as psychotic and self-centred as in the past, its expressive and communicative quality may betray a more transitional level. The child's exerting of pressure on people instead of physical objects may signal an entry into a more interpersonal, less autistic, world. (See examples in Alvarez and Reid (1999).)

Our responses as therapists must therefore also vary, and will depend on monitoring of both our countertransference and our perceptions: similar developments up the continuum toward transitional play can be seen in some abused perverted children and adolescents, and our technique can take account of this. We can sometimes be very easily shocked at the level of developmental delay in older sexual offenders. One 15-year-old boy, anally abused throughout his childhood, always chose, either openly or more disguisedly, to exhibit his (clothed) bottom to his therapist. He seemed convinced that that was all an adult could possibly be interested in about him. One day, he began instead to play a kind of simple peekaboo game, where he jumped out from behind a curtain with a triumphant yelp. It was important *not* to interpret sexual seductiveness or excitement but, instead, to comment on the fact that he needed to be sure that the therapist was surprised and delighted to find him once again after the break between sessions.

Such young people have a deep and, given their experience, realistic conviction that no one is interested in them in their own right – only as sexual objects. Teasing games of an ordinary kind – ordinary, that is, for a three-year-old – may begin to emerge in a 15-year-old. But whatever the accompanying sexual charge, these might, in this patient population, need to be seen in their non-sexual, but nevertheless exciting, *other* light. It is also difficult, but nevertheless very important, for the therapist to be able to find and amplify the glimmerings of a capacity for liking, pleasure, enjoyment and even excitement (which such patients may disguise under much stranger and more apparently perverse forms; see Cottis (2009) and Woods (2003)).

But what happens when the therapist fails to find such glimmerings, in either the patient or herself – when, for example, Billy (described in Chapter 7) was sticking the pin infinitely slowly into the teddy's eye? Until that moment, his cruelty to the teddy had seemed to be fuelled mostly by desperate, persecutory phantasies of a desire for revenge – affect-laden and needing someone else to play the part of the victim. But in that session there was something different – a cold hardness and pleasure (and, at one point, a beginning trace of sexual excitement) – to which I felt I should not be too masochistically receptive. I certainly interpreted how much he was enjoying his cruelty, but I also refused to play my usual part of crying and begging as teddy. I tried to lower the level of excitement by speaking coolly, without condemnation.

With another, similar child, where the cruel play had definitely become sometimes perversely exciting, but often simply casually habitual, I tried to show her that she was convinced I found her cruelty as exciting as she did. But I also began to let her know, as did her parents, that it had become boring. It would be a mistake to do this too early on, before the child had had sufficient opportunity to process and project pain, but it would also be a mistake to let the cruelty go on for too long. When Ruth got over-excited in her cruel play toward me and my baby, I did something similar. In fact, when she calmed down, I suggested a less sensual way of showing her now quite anxious friendliness.

In cases where the sadism in the sessions is extremely repetitive, it is certainly not enough to interpret addiction as defensive (even if it began that way years before). But moving from an explanatory level to a descriptive level, whatever emotional courage it takes for the therapist (as in Chapter 6), may not always be enough. If the child or adolescent is excited by his aggression, we may need to beware of either colluding or condemning too emotionally and to begin to evince something closer to a cool boredom. I said in Chapter 6 that we need to have the courage to look evil in the eye, but it also takes courage to look addictive excitement in the eye and to face the horror we are meant to see. But where it has become addictively chronic, we need to be free to communicate our boredom and unwillingness to play the sado-masochistic game while seeking to show that the patient may also be bored but may not know how to stop, and certainly may not know how to move on to something equally interesting but different. The same holds true for repetitive instances of casual brutality, and here, too, I think our tone of voice matters enormously. We can even sometimes actively discourage the play and insist on something with more meaning. (I would only do this when the play is clearly dead and addictive, not when there is still a paranoid persecutory meaning.) With children who have been abused and tortured, are not yet fully hardened psychopaths, but are in identification with the torturer, it is sometimes better to show them that we know it is not them, and ask who they are being today.

Discussion: can we still be psychoanalytically minded and play with the child, or even innovate and rouse the desire to play?

Clearly, Ruth had at least a conception of an interested figure. Other children may have faint traces of what Bion (1962b) calls a 'preconception' of such a figure, but life may not have provided them with sufficient 'realizations' to produce a real conception that people and the world, and what you can do with them, matter and can be interesting. For such children, Winnicott's idea that important psychological transformations can take place *via the process of play itself* is highly relevant. Winnicott, like the developmentalists, stressed the importance of the more creative and light-hearted element in playfulness, of the free use of the imagination. But he also believed, as Sanville (1991, p. xi) put it, that 'play is serious business'. He wrote: 'where playing is not possible then the work done by the therapist is directed towards bringing the patient from a state of not being able to play into a state of being able to play' (Winnicott, 1971, p. 38).

Earlier in this book, I mentioned the horribly abused little boy who had no idea how to play at first and one day was delighted to 'have an idea' about what he and his therapist could play. It is important to note that such children have frequently been not only abused but very neglected and deprived of ordinary opportunities for stimulation of the imagination. A few days later, as he returned to his foster mother after the session, this child said proudly, 'I made up a story.' Discovering, first, that one's mind has things called 'thoughts' in it – ideas that come on demand or sometimes even uninvited – and that one has the power to *make stories* is not only emotionally strengthening but cognitively expanding.

With certain children who have great difficulty in knowing how to play, due to either autism or deprivation, the therapist may find herself amplifying or enriching the play, even introducing innovations. One therapist recently saw her patient (Johnny) getting stuck at the sink in some water play that was becoming autistic and dead. She added some dolls to the edge of the sink and made them jump in with fear and excitement, and Johnny latched on to this idea and joined in using the dolls with great pleasure. This, as Reid (1988) has pointed out, would be a mistake with an avoidant autistic child who could very easily feel intruded on by such activity, but it accords with her concepts of generation of interest and demonstration of potential in play with a certain sort of passive child with autism. The therapist's introduction of new material to this mildly autistic child involved far more than reflection and description, but it was very effective.

Jesse, an autistic patient of mine, had been making somewhat better contact with me in recent months. He was also somewhat better able to play out stories with longer dramatic sequences and even, occasionally, to let me know what was happening in the narratives. One day, Indiana Jones was rescuing a girl doll from a cage, but I was being told nothing and totally ignored, more as I had been in the past. After about twenty minutes of my commenting and showing interest, I pointed out that I was apparently quite invisible today. This somewhat reflective comment, which had often reached him before, elicited no response. I then commented that I was just like that girl in the cage, but this did not seem to get through to him, either. Eventually I began to say that I wished Indiana Jones would come and rescue me, as I was so lonely with no one to play with. Jesse's response was immediate and warm, and he remained much less cut-off for the rest of the session. It seemed that it was my expression of emotion on behalf of either an imprisoned part of himself or his internal object that managed to reach him. I think we still have much to learn about how to reach autistic or dissociated patients – without, of course, becoming a nag.

Jesse was autistic, but the therapist's emotional initiative can also be a necessary strategy with non-autistic children who have been too rigid or too neglected to learn how to play. We may need to play peekaboo with an eight-year-old, and to offer a tactful 'Wow!' at an attempt at magic revelations even with a child who is chronologically too old for such games. There is something about the playfulness involved that can save everyone's dignity: that is, it avoids the child's concluding that we are so stupid as to be genuinely fooled by the magic trickery, yet it allows him to enjoy the power to have a possibly much-needed impact on someone.

At these levels of work, we can turn to Bion's theory of thinking. As I have pointed out (possibly all too often), Bion (1962b) hypothesized 'alpha function', a function of the mind that made thoughts 'thinkable'. He noted that thoughts precede thinking – that each thought needs to be thought about and dwelt upon (we might add 'played with') in order for it to be digested, processed and made useful for further thinking and for relating to other thoughts. Grotstein (2000, p. 299), however, has pointed out the importance of alpha function *in the mother*. That is, the mother (or father) of the normal infant also needs to be able to play if the child is to learn to be free to play. At times, we may need to rouse the desire to play first with people, next with toys and then with ideas.

Conclusion

I have tried to demonstrate the significance of play and the imagination for mental growth, and to describe some of the ways in which the therapist can facilitate this. I have extended Winnicott's and Segal's theories of symbol formation to include symbolically empty play and addictive or perverse play: in these latter situations, the therapist may approach different types of pathological play with differing levels of engagement. That is, much of the time, we can simply interpret or describe the play, but at other times we may need to play with, or on behalf of, the child. Finally, in some cases, we might need to go further and initiate play, innovate and rouse the desire to play. In these latter modes of intensified techniques, the therapist no longer simply searches for meaning but *insists* on meaning. As Slade (1987) has written, for certain children, we may need to make meaning.

Chapter 12

Finding the wavelength

Tools in communication with children with autism

Introduction

In this chapter I shall describe the intensified use of some infantile, maternal and paternal countertransferences that arose in my work with a nine-year-old boy with autism who had virtually no language. Alongside the more usual psychoanalytic explanatory and reflective comments, I came to use a kind of 'motherese' when I begged him to pay attention to me, rather than to his autistic figures. (For a fuller discussion of the previous clinical use of this term, borrowed from developmental research (Trevarthen and Marwick, 1986), see Alvarez (1996).) I also, however, came to realize that I was also using a kind of 'fatherese' when I amplified upon, and invited him to take note of, the strength and assertiveness that were buried in some of his autistic repetitive movements. This more emotional manner of speaking on my part involved the kind of work I have described previously (Alvarez, 1996, 1999) as being developmentally informed. In addition, I used a second kind of 'fatherese' tone in my firm dismissal of his more complacent, omnipotent activities. He was a child who at times was all too comfortable in and with his autism and had little interest in other human beings, especially when they were talking to him.

Listening is nevertheless a complex art. A few years ago, there was a series of letters in *The Times* on the subject of blackbirds and their song. Here is one from 14 June 2000:

> Sir – Blackbirds are joyful in May and sing in A major. In July, they are content and sing in F major. I've waited 68 years to say this, Beethoven's Seventh and Sixth Symphonies supporting my theory.
>
> Sincerely, D.F. Clarke.

This writer is clearly a good listener and seems to like listening. The Portuguese poet Fernando Pessoa (1981) has a rather different attitude to listening: he insists that he needs *silence* – not song – in order to listen. Children with autism are notoriously poor listeners; indeed, they are often thought to be deaf. The established triad of symptoms includes, as well as impairments in social relatedness and the use of the imagination, impairments in communication and language development. It is vital to identify symptoms, and to have verified that they occur in a triad, yet a nosology that relies too exclusively on a one-person psychology – that is, one that sticks to describing attributes of the child's self – may tell only part of the story. We may find that a fuller descriptive psychology of autism is provided by a two- (and eventually three-)person psychology. Such an approach involves a study of intra-personal relations: in a model of the mind that involves a two-person psychology, the mind contains not just a self with particular qualities and orientations and possible deficits, it also contains a relation to, and a relationship with, what are called 'internal objects' (Klein, 1959) or 'representational models' (Bowlby, 1988), and these may also contain deficits. A more personal, intra-personal view of autism carries the implication that the self is in an emotional, dynamic relationship with its internal representations, figures, objects – no matter how skewed, deficient or odd this relationship may be. (There is no aetiological implication here: it is the child's inner world of figures and representations that is at issue. Many psychoanalysts use the term 'internal object', rather than 'representation', as the latter may sometimes be taken to imply an exact copy of external figures, whereas the former carries no such implication. Internal objects are thought to be amalgams of both inner and outer factors.) If the child treats us as a piece of furniture, he may be *seeing* us as something like a piece of furniture, and may also *feel as though we are like* a piece of furniture. If he does not listen to us, that may be partly because he does not have the habit of listening, but it may also be because he finds our talk uninteresting, or intrusive, with too few of Pessoa's silences. How, then, are we to cease our song and still be heard? Also, if he does not talk to us, it may be partly because he does not think we are worth the effort of speaking to, or because he feels our listening capacities are limited. Or else he may feel we want to pull his words out of him so that, in some sort of terrible way, they will become ours and no longer his. His 'theory of mind' (Leslie, 1987) may assert that minds are basically unmindful. This can do major damage to processes of introjection and learning from other people, and the subsequent internalizations that lead to cognitive growth.

Yet symptomatology and pathology are not everything: each person with autism can usually be found to have an intact, non-autistic part of the personality interwoven with their autism. Bion described the importance, in psychoanalytic work with psychotic patients, of making contact with the 'non-psychotic part of the personality' (Bion, 1957a). There is also now a growing body of research on 'spared function' in autism (Hobson and Lee, 1999). For all its apparent stasis, the autistic condition is less static and more mutable than it sometimes appears. While a micro-second's interested glance by a child at a person or a new toy may be followed by an instantaneous return to old rituals, the quality of the child's glance may nevertheless offer a clue, a faint signal that can be amplified and built upon tactfully. It is important to assess what the developmental level is at which this apparently more normal part of the self may be operating. The child's chronological age may be five or ten years, but, because of habitual lifelong interference from the autism, the healthy, related, object-seeking part may be functioning at ten months or even three weeks of age. Traces of early preconceptions (Bion, 1962b) – or of not so much a 'theory of mind' (Leslie, 1987) or of person (Hobson, 1993) but a proto-theory of mind or a proto-sense of person – may still be detectable. It is on this foundation that a treatment – precisely calibrated to the level of emotional communication of which the child is capable – may build (Alvarez and Reid, 1999).

Normal infant development and proto-language

William, 13 months old, heard his father getting up at 5 a.m. outside his door. William called, 'Ey!' The father said it sounded like, 'Hey! What are you doing? Where the *heck* are you going?' He opened the baby's bedroom door, and was greeted with another demanding 'Ey!' In order not to wake his wife, the father whispered, 'I'm going to work, William. You go back to sleep now.' William said, 'Awhhhh,' and went back to sleep.

From the moment of birth – as Klein maintained and as developmental psychology research has subsequently demonstrated – normal babies are extremely precocious socially (Klein, 1959, p. 249; Newson, 1977, p. 49). They have all the basic equipment they require to begin to engage in face-to-face, interpersonal communication – initially of a non-verbal kind. They prefer to look at face-like patterns and to listen to the sound of the human voice, and they have a remarkable capacity for finely tuned interpersonal exchanges (Beebe *et al.*, 1985; Stern, 1985, p. 40; Trevarthen and Aitken, 2001). Clearly, emotional communication involves a whole orchestra of 'instruments' in which eye gaze (Fogel, 1977; Koulomzin *et al.*, 2002), emotional engagement (Demos, 1986), level of attention and interest, expressive bodily gestures (Hobson, 1993) and vocalizations (Trevarthen and Aitken, 2001) all play their part. Most of these instruments are used both expressively and then communicatively; or, to put it in psychoanalytic terms, via different types of projective identification. They are also used, however, for purposes of introjection and internalization.

Language and triadic skills involving visual regard

Toward the end of the first year of life, infants begin to extend the use of an earlier skill: the capacity for gaze monitoring. Scaife and Bruner (1975) have shown that even very young infants will turn their heads to follow the mother's line of regard. In the last quarter of the first year, following the trajectory of another's gaze and gazing at the object of the gaze are intensified, as the baby is motivated to keep track of his mother and her comings and goings. This is followed, between the ninth and fourteenth month, by the emergence of the more proactive activity of proto-declarative pointing (Scaife and Bruner, 1975). Proto-imperative pointing implies something like, 'Give me that banana!' but proto-declarative pointing stresses how *interesting* an object is – something like, 'Wow, look at the size of that lorry!'

Bruner (1983) was one of the first to point out that language arose in the context of interactions between infant and caregiver. (And see Urwin (2002) for a discussion of language development as an emotional process.) Burhouse (2001) has offered suggestions as to the emotional preconditions, which might explain why gaze monitoring seems to precede proto-declarative pointing. She points out that the baby has learned to value the mother's return of gaze during the early months of face-to-face, dyadic mutual gazing, and this interest in and valuing of her attention lead the baby to follow her gaze when it goes to someone such as an older sister. Eventually, the baby finds active ways of getting this attention back, through communicative pointing and expressive sounds. These are emotionally laden events, and the grammar of emotional events structures language. There are huge differences in communicative intention between a 'Hey there!', a 'C'mon, give us a smile', an 'Oh, look at the lovely bright sun!', a teasing 'I'm coming to catch *you*!', a 'You've been a very naughty boy!', an 'Oh, you really like that banana puree, don't you, oh yes, mmh-mmh' and an imperative 'Don't touch that socket – it is *very* dangerous!'

Language, as Bruner (1983) taught, always emerges *in contexts* and, as developmentalists have shown, it is accompanied by emotion (Demos, 1986). Burhouse (2001) describes a moment when the baby seems to be both aware of and thinking about the fact that her mother is talking to and looking at her sibling, not her. Psychoanalytic theorists and developmentalists alike have suggested that early two-person relationships lay the foundation for the later three-person social capacities (Klein, 1945; Trevarthen and Hubley, 1978). More recently, Striano and Rochat (1999) have demonstrated empirically that the link between triadic social competence and earlier dyadic competence in infancy is indeed a developmental one. You do not follow the trajectory of someone's gaze unless you find his gaze *worth having in the first place*. But it is also true that you do not bother to notice whether someone is talking to someone else, and feel curious about what they are saying, unless you have first been interested in their vocal communications to you.

It is interesting that so much of this work on proto-declarative pointing refers to the infant's visual regard. I assume it is easier to measure the direction of a child's visual gaze than to assess what he is listening to when he suddenly quiets. An older child can say, 'What's that [noise]?' A pre-verbal child can only attend and wonder. This may be why so much of the research on vocalizations in the baby concern vocal *dialogues* between mother and baby, which are easier to record than a quiet listening stance. This is in no way to underestimate the brilliance of the methods used by Stern, Trevarthen, Beebe and Tronick, and their findings about the profoundly interpersonal nature of early pre-verbal dialogue; and, in Beebe's and Tronick's work, the additional importance of the intra-personal element – the baby's tendency to regulate himself as well as his relationship (Beebe *et al.*, 1985; Stern, 1985; Trevarthen, 2001; Tronick, 2007).

Therapeutic implications of impairments in communication: getting on the right developmental wavelength

The question of the psychoanalytic treatment of children with autism has been surrounded by controversy. Some psychoanalysts and psychotherapists have themselves described the need for changes in technique with these children (Alvarez, 1992; Alvarez and Reid, 1999; Meltzer *et al.*, 1975; Tustin, 1992). The impairments in symbolic capacity, play and language make an understanding of more ordinary explanatory interpretations very difficult for them. Where the autistic symptomatology is especially severe, and where not only the child's sense of the existence of other people but his sense of self are weak, the concepts of transference and countertransference may *seem* too advanced: transference may seem to be non-existent, and a countertransference of frustration or despair in the therapist can lead to indifference. Yet, close observation may begin to reveal faint or disordered signs of relatedness, which can then be amplified.

Regardless of aetiology, though, a disorder of the capacity for social interaction may require and benefit from a treatment which functions via the process of social interaction itself. Such a relationship will need to take account of the nature and severity of the psychopathology and the particular developmental level at which the non-autistic part of the child is functioning. The therapeutic approach is three-pronged: it addresses the child's personality, the autistic symptomatology (disorder and sometimes deviance), and the intact or spared non-autistic part of the child, however developmentally delayed this may be (Alvarez and Reid, 1999). The psychotherapy is thus psychoanalytically, psychopathologically and developmentally informed.

The psychoanalytic perspective offers the close observation of the transference and countertransference. This can alert the therapist to personality features in the child that accompany, and may act to exacerbate or reduce, his autism. (Some children with autism develop quite deviant personalities that are in no way an essential feature of the autism itself.) The psychoanalytic theory of the need and capacity of every ordinary child first to relate intensely to, and gradually to identify with, both of his parents contributes greatly to the understanding of normal child development. So does the theory of the Oedipus complex, the understanding of the ordinary child's disturbance at, but also enormous interest in and stimulation by, those aspects of the parental couple's relationship that exist independently of him (Houzel, 2001; Rhode, 2001).

The psychopathological perspective, described in many previous chapters, helps the therapist to understand the power and pull of autistic repetitive behaviours, and the ways in which (as psychoanalysts, too, have suggested) addictive and concrete non-symbolic behaviours differ profoundly from simple neurotic mechanisms and defences (Joseph, 1982; Kanner, 1944; Tustin, 1992).

Clinically intuitive glimpses into the child's fleeting interest in and even desire for contact can be confirmed and supplemented by the study of very young infants, by both the methods of naturalistic observation (Miller *et al.*, 1989) and developmental research. We can try to identify and facilitate the precursors of social relatedness: the technique draws on findings into the ways in which mothers communicate with their babies, and into how this facilitates the infant's capacity for communication and relatedness. The developmental research emphasizes a number of factors: the normal baby's need for his level of stimulation and arousal to be carefully modulated (Brazelton *et al.*, 1974; Dawson and Lewy, 1989) and his attention channelled; the power of 'motherese' (softer, higher inflections with particular adagio rhythms during pre-speech/pre-music dialogues; Trevarthen, 2001) and particular grammars (coaxing rather than imperatives; Murray, 1991); differing proximity of faces at different ages for eliciting eye contact (Papousek and Papousek, 1975); and, depending on developmental level, the child's readiness for primary intersubjectivity (face-to-face communication and play in a dyadic situation) versus secondary intersubjectivity (shared play with objects, where the baby glances at the caregiver seeking moments of 'joint attention' to a toy, for example – a triadic situation; Trevarthen and Hubley, 1978). One severely autistic and developmentally delayed child whom I treated was found to be functioning on one part of a developmental scale at the age of one month (Alvarez and Lee, 2004, 2010).

Many severely autistic children have never played, nor developed a capacity for joint attention (Baron-Cohen *et al.*, 1992). They may have no language at all; worse, they may never have babbled playfully. It may be a real achievement in the therapy when the non-speaking child begins to play with sounds and make sounds that are more contoured than before. The technical issues for the psychotherapist are difficult: how can we reach a child with little or no language? How should we talk to such a child?

I now want to describe work with a child where the use of both 'motherese' and something that might be called 'fatherese' combined to facilitate communication between us and to help his communicative capacities to grow. In both situations I often found that I had to contain and dramatize feelings that were either unfamiliar or unmanageable for Joseph. Yet he showed growing interest in my reactions.

Joseph

Joseph was referred to me at the age of eight by his music therapist. He had been born two weeks overdue and had been induced. His older brothers were normal. Joseph was a placid baby – happy to be held by anybody – and he made eye contact until about the age of three. His parents suspected something might be wrong only when they tried to toilet train him at the age of two and he seemed not to understand. When they started to try to put pressure on him to communicate, he 'closed down', and eye contact reduced. He was always content, but he cut himself off and would not play with other children. He had always been tactile, cuddly, and loved being sung to. He could sing numerous songs, but his spoken language was very limited. Joseph's mother wrote that his early pretend play was good: from the age of two years he held two dolls facing each other and made them have 'conversations' with each other and dance together. Joseph did this in his sessions with me, but for much of the time the quality was very closed and shut off, and I think by then it was no longer real pretend play. It was too *real* for him: he seemed to believe he really was those people talking and playing together. Most of the language I heard in the early sessions was of this private type – conversations between characters from his favourite DVDs, lively, interested, yet very repetitive and, for much of the time, impossible to understand. Occasionally a question, or an exclamation, could be heard. But to his parents and me, the only real word I heard directed to them or me was when we asked Joseph if he would like to use the toilet, and he responded with an excessively light, quite disembodied 'No'. It was so light and impersonal, un-aimed and unlocatable, that you could easily imagine you had not heard it.

I saw Joseph together with his parents for three consultations. He occasionally responded to his mother's songs, in the sense of joining in on the last word, but much of his positive connection with her was through cuddling. He was a big eight-year-old, and I began to note how easy it was to see him as younger than his age, and to want to be protective of him: he was an attractive boy, with a sweet, rather unformed face, and a very loose-limbed body, which in the room was much of the time horizontally laid out on the couch, half in his mother's lap. He examined toys a little, but avoided most suggestions or directives from her or me regarding any play activity. When walking, he seemed to drag his arms and legs, and especially his feet, after him, as though they did not belong to him. I was cheered by more signs of alertness and life in a teasing game he began to play, in which he said, suddenly, 'Night-night,' and then liked it when I did an exaggerated startle and expressed my disappointment that he was disappearing under the blanket *again*. He made a little fleeting eye contact after these moments.

It was clear that Joseph was a very loved child, but there was also a sense in which he had never really woken up to the world. He seemed to need to discover his bones and muscles, his verticality (his pleasure in standing and stretching up into the world, to jump, and his capacity to move forward and explore it). There was far too much passivity in his life, and yet, as he so easily collapsed into a sort of panicky temper-tantrum when challenged or stretched, it was easy for everyone to suppose that his autism had made him far too delicate for ordinary life and ordinary demands. On the other hand, it was clear that both his parents and the school were able to be firm about certain things, as Joseph was, in many respects, a reasonable and easy-going child.

After roughly two months of psychotherapy, I had the impression that the talk between his favourite DVD characters, or between the toy animals, was not always as totally absorbing to Joseph as it seemed – that he was often actually quite aware of my attention on him as he carried out these repetitive activities. I also began to think he was enjoying my feelings of exclusion, so I began to dramatize my countertransference: 'Oh, Joseph won't talk to me. It's not fair. Nobody will talk to me, and they are having such a good time over there talking to each other.'

I also sometimes added, 'Oh, please talk to *me*, Joseph, not to them!' This was all quite emotional – coaxing/pleading/protesting, definitely using my infantile or maternal countertransference in an intensified manner. I was beginning to suspect that he thought of talking as something other people did together, with a third always excluded, but that he had no idea of the real pleasures of face-to-face talking in a twosome. I felt I needed to give the third a voice, and yet attract him back to real relationships. One day, after my coaxing, he looked straight at me, put his head up and back, started to shake it just like a toddler, and said, 'No! Nononononono!' – really relishing his power to tease and thwart me. But this had at least a bit of give and take: he was, after all, looking at me, and it was a genuine 'no', with some real *oomph* in it. Like his 'Night-night', it was full of mischief, and it made me laugh.

For years afterwards, Joseph's main form of greeting me – sometimes early, sometimes later in the session – was a musical 'na-na-na-na'. It was witty, and infinitely tender, and he always preferred that I imitate it back to him, rather than say, 'Hi' or 'Hello', or go on to push for a 'Hi' or a 'Hello' from him. In fact, he occasionally did utter a 'Hi, Anne', but always grudgingly, as though I were pulling his teeth, and I told him this. The 'na-na-na-na' was far more articulate, generous and warm, but it was still a very private and restricted language between just us two, and it developed very little over the years.

Not all of my countertransferences were positive. I sometimes found myself feeling very annoyed by Joseph's complacent assumption that only he and his shadow were interesting, or that he was not really bored silly by his unending conversations, or that he knew what was behind a particular wall in the room. Eventually, I felt our relationship was strong enough for me to begin to challenge these assumptions. I began saying things like 'Oh no, you *do not* know what is behind that wall. You'd love to know, but you don't.' I said it strongly but kept it lively, fun and rhythmical, so it accompanied or responded to his sing-song style. Except that his was high and expressive, whereas I was bringing him down with my voice to a more earthbound but, I hoped, more interesting place. It was flatter and lower than his, but still quite humorous. Often I combined the insistence that nothing interesting was happening there – behind the wall – with exasperated coaxing. (Two level-three intensities were being used at once.) I also persisted with the idea that his talk was *not* real, and that I knew he was yearning to talk in a real way. The people in his pretend conversations always seemed to be having fun – or at least a dramatic and interesting time. I stressed that in order to become *like* someone, he had to understand that he could not *be* that person. Joseph was all too certain that he *was* that lively couple.

To develop, you also have to feel that other people give you permission to be like them. When he was very wild and excited, I would echo the excited/aggressive element in his utterances. If there were sudden growls and stamping of feet, I copied and amplified both, which delighted him. I felt he needed to discover his musculature as well as his own boy's voice. I also encouraged the toy animals to take longer journeys. They were often sitting around kissing each other most tenderly, but they never went for even a simple walk. As I said in Chapter 9, I am certain that even Antony and Cleopatra went out for a breath of fresh air sometimes! I had frequently accompanied the animals' large, rather assertive steps (they always remained in the same place, or moved in tiny circles) with even more assertive stamps of my own feet, but eventually I began to get a bit tougher over their lack of adventurousness. I began to insist that they were not scared. They wanted to go further. It was Joseph who was holding them back. He began to climb them up the back of the sofa and, unlike the days when all I could see was their backs, placed them to face me from the top, just like a toddler who has climbed his first steps.

As the first year progressed, Joseph took ever more pleasure in discovering his deeper voice, and a somewhat more powerful and muscular self. His parents reported that he was making more eye contact and was occasionally using spontaneous speech at home. Not long after the end of the second year, he began to engage in what I think was real pretend play. He lay on the couch and shouted, 'Yee-ikes. Help, save me!' as he 'fell' on to the rug. Although this scene may have come from one of his videos, it was not carried out in isolation, as in the doll conversations where he usually kept his back to me. Here, he fell off the couch right in front of me, looking at me often. And, if I were too slow to call out, 'Help, this poor boy is falling off the cliff. We've got to rescue him. Hurry, hurry!' he would pull my arm to get it to reach out to his. The sequence was repeated but was never boring, perhaps because of Joseph's delight in the high drama. Certainly, my involvement in the game was quite intense, too: lack of a capacity for pretend play and for joint attention are early markers for autism, so it is moving and cheering when such pretend play and joint attention begin, however immature they may be in relation to the chronological age of the child. The game seemed heavy with meaning. Sometimes I told him that I agreed – he did indeed need rescuing from his self-imposed autistic isolation and to be brought on to firmer ground where there were other real people.

Many years ago, I heard Frances Salo give a paper in which she said 'Wow!' at the sight of a picture drawn by a deprived little boy with a rejecting mother. (Please note that Joseph was not the child of a rejecting mother, but he was certainly deprived by his autism.) Salo's child had drawn his first bold picture. At the time, I thought her response was very unpsychoanalytic. Now, I think it was repairing a deficit in the child's internal object. Trevarthen (2001) has written about the infant's need to feel proud – that is, 'chuffed', like the choughing of a bird – when the mother is delighted with his cleverness. On one occasion, Joseph was making a big splash in the sink, and kept saying, '*Werh.*' I repeated it appreciatively, and congratulated him on the big splashes. But then I remembered that a few weeks before I had said, '*Wow!*' every time he had made a big splash. So I began to say '*Wow!*' again and realized, first, that he was delighted that I had finally got it, and then that he was struggling to make his word sound even more like mine. I noticed that he was watching my lips and really trying to imitate them. I found myself saying 'lovely' and 'clever', because I felt real love at those moments for him and for his generosity in finally sticking his neck out. He got nearer and nearer to the '*Wow!*' sound, and it is not an easy sound to make.

Discussion and conclusion

The technical issues in talking to a child like Joseph are difficult. Needless to say, I have only cited parts of sessions where I think I managed to find a way of being heard and encouraging proto-speech between us. Working with these children is never easy, and the power of their autism, particularly when treatment starts late, is awesome. However, it is interesting to think about how to talk to these children, and why particular methods may be more useful than others.

I think there were many different motives for Joseph's repetitive talk. Sometimes he seemed totally absorbed in it but, as I said, I began to think that at times he was definitely monitoring my response to it. And he became less autistic when I gave urgent voice to this excluded third. This suggests that there was a communicative element in the projection at such moments. Or should we call it a proto-communication? He may not have expected a response, but he recognized it and seemed delighted by it when he got it. At other moments, when I felt his 'talking' was more arrogantly self-indulgent, I challenged it. I think he needed *both* the more receptive coaxing 'motherese' from me *and* the more challenging 'fatherese'. There seem to have been two aspects to the father's voice in the room: first, a father who declines to indulge omnipotence, makes demands on his child to learn and grow, and makes it clear that the child is not the same as the grown-ups; and, second, the father who invites and permits identification (with the strong voice and the potency of the stamping). Both worked only when I got the tone right. I suspect that when I challenged him too strictly, it may not have permitted the kind of identification he needed with a strong father. What seemed to work better was a firm, slightly bored tone or a more humorous teasing. Some identification processes seemed to be beginning with his deeper growls, strong stamping and standing tall. Some identification with a father certainly aids the tolerance of Oedipal rivalries, and enables omnipotent methods to be replaced by a more realistic sense of agency and potency.

I have described elsewhere the need to approach the child with autism on the right band of intensity (Alvarez, 1999), but it is interesting that Barrows (2002) has been even more specific in introducing aggressive play to a child with autism.

To return to the more receptive or maternal function, as I have said, Bion (1962b) described this in terms of the mother's 'containment' of the baby's distress which had been projected into her and then transformed there by her capacity to think about and process feelings. But as developmentalists like Stern (1985) and Trevarthen and Aitken (2001) remind us, these processes do not concern only moments of distress. Babies need to impress, to delight, to bring a light to the parents' eyes, to surprise and astonish them, to make them laugh; and Joseph loved it when I laughed at him (or with him). But they also need to be given room, space and time in which to do all this. We all may need to learn to keep our distance, know our place, wait our turn, and bide our time – and, especially important, respect the child's space and timing. I think it was important for Joseph that I could feel strongly but then hold the experience of being left out, unwanted, helpless and, especially, powerless, and give him space and time to feel that he had the power to keep me waiting. Of course, such a technique risks being experienced as masochistically colluding with omnipotence: it needed vigilant monitoring on my part, so when it felt more self-indulgent on his part, I could be firmer.

Elsewhere (Alvarez, 2010b) I have described an adolescent girl in the throes of a depressive episode that included characteristics of the addictive quality described by Freud and Abraham in their cases of melancholia, which they differentiated from real mourning. I found that attaining a balance between my sympathy for my patient's real grief and my growing impatience with her tendency to wallow in misery was very difficult but necessary. It was important not to get over-excited and over-concerned by her upset but also, eventually, sometimes to convey a kind of dry weariness over the tenacity with which she clung to her symptoms.

I want to mention another point concerning the strength of my voice when I coaxed Joseph to talk to me, rather than to his imaginary (or delusional) friends. There was a process of 'reclamation' at such moments, possibly because Joseph did not really believe his objects minded when he disappeared (Alvarez, 1992). Even the most loving and devoted parents, teachers and therapists can become very demoralized and give up a little under such conditions. Joseph did seem to appreciate my staying power, but only when I kept it mock-desperate, playful/needy. As soon as there was a hint of unprocessed frustration or directive pulling on my part, he retreated. (His teachers independently developed similar non-controlling methods with him.) I also think the drama in my voice got through to the developmentally delayed proto-speaker in him. (These intensified elements in the technique were informed by developmental thinking and also by awareness of the powerful hold of the repetitive preoccupations. The technique was by no means strictly, classically psychoanalytic.) We have to find ways of helping these children to attend to us, and have to sustain their attention; and emotionally heightened interest is central to this process. (See Beebe and Lachmann (1994) on their third principle of saliency – heightened affective moments.)

In conclusion, it is important to say that Joseph had dedicated parents, teachers and speech and music therapists with whom I liaised regularly, so this was a cooperative effort. I have simply tried to outline some techniques and concepts that seem to have been helpful in my particular part of the work.

Chapter 13

Further reflections

Countertransference, the paranoid and schizoid positions, and some speculations on parallels with neuroscience

Introduction: the level of mental disturbance and mental illness in children and adolescents

This final chapter is an attempt to integrate ideas outlined in the book with some of my more recent thoughts. I have hoped to contribute to the literature on child and adolescent psychotherapy relevant to the cases we are seeing in this new millennium. Many of these patients are extremely dangerous to others as well as to themselves. Without treatment, or with treatment that ends prematurely, some are at grave risk of serious mental illness. One adolescent who was beginning to emerge from a breakdown and an over-intense relationship with a psychotic mother had to terminate her therapy when social services cut the funding. She was 15 and, after a year's treatment, had matured somewhat – perhaps to something like age three or four – in her emotional development. Her despair was acute and, for her, termination might have been terminal. Children in treatment now are not only more disturbed and damaged than those referred half a century ago; they are often more emotionally and cognitively delayed as a result of both abuse and neglect. This book has attempted to systematize some clinical reflections after listening to generations of therapists' struggles to reach them and help them, occasionally using methods that are too traditional to do so. Although many of the cases were helped by the more traditional approach described at the explanatory level, some were not. So, to my mind, it is time to begin a closer study of how we – both patients and therapists – manage to come to think new thoughts. I think in psychoanalysis we still have much to learn about the nature of introjections, internalization and identification.

Re-examining the paranoid-schizoid position

First, a word about Klein's concept of the paranoid-schizoid position: it is well known that Klein decided to add to her concept of the paranoid position (1946) the ideas of Fairbairn (1952) and Winnicott (1945) on the schizoid position. She saw that schizoid withdrawal from feeling, with states of fragmentation and unintegration, were characteristic of these more disturbed states of mind in adults but also, in slightly different ways, in very young babies (Klein, 1946; Likierman, 2001). The reader will note that in Figure A2, where the sense of badness outweighs the sense of goodness, I have termed the lower section the 'paranoid position', not the 'paranoid-schizoid position'. In Figure A3, where the sense of goodness and badness are both weak, I have termed the lower section the 'schizoid position'. This is very over-simplified, because both autistic children and neglected children are different from schizoid or dissociated children. Yet I think that some sub-types of these conditions do have something in common in terms of their deficit. These more pathological affectless states, described in Chapter 1 and Part III, do differ from even the most persecuted of states of mind. So I have divided the more persecuted or paranoid states from those characterized either by deficit or by dissociation so chronic that it amounts to a deficit. Of course, schizoid and paranoid elements may coalesce in the same patient, but the diagnostic manuals themselves distinguish between paranoid types of schizophrenia characterized by disorganization of speech, behaviour and affect, and those paranoid types that are more organized (APA, 1994, p. 149).

However, child psychotherapists face more problems than persecutory anxiety, fragmentation and under-integration. Clinical depression and sometimes chronic despair are major issues, too. In 2005, the National Health Service instructed its general practitioners to cease giving anti-depressants to children under the age of 18. Apparently, there was an increased risk of suicide among the 40,000 children with depression, anxiety or other problems who were taking such drugs. Three months of counselling was recommended for those with moderate depression – but, of course, there were not enough counsellors (*Guardian*, 28 September 2005, p. 3). Trowell *et al.*'s (2003) research on depression in young adolescents warns us to take seriously what it may be like to have not only internal objects who are felt to be too fragile and depressed to be criticized but possibly external real ones. Some patients seem to have had nowhere to put blame other than on to themselves. At the time of writing, a multi-site study (18 child and adolescent mental health clinics in England) was examining the impact of three different treatments – psychoanalytic psychotherapy, cognitive behavioural therapy and special clinical care – on 540 depressed adolescents. In particular, it was exploring the sleeper effect in terms of prevention of relapse after one year (Nick Midgley, personal communication, 2011).

In 2010, it was reported that general practitioners were demanding more therapy for mentally ill children: 78 per cent of doctors in the survey said that they could rarely get help within the two months' prescribed waiting time. A 16-year-old rape victim had started self-harming after being refused help, while another girl, who had seen her sibling burn to death in a car, was offered an appointment with the mental health service in six months' time (*Observer*, 21 March 2010, p. 21). To anyone who works with children, it will also be no surprise that up to 80 per cent of crime in the UK is caused by people who had behavioural problems as children and teenagers. A report published by the Sainsbury Centre for Mental Health argued that early intervention programmes could significantly lower crime levels. And not only crime – childhood mental health problems can result in poor educational achievement, unemployment, low earnings, teenage pregnancies and marital problems (*Guardian*, 23 November 2009, p. 7). One group of researchers has suggested that pre-school disruptive behaviour needs careful study, and fine distinctions need to be made between more normal types of reactive aggression and those that seem more deliberate and calculating. Careful psychoanalytic clinicians make such distinctions all the time, and it is heartening to see these researchers insisting that current psychiatric classifications for children are too crude and therefore still inadequate to the task of good assessment of the needs and suffering of the child and the risks he presents (Wakschlag *et al.*, 2010). DeJong (2010) has suggested that the current classification system, *DSM-IV* (APA, 1994), inadequately captures the range and type of psychopathology seen in the 'in care' population of children. As mentioned in Chapter 5, Van der Kolk (2009), an expert in child abuse, has suggested that *DSM-V* should include a new diagnostic entity that he terms 'Developmental Trauma Disorder'. And see Reid's (1999a) proposal that children with an 'Autistic Post-Traumatic Developmental Disorder' may make up an important sub-group of youngsters with autism.

Early intervention for all these conditions is vital but extremely rare, and the funding for Sure Start Centres was radically reduced in 2011. Much of the time, help does not arrive until much later in childhood or adolescence, when depressed or cynical habits of mind may be well entrenched and development distorted. Parents or carers will be offered help with parenting issues, but the child or adolescent may well need individual psychotherapy for himself. Although there are just over 800 child and adolescent psychotherapists in the UK, the children we are treating are, as I said, increasingly more disturbed and/or developmentally delayed. Traditional psychoanalytic psychotherapy, however, mostly still works. A recent meta-analysis of the effectiveness of long-term psychodynamic therapy showed that it was a more effective treatment for complex disorders than other, shorter forms of treatment (Leichsenring and Rabung, 2008). Another author pointed out that non-psychodynamic therapies may be effective in part because the more skilled practitioners utilize techniques that have long been central to psychodynamic theory and practice (Shedler, 2010). My own view is that, if we wait long enough – and if the practitioners of all the differing treatments have sufficient integrity, honesty and, above all, humility – we begin to see more overlaps where practitioners are truly learning from their subject matter, the patients. It is interesting, for example, that some of the cognitive behaviour therapists are now turning their attention to the relationship between the patient and therapist, just as Freud did as long ago as 1905. Research by Chiu *et al.* (2009) suggests that the quality of the child–therapist alliance assessed early in treatment was differentially associated with symptom reduction at mid- and post-treatment.

But I think it is also true that psychoanalysts have had to learn to know when symptoms have deep symbolic meaningfulness and when – as in the case of some psychotic preoccupations, some addictive behaviours and some autistic repetitive behaviours – they do not (Alvarez, 1992; Joseph, 1982; Segal, 1957; Tustin, 1980). Such processes have become habitual and are more like a 'bad habit', with the patient becoming what Reid has termed 'stuck'. As I said in Part III, this may require different analytic techniques. CBT is documented as having helped numerous patients with obsessive-compulsive disorder, depression and anxiety, and it is my guess that this happens where the symptom has outworn its motivational usefulness. Where it has not, I believe the patients need psychoanalytic psychotherapy. It is also true that music therapists and other arts therapists, including movement therapists, have much to offer to these damaged people, and these therapists make much use of the descriptive and amplifying level I have described in psychoanalytic work (Bloom, 2006; Robarts, 2009).

The danger of 'manualizing' psychotherapy

In spite of some of the generalizations regarding sub-types of conditions in this book, it is not a manual. I have suggested that the continuum of ways of ascribing meaning to our patients' play or words can be seen to contain three discernible levels, and this may seem to be recommending that the vast complexity of therapeutic work can be reduced to something like a manual or a recipe book. But that cannot be done: our work as clinicians can never be condensed in such a way. Psychotherapy, as a clinical practice, is an art and craft (although its effects can be measured scientifically). Each patient is different from all the others, and different from himself a few minutes – or even a few seconds – earlier. Moreover, the interaction between patient and therapist is different at each moment. Yet there are patterns and recurrences of patterns; states of mind, however fleeting at first, do, in time, coalesce, even harden, into enduring traits of personality. These may include regularly returning feelings of love or hate, difficulties in containment and regulation of excitement, defences, addictive and habitual behaviours, or tendencies to perverse excitement. They may also include states of despair or dissociation. A further possible outcome is the blunting of mind and feeling, and the stunting of brain growth with its attendant emotional and cognitive delay, which can result from emotional neglect (Music, 2009; Perry, 2002). Also, Strathearn et al. (2001) found neglect to be the most significant predictor of cognitive impairment, and their data showed a significant drop in cognitive functioning in the first three years of life in those children experiencing neglect.

Children and adolescents with this history fail to pay attention not because they are defending themselves against thinking, nor because they are suspicious of and hate teachers, but simply because they expect nothing of interest to emerge from an encounter with another person. Something similar may be seen in a type of autism, where the autism has turned the child away, in earliest infancy, from the world of other human beings to his own repetitive preoccupations with inanimate objects.

Countertransference

I am aware that my attempt to group some of these conditions into differing levels of pathology may seem crude. However, I believe that the idea of a continuum of levels of functioning in ego, self and the internal objects may provide some degree of structure to our thinking about how best to reach such children. And this is no mere matter of finding the right words. Usually, the feelings in our countertransference have to come first (although, very occasionally, it can be the other way round, as I shall illustrate later in an afterthought regarding some work with Robbie). The transference and countertransference emotional encounters, especially with more ill patients, are intense and often overpowering. Conversely, and more worryingly, they are sometimes seriously underpowering: nothing seems to matter and our meeting with a particular patient may seem to be bereft of meaning for both parties. These various states of mind and feeling – or lack of it – are taken very seriously by those therapists who work psychoanalytically. Bion taught that if you are bored, study the boredom. (And see Bergstein (2009) on the relationship of boredom to encapsulated parts of the psyche.) Transference and countertransference do not interfere with the work – they are the work's most vital instruments. But although the containment and processing of our countertransference feelings, even without the 'right' words, may often be enough to enable the patient to feel understood and to get something from that moment of encounter, this is not always the case. Sometimes the elements in something Bion called 'transformation' – the stage beyond containment, where the feeling in the analyst is returned in a transformed manner to the patient – are more essential than they are at other times. This is because an emotional experience is transformable in innumerable ways. I have suggested that with the most pathological of cases – states of extreme chronic dissociation, emptiness or perverse attachments to inhuman, non-human or sado-masochistic objects – we may need to use the intensity of our feelings – or else our intense alarm about our lack of feeling – in inten*sified* ways.

Further examples of intensified work

In Chapters 1, 11 and 12 I gave several examples of children coming to life at such moments, but here are three more that may serve to illustrate – and probably complicate the understanding of – this phenomenon. In Chapter 1 I mentioned the period in his teens when Robbie often arrived in a very agitated, almost psychotic state. By the time he was in his twenties, he was much more independent, less engaged in his ritualistic talk and altogether saner. His conversation now made sense, but it had become terribly compliant and dull. He would, for example, begin the session by telling me that he had helped his father sweep the leaves in the garden the day before. (In the transference, he was telling me what he thought I wanted to hear and, although I had interpreted this many times, it had had little effect. He tended to hear it as a confirmation that that was what he should do.) However, I had recently begun to notice that I greeted him at the start of the session in a very different manner from the way I greeted Samuel (a much more severely autistic patient whom I also saw at the clinic). Samuel was a very embittered, frustrated child, but nevertheless full of a powerful, compressed vitality. I began to notice that when I greeted him, my eyes were probably alight with some kind of energized anticipation; whereas, when I greeted Robbie, although I was relieved at the signs of his sanity, my eyes were probably dull. I worried about this a good deal, wondering what I could do about my countertransference.

One day Robbie came in, glanced at the brass doorknob, which we passed on the way to the consulting room, and said, longingly, 'I want to be that doorknob.' My heart sank, as this remark was very similar to an autistic repetition of his from a decade earlier, when he used to 'want to be the weathervane'. I never really understood at the time, as I believe I understand now, that he wanted to be *someone* or *something* that people watched, followed and admired. In the film *On the Waterfront*, Marlon Brando's character says to his brother, 'I could have been a contender.' Robbie wanted to be a contender, but, in those early years of child analysis, I had taken it not just in too part-object a way as an identification with a penis or breast but as something an Oedipal child had to learn to relinquish. In those years, I did not understand that, in his pre-Oedipal self, Robbie had a *rightful need* to be admired, as all babies do.

In any case, as I followed him down the hall, with my heart sinking, I realized that he had spoken in a quite emotional way. There had been nothing autistic about it. So, when we reached the consulting room, I asked him why he wanted to be the doorknob. He answered slowly, 'Because . . . it's so shiny.' (It was brass.) I started to think about research cited by Allan Schore (1994) about how the pupils of people's eyes enlarge when they look lovingly at a baby or a lover, and that this allows more light to get in and hit the retinas. Thus, when observers of infants – or clinicians – assert that someone's eyes lit up, they are describing a physiological fact. I found myself thinking of the need and right every baby has to bring a light to their mother's or father's eyes. I said to Robbie (who was only coming up to London once a month by now): 'I know what I should have said at the door, Robbie. I should have said, "How lovely to see you. I haven't seen you for a whole month!"' As I said this, my feelings toward him changed: I was quite moved. And, as I spoke, he became enlivened, too: his eyes lit up and colour came into his cheeks. I learned subsequently to be extremely vigilant about my own counter-transference and about the quality of the eye contact I maintained with him, and I believe it helped him to find ways to feel alive *other than* the old autistic perverse excitements.

It is worth noting that although we usually think of the countertransference as coming first and therefore dictating the words we use – that is, containment leading on to transformation – on this occasion it was the other way round. My thinking and my words helped me to change my feelings. With very disturbing psycho-pathic patients, I have often noticed my voice go high when I am having difficulty facing some particularly horrifying cruelty or brutality in a child's play or his treatment of me. If I then struggle to lower my voice to something more in touch with the dark place he is in, my mood seems to be able to follow him into his emotional cemetery. He then feels a little more understood and somewhat less contemptuous.

A second example: Jesse, an eight-year-old autistic boy who had become generally more related to people in recent months, came back to his first session after the Christmas break. He burst into the playroom, looked at his toys, and said, 'There are . . . there are . . . too many toys, I want some others. I want to get into that cupboard!' When he had first come, the year before, his phantasy had been that I had offered too few – there were much better toys in that cupboard. In the past, I had interpreted sibling rivalry and idealization of what lay hidden, but something about his hesitation made me think differently. He then said, 'I know what I need. An axe. Could you get me an axe? Do you have an axe anywhere in this house I could use?' There was definitely eagerness, and eager anticipation, but also bewilderment. I felt that he knew he wanted *something*, but he did not know what it was. This time I said, 'I think what you want is for me to give you an instrument all right, but one that will help you find a way of having a good time here with me today.' He stopped his demands at once and started to play, making good contact for most of the session.

I think I sensed that he was glad to be back, even glad to see me, but did not know what to do with that feeling. I do not think I was being simply evasive, or inviting Jesse to be distracted from his desires or his aggression. Although the phantasy of the cupboard's contents may have had some degree of unconscious significance regarding the inside of his maternal object's body, his relation to his object's mental/emotional qualities required more attention. An already connected child functioning at a symbolic level who wants more than his share presents a different problem and we can interpret unconscious rivalry and intrusive desires there. But this, I think, was closer to a symbolic equation (Segal, 1957) or autistic object (Tustin, 1980), and Jesse needed reminding of the existence of an interpersonal world of human beings and *what could be done with them.*

Where the internal world of human mindful objects does not beckon – that is, where there is a deficit in the internal object – we may need to spell out something about the potential, the possibility, the options, that could lie ahead. Luisa Carbone (personal communication, 2011) has wondered why I did not discuss Jesse's phantasy that he needed something as powerful as an axe to get through. This is an important question, but I think that (possibly only through luck) I managed to convey that the instrument was to hand, and it did not have to be an axe. Perhaps something in his eager desperation warned me that I needed to offer the instrument of interpersonal interaction quickly or I would lose him. In the majority of situations with other patients, however, the therapist's willingness to accept and acknowledge the negative transference (in this case that I was some sort of withholding and impermeable object) acts as a lifeline to the patient. (See Chapters 6 and 7 for several examples of this.)

In this above example with Jesse, although I was certainly stressing the importance of his transference relation to me, I seem to have made an interpretation along fairly classical analytic lines: 'You think you want *that*, but you really want *this*.' But I think I was going further in offering a conception to meet what was only a preconception in him. In Chapter 11, I described the way in which, a few weeks later, something even more intensified seemed to be needed. When my reflective interpretations failed to reach him, and I finally cried emotionally that I wished Indiana Jones would come and rescue *me*, Jesse warmed up and stayed in contact thereafter.

Some possible parallels with neuroscience

In the Introduction I drew attention to the fact that there has been much discussion in recent decades about the existence of two levels of analytic work: that is, of insight versus other more primary levels of understanding (containment, attunement and empathy, for example). Some authors have suggested that these two methods of work involve different areas of the brain (Schore, 2003; Siegel, 1999). This follows from the fact that much attention in neuroscience has begun to be paid to the differing functions of the left and right hemispheres, with the left having more to do with linear sequentiality and ordinary grammatical language and the right dominant for emotional and social processing and emotive, expressive language, including metaphor and exclamation. The right brain has a growth spurt in the first 18 months of life, whereas the left has its surge after 18 months. The stress regarding the right brain now is not on emotional *and* social development, but on socio-emotional processing, because it is increasingly recognized that emotional life and development are borne out of interactions with other human beings, and that the effect of emotional abuse and neglect on infants' brains is devastating (Murray and Cooper, 1997; Perry, 2002; Perry *et al.*, 1995). But the child's (and even the adult's) brain continues to be characterized by plasticity, and environmental experience that alters the mind, including that provided by psychotherapy, may be altering the brain, too (see Sonuga-Barke, 2010). These authors imply that the level of pathology and of emotional development determines the nature of the appropriate treatment.

Schore (2003) suggests a formulation of a treatment model that is matched to the developmental level of the patient. When there is damage and deficit in right-brain processing, he stresses the need for vitalizing attunements between the therapist's and the patient's right brains, what he says Buck (1994, p. 266) calls a 'conversation between limbic systems'. Schore (2003, p. 281), however – in common with the more classical psychoanalytic aims – adds that 'a directing of therapeutic technique towards the elevation of emotions from a primitive pre-symbolic sensorimotor level of experience to a mature symbolic representational level, and a creation of a self-reflective position that can appraise the significance and meaning of these affects' are also needed.

Siegel (1999, p. 237) describes the type of patient in whom right-hemisphere information processing may be disassociated from that of the left hemisphere in order to maintain functioning. Words and feelings are not connected. In such a case, he states, 'we can envision strategies of moving toward growth and development as initially involving right-hemisphere-to-right-hemisphere communication between two people. Eventually, further internal change may be brought about by a process facilitating integration of the right and left hemispheres within the individual.' Thus, like Schore, he describes two stages in the work with more damaged patients. Divino and Moore (2010) have suggested that psychoanalytic technique has lagged behind the new findings regarding the neurobiology of interpersonal experience: they suggest ways of incorporating this into training, discussing the effect of trauma while taking care not to traumatize their students.

Further research will be needed to establish the veracity of these speculations about the link between brain development and technique. However, I have complicated the issue in this book by adding the notion of a third level of work. This involves neither left-brain sequential thinking about alternative meanings nor the descriptive and amplifying right-brain level regarding the emotional whatness (the qualitative nature) of experience, but rather the therapist's insistence on meaning itself in situations where there seems to be no affect and nothing matters. I have wondered about what brain science might have to offer in order to understand these moments.

Gerhardt, following Schore, tells us that when the mother smiles, the baby's nervous system is pleasantly aroused and his heart rate increases. These processes trigger a biochemical response: 'endogenous' or homemade opioids. As natural opioids, they also make you feel good. She adds, however, that another neurotransmitter called dopamine is simultaneously released from the brainstem, and, 'like the opioids, it makes its way up to the prefrontal cortex. Both neurochemicals enhance the uptake of glucose there, helping new tissue to grow in the prefrontal brain' (Gerhardt, 2004, pp. 41–42).

Biven, too, has pointed out that there are two major ways of feeling good, but she stresses the difference between them. One is evoked by the opioids, which give feelings of pleasure and happiness; the other is evoked by the dopamine system, which generates curiosity and anticipatory excitement – it is energizing and stimulating. She suggests that Panksepp's ideas about what he calls the 'seeking system' in the brain are of great interest (Lucy Biven, personal communication, 2010). Panksepp distinguishes this system from attachment, sex and hunger, although he points out it can and does combine with these other systems (Panksepp, 1998; Panksepp and Biven, 2011). His descriptions correspond somewhat to Bion's concept of K – the desire to get to know someone or something, not to *have* knowledge (Bion, 1962b).

I think that the sense of wonder plays a part here. Stern (2010) suggests that it is not only the content of mental/emotional life that matters; the quality of the forms of expression and of experience also requires greater study. He thinks the neuroscience underpinning of this may lie in the arousal system, which is providing the force behind and under all mental/emotional activity – a force that pushes sex, hunger, attachment and so on into action, that triggers the emotions, sharpens the attention, starts cognitions, and initiates movement. Solms (2000, pp. 618–619) has suggested that this seems very close to what Freud called the life instinct, or the life force, or even the drives!

Panksepp (1998, p. 144) himself writes of Leonard, a grown man whose dopamine circuits were destroyed in childhood. Only after the introduction of L-dopa by Oliver Sacks could he partake again of worldly delights. Panksepp says that we now know that ascending dopamine circuit tracts lie at the heart of powerful, affectively valenced neural systems that allow people and animals to operate smoothly and efficiently in all of their day-to-day pursuits. He suggests that 'intense interest, engaged curiosity, and eager anticipation' are the types of feelings that reflect arousal of this system in humans (p. 149).

A technical parallel

Interestingly, Panksepp (1998, p. 144) goes on to say,

> without the synaptic energy of dopamine, these potentials remain frozen, as it were, in an endless winter of discontent. Dopamine synapses resemble gatekeepers rather than couriers that convey detailed messages. When they are not active at their posts, many potentials of the brain cannot be readily manifested in thought or actions. Without dopamine, only the strongest emotional messages instigate behavior.

This is the seeking system. Panksepp suggests that it underlies all systems, makes you reach out for things. It engenders feelings of pleasurable anticipation, excitement and euphoria at the extreme. He points out that if the capability of the dopamine system is too high, the person goes over the top in self-enhancement.

Biven (personal communication, 2010) has suggested that emotional neglect might lead to atrophy of those seeking structures, which therefore do not generate enough dopamine activity. There is a difference between a feeling that I want something and a feeling that indicates that I can also reach out and get it, or at least try. This may be connected with the sense of agency so lacking in despairing children (discussed in Chapters 2 and 5). Perhaps this is connected with the awareness of 'live company' – the 'other' is both accessible and impressible.

I have suggested that there are certain states of mind (and perhaps states of brain) where a more intensive, vitalizing insistence on meaning is required because it creates what some developmentalists call a 'heightened affective moment' (Beebe and Lachmann, 1994). The pulse and pitch of our voices change at such moments of urgency, where we 'reclaim' our patients into the world of meaning. Some research has found that the insistent rhythms of music can increase the synthesis of dopamine in animals (Panksepp, 1998, p. 131). Gampel (2005, p. 17) has pointed out that such reclamatory work is a question of activity not in the sense of doing but in the sense of being. She states that we add an emotional soundtrack to the child's cut-off and shut-in life.

Lanyado and Horne (2006), writing about technique from the point of view of the British independent tradition, cite many examples where playfulness, humour, spontaneity and intuition were central to achieving or maintaining contact with very disturbed, often unreachable children and adolescents. In many ways, I agree with them, because I would rather we use our heart than imagine that we are being 'psychoanalytic' simply by being reserved and maintaining a neutral and/or containing and reflective attitude. Many authors, including Kleinians, emphasize the importance of reflection needing to arise *out of countertransference* feeling (e.g., Feldman, 2004). Yet I think it takes decades to make a psychoanalyst – that is, someone who can use his countertransference both analytically and effectively. If a deprived child comes in complaining of a scraped knee and we rush to say that he feels hurt by tomorrow's break in treatment (even if that is so), the child may experience us as cruel or indifferent to his actual, physical hurt. He may not be able to manage that symbolic jump to tomorrow, yet he may hear the sympathy when we say, 'Oh, that does look sore.' Then we might add, 'And, on top of all that, I am leaving you tomorrow. Not fair!'

I would rather we hang on to our natural instincts of human sympathy and spontaneous Winnicottian intuitive responses than carry out pseudo-psychoanalysis with children totally incapable – as yet – of symbol formation. Little moments of adding meaning (alpha function) can provide the building bricks of symbol formation, and too many proscriptions against advice-giving and against enactments of maternal or paternal countertransferences may inhibit some ordinary humanity, which could arrive with a 'minimal dose' (Strachey, 1934) of thinking attached – and eventually thereby lead to enhanced symbolic functions.

So I am definitely not arguing against spontaneous, intuitive reactions from the therapist. I simply wish to emphasize the importance of studying why such an intuitive response might have been effective at one moment but unnecessary – or, worse, intrusive or premature – at another. We must *aim* to feel and think, preferably at the same time, but there is often a time delay (Pick, 1985). There is, however, no substitute for the close and honest examination of both our own countertransference feelings and our patient's transference feelings. If we find the child unappealing and distasteful, and even dread seeing her, we have to examine this and find out what it is about her facial expression, gait, behaviour or manner that evokes this in us. Only then can we begin to get through to her feelings of unlikeability and unlovability, then to the things she does to evoke this, finally to find glimmerings of the likeable and lovable child she might – and could – become.

The transference

This illustrates the vital importance of staying in touch with the transference. I believe that it is in the transference relationship that personal history can be rewritten. This does not mean that we do not need support from the network of carers and educators, nor that they do not need close liaison and support from us and our colleagues. (See Klauber (1999), Reid (1999b) and Rustin (1998) on the importance of work with the parents of a child in treatment. Rustin describes four different categories of such work, each realizing a different aim.) So, while I am in no way suggesting that the child can be treated without parallel support or even treatment for the parents or carers, I am stressing that the power of the relationship between patient and therapist is the primary healing ground of the internal world.

This view can be hard to maintain when we know that the child has had, or is even still having, terrible experiences in the external world. Many therapists feel compelled to mention these external factors frequently. In my view, timing is all-important, because the child may need, for a moment, to have a completely different experience in the therapy with the therapist, and a reference to outside horrors (or recent external misconducts on the part of the child) can interfere profoundly with new, possibly healthy introjections of a different sort of parental object or a different sort of self. A child may burst into a session after an unexpected three-week break from therapy, saying longingly, 'I want to see my real mother!' (The mother from whom she had long ago been removed, a woman who had been extremely abusive and neglectful.) There are, I believe, ways of being respectful to the actual mother's importance while tactfully pointing out that the child may *also* want to get together with me (someone she has not seen for three weeks) today. That is, one can hitch a lift into the transference without setting oneself up as the only person of importance in the patient's life. This requires great tact, delicacy and modesty. It is not a question of interpreting everything in the transference – for example, when an adolescent boy finds a new girlfriend he likes – by assuming that she 'stands for' us. Rather, it is a question of listening to implications for what is happening in the relationship between us, and responding accordingly and, to repeat, tactfully. Judith Edwards reminded me recently of arguments she and I used to have about how much to talk about the transference with adolescent patients. I wanted more; she wanted less. She reminded me that Marinella Lia, an analyst from Turin, had suggested one could say, 'Today I am a little like your Leonora in your mind' – that is, let the girlfriend be the primary object, and yourself the secondary (as reported in Edwards, 1994).

Winnicott taught us to respect the paradox of the transitional area, and I think there are parallels with the newer, more containing attitude to projective identifications into the person of the analyst. Sometimes the child projects aspects of his inner world into the toy materials on the table, sometimes into the person in the room with him. The transitional area can be an extremely adequate container, particularly for paranoid or very schizoid patients who cannot handle the intensity of a human relationship, and here we may need to be careful not to overdo the transference interpretations, while remaining aware of its great significance for ourselves in the room.

The setting

This book is not an introduction to child psychotherapy, but I may need to say what may not be obvious to every reader: that every technical modification advocated here needs to be carried out in the context of a reliable, regular setting for the therapy. Child psychoanalysts and child psychotherapists stress the importance of the regularity and consistency of appointments, with sessions always taking place in the same room and the therapeutic work needing to take account of the emotional havoc when disruptions to time and space do occur (Rustin, 1997). The room and the building matter.

On returning to the Tavistock Clinic in the late 1980s, I had the strange experience that my belief in the power of transference to the person of the therapist (and in the difficulty patients had in changing therapists after a consultation) had to be fine tuned. When I was the consultant on a case at the Tavistock and had to pass the child on to another worker, I had to take account of the fact that it was nothing like so difficult as it had been in private practice: there was a transference to the building, the waiting room, the receptionists, and I was still remaining as the case manager – as a sort of grandmother figure. This is very different from passing on a case in private practice to a therapist in a different geographical location. I have subsequently learned that it is often a good idea in private work to accompany the family to the first meeting at the new setting to enable the link to hold. The timing and space of the setting are precious. Bucci (2001) has suggested that there is a sub- (not pre-)symbolic function that is neither archaic nor primitive but operates alongside symbolic processes throughout normal rational life. To me, this seems rather close to the Kleinian idea that unconscious phantasy can accompany and infuse reality-thinking, and seems to be relevant to this issue of our bodily sense of our relation to our physical environment.

In conclusion, I have tried to show that there are several important preconditions necessary to the achievement of the final integrations of the depressive position. Of course, in family life, society, culture, poetry and the other arts, there may be powerful integrating forces at work – that is, integrations not only between one part of the mind and another, but between the body and mind. Al Alvarez has written about the way in which the poet John Donne could make his readers sit up and attend. He writes, 'In a poem called "The Blossom", Donne spoke of "my naked, thinking heart" . . . [T]hat seems to describe exactly what he expresses in his best poems: you can hear his heart beat *and you* can hear him think, as though they were one and the same process' (Al Alvarez, 2005, p. 55). Well, although we might not be poets, when we attend to our deepest feelings and manage to contain and transform them, we might find words informed and accompanied by feelings and at least aim to reach for our own and our patients' 'naked, thinking' hearts.

Appendix

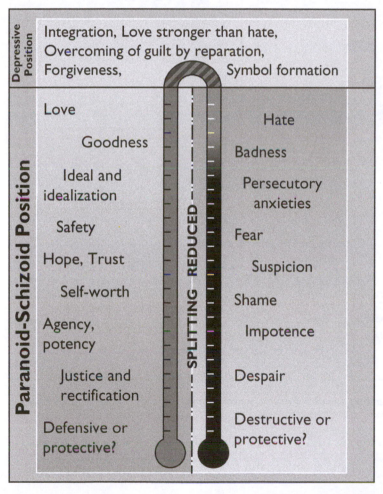

Figure A1 Integrated/concerned states: moments when the sense of goodness is stronger than badness

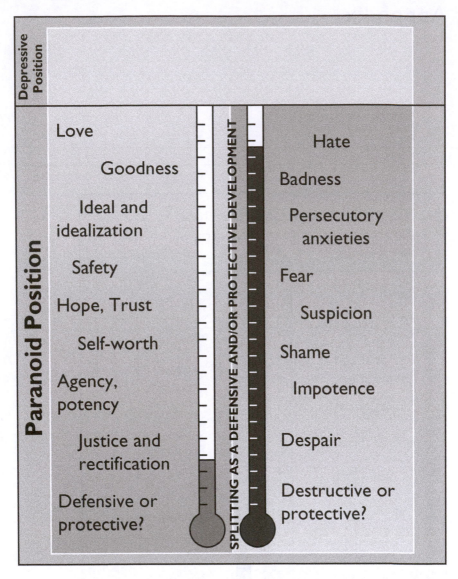

Figure A2 Paranoid and/or persecuted states: moments when the sense of goodness is too
weak to overcome badness

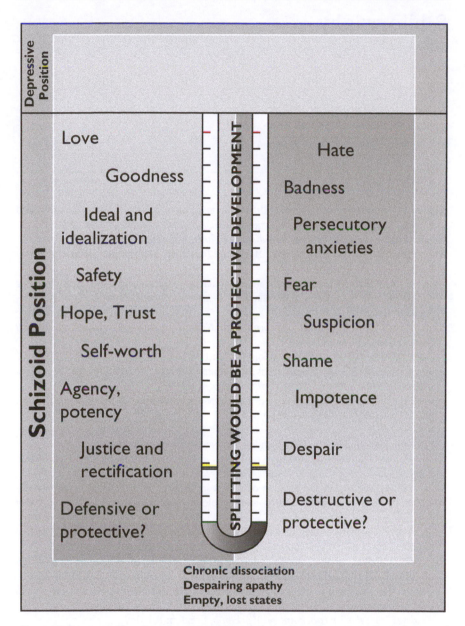

Figure A3 Empty and/or dissociated states: moments when the senses of goodness and badness are both extremely weak

Bibliography

Abello, N. and Perez-Sanchez, M. (1981) 'Concerning narcissism, homosexuality, and Oedipus: clinical observations', *Revue Francaise de Psychanalyse*, 45, 4: 767–775.

Acquarone, S. (ed.) (2007) *Signs of Autism in Infants*, London: Karnac.

Alexander, P.F. (2008) *Les Murray: A Life in Progress*, Melbourne: Open University Press.

Alhanati, S. (2002) 'Current trends in molecular genetic research of affective states and psychiatric disorders'. In S. Alhanati, *Primitive Mental States*, Vol. II, London: Karnac.

Alvarez, Al (1995) *Night: An Exploration of Night Life, Night Language, Sleep and Dreams*, London: Jonathan Cape.

—— (2005) *The Writer's Voice*, London: Bloomsbury.

Alvarez, Anne (1980) 'Two regenerative situations in autism: reclamation and becoming vertebrate', *Journal of Child Psychotherapy*, 6, 1: 69–80.

—— (1988) 'Beyond the unpleasure principle: some preconditions for thinking through play', *Journal of Child Psychotherapy*, 14, 2: 1–14.

—— (1992) *Live Company: Psychoanalytic Psychotherapy with Autistic, Borderline, Deprived and Abused Children*, London and New York: Routledge.

—— (1995) 'Motiveless malignity: problems in the psychotherapy of psychopathic patients', *Journal of Child Psychotherapy*, 21, 2: 167–182.

—— (1996) 'Addressing the element of deficit in children with autism: psychotherapy which is both psychoanalytically and developmentally informed', *Clinical Child Psychology and Psychiatry*, 1, 4: 525–537.

—— (1997) 'Projective identification as a communication: its grammar in borderline psychotic children', *Psychoanalytic Dialogues*, 7, 6: 753–768.

—— (1998) 'Failures to link: attacks or defects? Some questions concerning the thinkability of Oedipal and pre-Oedipal thoughts', *Journal of Child Psychotherapy*, 24, 2: 213–231.

—— (1999) 'Addressing the deficit: developmentally informed psychotherapy with passive, "undrawn" children'. In A. Alvarez and S. Reid (eds) *Autism and Personality: Findings from the Tavistock Autism Workshop*, London: Routledge.

—— (2004) 'Issues in assessment: Asperger's Syndrome and personality'. In M. Rhode and T. Klauber (eds) *The Many Faces of Asperger's Syndrome*, London: Karnac.

—— (2006a) 'Narzissmus und das dumme object- Entwertung oder Missachtung? Mit einer anmerkung zum Suchtigen und zum manifesten Narzissmus'. In O.F. Kernberg and H.P. Hartmann (eds) *Narzissmus: grundlagen – Storungsbilder-Therapie*, Stuttgart: Schattauer.

—— (2006b) 'Some questions concerning states of fragmentation: unintegration, under-integration, disintegration, and the nature of early integrations', *Journal of Child Psychotherapy*, 32, 2: 158–180.

—— (2010a) 'Levels of analytic work and levels of pathology: the work of calibration', *International Journal of Psychoanalysis*, 91, 4: 859–878.

—— (2010b) 'Mourning and melancholia in childhood and adolescence: some reflections on the role of the internal object'. In E. McGinley and A. Varchevker (eds) *Enduring Loss: Mourning, Depression and Narcissism throughout the Life Cycle*, London: Karnac.

Alvarez, A. and Furgiuele, P. (1997) 'Speculations on components in the infant's sense of agency: the sense of abundance and the capacity to think in parentheses'. In S. Reid (ed.) *Developments in Infant Observation: The Tavistock Model*, London: Routledge.

Alvarez, A. and Lee, A. (2004) 'Early forms of relatedness in autism', *Clinical Child Psychology and Psychiatry*, 9, 4: 499–518.

—— (2010) 'Interpersonal relatedness in children with autism: clinical complexity versus scientific simplicity?' In A. Midgley, J. Anderson, E. Grainger, T. Nesic-Vuckovic and C. Urwin (eds) *Child Psychotherapy and Research*, New York: Routledge.

Alvarez, A. and Reid, S. (eds) (1999) *Autism and Personality: Findings from the Tavistock Autism Workshop*, London: Routledge.

American Psychiatric Association [APA] (1994) *Diagnostic and Statistical Manual of Mental Health Disorders* (4th edn) [*DSM-IV*], Washington, DC: American Psychiatric Association.

Anderson, J. (2003) 'The mythic significance of risk-taking, dangerous behaviour', *Journal of Child Psychotherapy*, 29, 1: 75–91.

Balint, M. (1968) *The Basic Fault: Therapeutic Aspects of Regression*, London: Tavistock.

Baron-Cohen, S., Allen, J. and Gillberg, C. (1992) 'Can autism be detected at 18 months? The needle, the haystack, and the CHAT', *British Journal of Psychiatry*, 161: 839–843.

Barrows, P. (2002) 'Becoming verbal: autism, trauma and playfulness', *Journal of Child Psychotherapy*, 28, 1: 53–72.

Bartram, P. (1999) 'Sean: from solitary invulnerability to the beginnings of reciprocity at very early infantile levels'. In A. Alvarez and S. Reid (eds) *Autism and Personality: Findings from the Tavistock Autism Workshop*, London: Routledge.

Bateman, A.W. (1998) 'Thick- and thin-skinned organisations and enactment in borderline and narcissistic disorders', *International Journal of Psychoanalysis*, 79: 13–25.

Beebe, B. and Lachmann, F.M. (1994) 'Representation and internalization in infancy: three principles of salience', *Psychoanalytic Psychology*, 11, 2: 127–165.

—— (2002) *Infant Research and Adult Treatment: Co-constructing Interactions*, New York: Analytic Press.

Beebe, B., Jaffe, J., Feldstein, S., Mays, K. and Alson, D. (1985) 'Interpersonal timing: the application of an adult dialogue model to mother–infant vocal and kinesic interactions'. In T.M. Field and N.A. Fox (eds) *Social Perception in Infants*, Norwood, NJ: Ablex.

Beebe, B., Jaffe, J., Lachmann, F., Feldstein, S., Crown, C. and Jasnow, M. (2000) 'Systems models in development and psychoanalysis: the case of vocal rhythm coordination and attachment', *Infant Mental Health Journal*, 21: 99–122.

Beren, P. (ed.) (1998) *Narcissistic Disorders in Childhood and Adolescence*, Northvale, NJ: Aronson.

Bergstein, A. (2009) 'On boredom: a close encounter with encapsulated parts of the psyche', *International Journal of Psychoanalysis*, 90: 613–631.

Bick, E. (1968) 'The experience of the skin in early object-relations'. In A. Briggs (ed.) *Surviving Space: Papers on Infant Observation*, London: Karnac Tavistock Clinic Series [also in M. Harris Williams (ed.) (1987) *Collected Papers of Martha Harris and Esther Bick*, Strathtay: Clunie].

Bion, W.R. (1950) 'The imaginary twin'. In W.R. Bion (1967) *Second Thoughts: Selected Papers on Psychoanalysis*, London: Heinemann.

—— (1955) 'Language and the schizophrenic'. In M. Klein, P. Heimann and R.E. Money-Kyrle (eds) *New Directions in Psycho-analysis: The Significance of Infant Conflict in the Pattern of Adult Behaviour*, London: Tavistock.

—— (1957a) 'Differentiation of the psychotic from the non-psychotic personalities', *International Journal of Psychoanalysis*, 38: 266–275 [also in W.R. Bion (1967) *Second Thoughts: Selected Papers on Psychoanalysis*, London: Heinemann].

—— (1957b) 'On arrogance'. In W.R. Bion (1967) *Second Thoughts: Selected Papers on Psychoanalysis*, London: Heinemann.

—— (1959) 'Attacks on linking'. In W.R. Bion (1967) *Second Thoughts: Selected Papers on Psychoanalysis*, London: Heinemann.

—— (1962a) 'A theory of thinking'. In W.R. Bion (1967) *Second Thoughts: Selected Papers on Psychoanalysis*, London: Heinemann.

—— (1962b) *Learning from Experience*, London: Heinemann.

—— (1963) *Elements of Psycho-analysis*, London: Heinemann.

—— (1965) *Transformations: Change from Learning to Growth*, London: Heinemann.

—— (1967) *Second Thoughts: Selected Papers on Psychoanalysis*, London: Heinemann.

—— (1974) *Development in Infancy*, San Francisco: W.H. Freeman and Co.

—— (1992) *Cogitations*, London: Karnac.

Blake, P. (2008) *Child and Adolescent Psychotherapy*, Sydney: IP Communications.

Blomberg, B. (2005) 'Time, space and the mind: psychotherapy with children with autism'. In D. Houzel and M. Rhode (eds) *Invisible Boundaries: Psychosis and Autism in Children and Adolescents*, London: Karnac.

Bloom, K. (2006) *The Embodied Self: Movement and Psychoanalysis*, London: Karnac.

Bonasia, R. (2001) 'The countertransference: erotic, erotised, and perverse', *International Journal of Psychoanalysis*, 82: 249–262.

Botella, C. and Botella, S. (2005) *The Work of Psychic Figurability: Mental States without Representation*, Hove: Brunner-Routledge.

Bower, T.G.R. (1974) *Development in Infancy* (2nd edn), San Francisco: W.H. Freeman and Co.

Bowlby, J. (1988) *A Secure Base: Clinical Applications of Attachment Theory*, London: Routledge.

Boyers, L.B. (1989) 'Counter-transference and technique in working with the regressed patient: further remarks', *International Journal of Psychoanalysis*, 70: 701–714.

Braten, S. (1987) 'Dialogic mind: the infant and the adult in proto-conversation'. In M. Carvallo (ed.) *Nature, Cognition and Systems*, Dordrecht and Boston: D. Reidel.

—— (ed.) (2007) *On Being Moved: From Mirror Neurons to Empathy*, Philadelphia, PA: John Benjamins.

Brazelton, T.B. and Nugent, J.K. (1995) *Neonatal Behavioral Assessment Scale* (3rd edn), London: Mackeith Press.

Brazelton, T.B., Koslowski, B. and Main, M. (1974) 'The origins of reciprocity: the early mother–infant interaction'. In M. Lewis and L.A. Rosenblum (eds) *The Effect of the Infant on its Caregivers*, London: Wiley.

Brendel, A. (2001) *Alfred Brendel on Music: Collected Essays*, London: Robson.

Britton, R. (1989) 'The missing link: parental sexuality in the Oedipus complex'. In J. Steiner (ed.) *The Oedipus Complex Today*, London: Karnac.

—— (1998) *Belief and Imagination: Explorations in Psychoanalysis*, London: Routledge.

—— (2003) *Sex, Death, and the Superego*, London: Karnac.

Brody, H. (1982) *Maps and Dreams*, London: Jill Norman and Hobhouse.

Brontë, E. (1965) *Wuthering Heights*, Harmondsworth: Penguin.

Broucek, F.J. (1979) 'Efficacy in infancy: a review of some experimental studies and their possible implications for clinical theory', *International Journal of Psychoanalysis*, 60: 311–316.

—— (1991) *Shame and the Self*, London: Guilford Press.

Bruner, J. (1968) *Processes of Cognitive Growth: Infancy*, Worcester, MA: Clark University Press.

—— (1972) 'Nature and uses of immaturity'. In J.S. Bruner, A. Jolly and K. Sylva (eds) (1976) *Play: Its Role in Development and Evolution*, Harmondsworth: Penguin.

—— (1983) 'From communicating to talking'. In J. Bruner, *Child's Talk: Learning to Use Language*, New York: Norton.

—— (1986) *Actual Minds, Possible Worlds*, Cambridge, MA: Harvard University Press.

Bruner, J.S. and Sherwood, V. (1976) 'Peekaboo and the learning of rule structures'. In J.S. Bruner, A. Jolly and K. Sylva (eds) *Play: Its Role in Development and Evolution*, Harmondsworth: Penguin.

Bruner, J.S., Jolly, A. and Sylva, K. (eds) (1976) *Play: Its Role in Development and Evolution*, Harmondsworth: Penguin.

Bucci, W. (2001) 'Pathways of emotional communication', *Psychoanalytic Inquiry*, 21: 40–70.

Buck, R. (1994) 'The neuropsychology of communication: spontaneous and symbolic aspects', *Journal of Pragmatics*, 22: 265–278.

Burhouse, A. (2001) 'Now we are two, going on three: triadic thinking and its link with development in the context of young child observations', *Infant Observation*, 4, 2: 51–67.

Caper, R. (1996) 'Play, experimentation and creativity', *International Journal of Psychoanalysis*, 77, 5: 859–870.

Chatwin, B. (1987) *The Songlines*, London: Jonathan Cape.

Chiu, A.W., McLeod, B.D., Har, K. and Wood, J.J. (2009) 'Child–therapist alliance and clinical outcomes in cognitive behavioural therapy for child anxiety disorders', *Journal of Child Psychology and Psychiatry*, 50, 6: 751–758.

Cohen, M. (2003) *Sent before My Time*, London: Karnac.

Collis, G.M. (1977) 'Visual co-orientation and maternal speech'. In H.R. Schaffer (ed.) *Studies in Mother–Infant Interaction*, London: Academic Press.

Cottis, T. (ed.) (2009) *Intellectual Disability, Trauma, and Psychotherapy*, London: Routledge.

Crapanzano, V. (2004) *Imaginative Horizons: An Essay in Literary-Philosophical Anthropology*, Chicago: University of Chicago Press.

Da Rocha Barros, E.M. (2002) 'An essay on dreaming, psychical working out and working through', *International Journal of Psychoanalysis*, 83, 5: 1083–1093.

Davies, J.M. (1998) 'Between the disclosure and foreclosure of erotic transference–countertransference: can psychoanalysis find a place for adult sexuality?', *Psychoanalytic Dialogues*, 8: 747–766.

Dawson, G. and Lewy, A. (1989) 'Reciprocal subcortical–cortical influences in autism: the role of attentional mechanisms'. In G. Dawson (ed.) *Autism, Nature, Diagnosis and Treatment*, New York: Guilford Press.

De Bellis, M.D., Keshavan, M.S., Clark, D.B., Casey, B.J., Giedd, J.N., Boring, A.M., Frustaci, K. and Ryan, N.D. (1999) 'Developmental traumatology part II: brain development', *Biological Psychiatry*, 45, 10: 1271–1284.

DeJong, M. (2010) 'Some reflections on the use of psychiatric diagnosis in the looked after or "in care" population', *Clinical Child Psychology and Psychiatry*, 15, 4: 589–599.

Demos, V. (1986) 'Crying in early infancy: an illustration of the motivational function of affect'. In T.B. Brazelton and M.W. Yogman (eds) *Affective Development in Infancy*, Norwood, NJ: Ablex.

Director, L. (2009) 'The enlivening object', *Contemporary Psychoanalysis*, 45, 1: 121–139.

Dissanayake, E. (2009) 'Root, leaf, blossom, or bole'. In S. Malloch and C. Trevarthen (eds) *Communicative Musicality: Exploring the Basis of Human Companionship*, Oxford: Oxford University Press.

Divino, C. and Moore, M.S. (2010) 'Integrating neurobiological findings into psycho-dynamic psychotherapy training and practice', *Psychoanalytic Dialogues*, 20: 1–19.

Docker-Drysdale, B. (1990) *The Provision of Primary Experience: Winnicottian Work with Children and Adolescents*, London: Free Association Books.

Dreyer, V. (2002) 'On some possible prerequisites of mental representation: a study of the child's pre-symbolic movement in relation to the development of an interpretative function'. Unpublished MA dissertation for the University of East London.

Dylan, B. (1987) 'Not dark yet'. On *Time out of Mind*, Columbia/Sony.

Edwards, J. (1994) 'On solid ground: the ongoing psychotherapeutic journey of an adolescent boy with autistic features', *Journal of Child Psychotherapy*, 20, 1: 57–84.

—— (2001) 'First love unfolding'. In J. Edwards (ed.) *Being Alive: Building on the Work of Anne Alvarez*, Hove: Brunner-Routledge.

Fairbairn, W.R.D. (1952) 'Schizoid factors of the personality'. In W.R.D. Fairbairn, *Psychoanalytic Studies of the Personality*, London: Tavistock/Routledge and Kegan Paul.

—— (1994) 'The nature of hysterical states'. In D.E. Scharff and E.F. Birtles (eds) *From Instinct to Self: Selected Papers of W.R.D. Fairbairn*, Northvale, NJ: Jason Aronson.

Feldman, M. (2004) 'Supporting psychic change: Betty Joseph'. In E. Hargreaves and A. Varchevker (eds) *In Pursuit of Psychic Change: The Betty Joseph Workshop*, London: Brunner-Routledge.

Ferris, S., McGauley, G. and Hughes, P. (2004) 'Attachment disorganization in infancy: relation to psychoanalytic understanding of development', *Psychoanalytic Psychotherapy*, 18, 2: 151–166.

Ferro, A. (1999) *The Bi-personal Field*, London: Routledge.

First, E. (2001) 'Liking *liking* doing'. In J. Edwards (ed.) *Being Alive: Building on the Work of Anne Alvarez*, Hove: Brunner-Routledge.

Fitzgerald, A. (2009) 'A psychoanalytic concept illustrated: will, must, may, can – revisiting the survival function of primitive omnipotence', *Infant Observation*, 12, 1: 43–61.

Fivaz-Depeursinge, E. and Corboz-Warnery, A. (1999) *The Primary Triangle: A Developmental Systems View of Mothers, Fathers, and Infants*, New York: Basic Books.

Fogel, A. (1977) 'Temporal organization in mother–infant face-to-face interaction'. In H.R. Schaffer (ed.) *Studies in Mother–Infant Interaction*, London: Academic Press.

—— (1993) 'Two principles of communication: co-regulation and framing'. In J. Nadel and L. Camaioni (eds) *New Perspectives in Early Communicative Development*, London: Routledge.

Fonagy, P. (1995) 'Playing with reality: the development of psychic reality and its malfunction in borderline personalities', *International Journal of Psychoanalysis*, 76: 39–44.

Fonagy, P. and Target, M. (1996) 'Playing with reality, I: Theory of mind and the normal development of psychic reality', *International Journal of Psychoanalysis*, 77: 217–233.

—— (1998) 'Mentalization and the changing aims of child psychoanalysis', *Psychoanalytic Dialogues*, 8, 1: 87–114.

Fonagy, P., Steele, M., Steele, H., Moran, G.S. and Higgitt, A.C. (1991) 'The capacity for understanding mental states: the reflective self in parent and child and its significance for security of attachment', *Infant Mental Health Journal*, 12: 201–218.

Fonseca, V.R.J.R.M. and Bussab, V.S.R. (2005) 'Trauma, deficit, defense: current trends in the psychoanalysis of children with pervasive developmental disorder'. Panel presented at the 44th IPA Congress, Rio De Janeiro, July.

Fordham, M. (1985) *Explorations into the Self, The Library of Analytic Psychology*, Vol. VII, London: Academic Press.

Freud, S. (1893–1895) *Studies on Hysteria*. In J. Strachey (ed.) (1966) *Standard Edition of the Complete Works of Sigmund Freud*, Vol. II, London: Hogarth.

—— (1905a) 'Fragment of an analysis of a case of hysteria'. In J. Strachey (ed.) (1966) *Standard Edition of the Complete Works of Sigmund Freud*, Vol. VII, London: Hogarth.

—— (1905b) 'Three essays on the theory of sexuality'. In J. Strachey (ed.) (1966) *Standard Edition of the Complete Works of Sigmund Freud*, Vol. VII, London: Hogarth.

—— (1909) 'Analysis of a phobia in a five-year-old boy'. In J. Strachey (ed.) (1966) *Standard Edition of the Complete Works of Sigmund Freud*, Vol. X, London: Hogarth.

—— (1911) 'Formulations on the two principles of mental functioning'. In J. Strachey (ed.) (1966) *Standard Edition of the Complete Works of Sigmund Freud*, Vol. XII, London: Hogarth.

—— (1916–1917) *Introductory Lectures on Psycho-analysis*. In J. Strachey (ed.) (1966) *Standard Edition of the Complete Works of Sigmund Freud*, Vols. XV and XVI, London: Hogarth.

—— (1917) *Mourning and Melancholia*. In J. Strachey (ed.) (1966) *Standard Edition of the Complete Works of Sigmund Freud*, Vol. XIV, London: Hogarth.

—— (1920) *Beyond the Pleasure Principle*. In J. Strachey (ed.) (1966) *Standard Edition of the Complete Works of Sigmund Freud*, Vol. XVIII, London: Hogarth.

—— (1930) 'Fetishism'. In J. Strachey (ed.) (1966) *Standard Edition of the Complete Works of Sigmund Freud*, Vol. XXI, London: Hogarth.

—— (1938) 'The theory of the instincts'. In J. Strachey (ed.) (1966) *Standard Edition of the Complete Works of Sigmund Freud*, Vol. XXIII, London: Hogarth.

Frick, P.J. and White, S.F. (2008) 'Research review: the importance of callous-unemotional traits for developmental models of aggressive and antisocial behaviour', *Journal of Consulting and Clinical Psychology*, 49, 4: 359–375.

Gabbard, G.O. (1989) 'Two subtypes of narcissistic personality disorder', *Bulletin of the Menninger Clinic*, 53, 6: 527–532.

—— (1994) 'Sexual excitement and countertransference love in the analyst', *Journal of the American Psychoanalytic Association*, 42:1083–1106.

Gampel, G. (2005) 'Foreword'. In A. Alvarez (2005) *Live Company* (Hebrew translation), Tel Aviv: Bookworm.

Gerhardt, S. (2004) *Why Love Matters: How Affection Shapes a Baby's Brain*, New York: Brunner-Routledge.

Gerrard, J. (2010) 'Seduction and betrayal', *British Journal of Psychotherapy*, 26, 1: 65–80.

—— (2011) *The Impossibility of Knowing*, London: Karnac.

Glover, E. (1928a) 'Lectures on technique in psycho-analysis', *International Journal of Psychoanalysis*, 9: 7–46.

—— (1928b) 'Lectures on technique in psycho-analysis', *International Journal of Psychoanalysis*, 9: 181–218.

Green, A. (1995) 'Has sexuality anything to do with psychoanalysis?', *International Journal of Psychoanalysis*, 76: 871–883.

—— (1997) *On Private Madness*, London: Karnac.

—— (2000) 'Science and science fiction in infant research'. In J. Sandler, A.M. Sandler and R. Davies (eds) *Clinical and Observational Psychoanalytic Research: Roots of a Controversy*, London: Karnac.

Greenspan, S.I. (1997) *Developmentally Based Psychotherapy*, Madison, CT: International Universities Press.

Grotstein, J. (1981a) *Splitting and Projective Identification*, London: Aronson.

—— (1981b) 'Wilfred R. Bion: the man, the psychoanalyst, the mystic. A perspective on his life and work'. In J. Grotstein (ed.) *Do I Dare Disturb the Universe? A Memorial to Wilfred R. Bion*, Beverly Hills, CA: Caesura Press.

—— (1983) 'Review of Tustin's *Autistic States in Children*', *International Review of Psychoanalysis*, 10: 491–498.

—— (2000) *Who is the Dreamer who Dreams the Dream: A Study of Psychic Presences*, Hillsdale, NJ: Analytic Press.

Haag, G. (1985) 'La mère et le bébé dans les deux moitiés du corps', *Neuropsychiatrie de L'enfance*, 33: 107–114.

Hamilton, V. (1982) *Narcissus and Oedipus: The Children of Psycho-analysis*, London: Routledge and Kegan Paul.

Hamilton, V.E. (2001) 'Foreword'. In J. Edwards (ed.) *Being Alive: Building on the Work of Anne Alvarez*, Hove: Brunner-Routledge.

Hand, H. (1997) 'The terrible surprise: the effect of trauma on a child's development'. Paper delivered to Psychoanalytic Section (Division 39) Spring Meeting of the American Psychological Association, Denver.

Hartmann, E. (1984) *The Nightmare*, New York: Basic Books.

Hawthorne, J. (2004) 'Training health professionals in the Neonatal Behavioral Assessment Scale (NBAS) and its use as an intervention', *The Signal, WAIMH* [*World Association for Infant Mental Health*] *Newsletter*, 12, 3–4: 1–5.

Herbert, Z. (1977) 'The envoy of Mr Cogito'. In *Selected Poems*, Oxford: Oxford University Press.

—— (1999) 'Chord'. In *Elegy for the Departure*, Hopewell, NJ: The Ecco Press.

Hinshelwood, R.D. (1989) *A Dictionary of Kleinian Thought*, London: Free Association Books.

Hobson, P. (1993) *Autism and the Development of Mind*, Hove: Lawrence Erlbaum.

—— (2002) *The Cradle of Thought*, London: Macmillan.

Hobson, R.P. and Lee, A. (1999) 'Imitation and identification in autism', *Journal of Child Psychology and Psychiatry*, 40: 649–659.

Hopkins, J. (1996) 'From baby games to let's pretend: the achievement of playing', *Journal of the British Association of Psychotherapy*, 31: 20–27.

Houzel, D. (2001) 'Bisexual qualities of the psychic envelope'. In J. Edwards (ed.) *Being Alive: Building on the Work of Anne Alvarez*, Hove: Brunner-Routledge.

Hughes, D.A. (1998) *Building the Bonds of Attachment: Awakening Love in Deeply Troubled Children*, Lanham, MD: Aronson.

Hughes, R. (2004) Lecture at the Royal Academy of Arts. Reported in *The Times*, 3 June.

Hurry, A. (ed.) (1998) *Psychoanalysis and Developmental Therapy*, London: Karnac.

Hutt, C. (1972) 'Exploration and play in children'. In J.S. Bruner, A. Jolly and K. Sylva (eds) (1976) *Play: Its Role in Development and Evolution*, Harmondsworth: Penguin.

Isaacs, S. (1948) 'The nature and function of phantasy', *International Journal of Psychoanalysis*, 29: 73–97.

—— (1991) 'Fifth discussion of scientific controversies'. In P. King and R. Steiner (eds) *The Freud–Klein Controversies 1941–45*, London: Tavistock/Routledge.

James, W. (1992) *Writings, 1878–1899*, New York: Library of America.

Jonas, H. (1974) *Philosophical Essays*, New York: Prentice-Hall.

Jones, E. (1967) *Sigmund Freud: Life and Work*, Vol. II: *Years of Maturity*, London: Hogarth.

Joseph, B. (1975) 'The patient who is difficult to reach'. In E.B. Spillius and M. Feldman (eds) (1989) *Psychic Equilibrium and Psychic Change: Selected Papers of Betty Joseph*, London: Routledge.

—— (1978) 'Different types of anxiety and their handling in the clinical situation'. In E.B. Spillius and M. Feldman (eds) (1989) *Psychic Equilibrium and Psychic Change: Selected Papers of Betty Joseph*, London: Routledge.

—— (1981) 'Towards the experiencing of psychic pain'. In E.B. Spillius and M. Feldman (eds) (1989) *Psychic Equilibrium and Psychic Change: Selected Papers of Betty Joseph*, London: Routledge.

—— (1982) 'Addiction to near death'. In E.B. Spillius and M. Feldman (eds) (1989) *Psychic Equilibrium and Psychic Change: Selected Papers of Betty Joseph*, London: Routledge.

—— (1983) 'On understanding and not understanding: some technical issues'. In E.B. Spillius and M. Feldman (eds) (1989) *Psychic Equilibrium and Psychic Change: Selected Papers of Betty Joseph*, London: Routledge.

—— (1998) 'Thinking about a playroom', *Journal of Child Psychotherapy*, 24, 3: 359–366.

Kanner, L. (1944) 'Early infantile autism', *Journal of Paediatrics*, 25: 211–217.

Kernberg, O. (1975) *Borderline Conditions and Pathological Narcissism*, Northvale, NJ: Jason Aronson.

Kernberg, P., Weiner, A.S. and Bardenstein, K.K. (eds) (2000) *Personality Disorders in Children and Adolescents*, New York: Basic Books.

Klauber, T. (1999) 'The significance of trauma and other factors in work with the parents of children with autism'. In A. Alvarez and S. Reid (eds) *Autism and Personality: Findings from the Tavistock Autism Workshop*, London: Routledge.

Klaus, M.H. and Kennell, J.H. (1982) *Parent–Infant Bonding*, London: C.H. Mosby.

Klein, M. (1923) 'The role of the school in the libidinal development of the child'. In M. Klein (1975) *The Writings of Melanie Klein*, Vol. I, London: Hogarth.
—— (1930) 'The importance of symbol-formation in the development of the ego'. In M. Klein (1975) *The Writings of Melanie Klein*, Vol. I, London: Hogarth.
—— (1932a) 'The psycho-analysis of children'. In M. Klein (1975) *The Writings of Melanie Klein*, Vol. II, London: Hogarth.
—— (1932b) 'The significance of early anxiety-situations in the development of the ego'. In M. Klein (1975) *The Writings of Melanie Klein*, Vol. I, London: Hogarth.
—— (1935) 'A contribution to the psychogenesis of manic-depressive states'. In M. Klein (1975) *The Writings of Melanie Klein*, Vol. III, London: Hogarth.
—— (1937) 'Love, guilt and reparation'. In M. Klein (1975) *The Writings of Melanie Klein*, Vol. I, London: Hogarth.
—— (1940) 'Mourning and its relation to manic-depressive states'. In M. Klein (1975) *The Writings of Melanie Klein*, Vol. III, London: Hogarth.
—— (1945) 'The Oedipus complex in the light of early anxieties'. In M. Klein (1975) *The Writings of Melanie Klein*, Vol. I, London: Hogarth [also in (1945) *International Journal of Psychoanalysis*, 26: 11–33].
—— (1946) 'Notes on some schizoid mechanisms'. In M. Klein (1975) *The Writings of Melanie Klein*, Vol. III, London: Hogarth [also in (1946) *International Journal of Psychoanalysis*, 27: 99–110].
—— (1952) 'Some theoretical conclusions regarding the emotional life of the infant'. In M. Klein (1975) *The Writings of Melanie Klein*, Vol. III, London: Hogarth.
—— (1955) 'On identification'. In M. Klein (1975) *The Writings of Melanie Klein*, Vol. III, London: Hogarth.
—— (1957) 'Envy and gratitude'. In M. Klein (1975) *The Writings of Melanie Klein*, Vol. III, London: Hogarth.
—— (1958) 'On the development of mental functioning', *International Journal of Psychoanalysis*, 39: 84–90.
—— (1959) 'Our adult world and its roots in infancy'. In M. Klein (1975) *The Writings of Melanie Klein*, Vol. III, London: Hogarth.
—— (1961) *Narrative of a Child Analysis*, London: Hogarth.
—— (1963) 'On the sense of loneliness'. In M. Klein (1975) *The Writings of Melanie Klein*, Vol. III, London: Hogarth.
Klein, M., Heimann, P., Isaacs, S. and Riviere, J. (1952) *Developments in Psychoanalysis*, London: Hogarth.
Kleitman, N. (1963) *Sleep and Wakefulness*, Chicago: University of Chicago Press.
Knoblauch, S. (2000) *The Musical Edge of Therapeutic Dialogue*, Hillsdale, NJ: Analytic Press.
Kohut, H. (1977) *The Restoration of the Self*, New York: International University Press.
—— (1985) *The Analysis of the Self*, New York: International University Press.
Koulomzin, M., Beebe, B., Anderson, S., Jaffe, J., Feldstein, S. and Crown, C. (2002) 'Infant gaze, head, face and self-touch differentiate secure vs. avoidant attachment at 1 year: a microanalytic approach', *Attachment and Human Development*, 4, 1: 3–24.
Kundera, M. (1982) *The Joke*, Harmonsdworth: Penguin.
Kut Rosenfeld, S. and Sprince, M. (1965) 'Some thoughts on the technical handling of borderline children', *Psychoanalytic Study of the Child*, 20: 495–517.
Lahr, J. (1995) 'King Tap', *New Yorker*, 17 April.
Lanyado, M. and Horne, A. (2006) *A Question of Technique*, Hove: Routledge.

Laplanche, J. and Pontalis, B. (1973) *The Language of Psychoanalysis*, London: Hogarth.

Laznik, M.C. (2009) 'The Lacanian theory of the drive: an examination of possible gains for research in autism', *Journal of the Centre for Freudian Analysis and Research*, 19: n.p.

Leichsenring, F. and Rabung, S. (2008) 'Effectiveness of long-term psychodynamic psychotherapy: a meta-analysis', *Journal of the American Medical Association*, 300: 1551–1565.

Leslie, A.M. (1987) 'Pretence and representation: the origins of theory of mind', *Psychological Review*, 94: 412–426.

Levi, P. (2001) *The Search for Roots*, London: Penguin.

Likierman, M. (2001) *Melanie Klein: Her Work in Context*, London: Continuum.

Lubbe, T. (ed.) (2000) *The Borderline Psychotic Child: A Selective Integration*, London: Routledge.

Lupinacci, M.A. (1998) 'Reflections on the early stages of the Oedipus complex: the parental couple in relation to psychoanalytic work', *Journal of Child Psychotherapy*, 24, 3: 409–422.

Lynd, H.M. (1958) *On Shame and the Search for Identity*, New York: Harcourt Brace and World.

Magagna, J., Bakalar, N., Cooper, H., Levy, J., Norman, C. and Shank, C. (eds) (2005) *Intimate Transformations: Babies with Their Families*, London: Karnac.

Mahler, M. (1968) *On Human Symbiosis and the Vicissitudes of Individuation*, New York: International University Press.

Mahler, M., Pine, F. and Bergman, A. (1975) *The Psychological Birth of the Human Infant*, New York: Basic Books.

Maiello, S. (1995) 'La voce: il suono madre'. In G. Buzzatti and A. Salvo (eds) *Corpo a Corpo: Madre e Figlia nella Psicoanalisi*, Bari: Laterza.

Main, M. (1991) 'Metacognitive knowledge, metacognitive monitoring, and singular (coherent) vs. multiple (incoherent) models of attachment'. In C.M. Parkes, J. Stevenson-Hinde and P. Marris (eds) *Attachment across the Life Cycle*, London: Routledge.

Malloch, S. and Trevarthen, C. (eds) (2009) *Communicative Musicality: Exploring the Basis of Human Companionship*, Oxford: Oxford University Press.

Maurer, D. and Salapatak, P. (1976) 'Developmental changes in the scanning of faces by young infants', *Child Development*, 47: 523–527.

McCarthy, C. (1992) *All the Pretty Horses*, New York: Knopf.

Meloy, J.R. (1996) *The Psychopathic Mind: Origin, Dynamics, Treatment*, London: Jason Aronson.

Meltzer, D. (1983) Dream-life: A Re-examination of the Psycho-analytical Theory and Technique, Strathtay: Clunie.

Meltzer, D. and Harris Williams, M. (1988) *The Apprehension of Beauty: The Role of Aesthetic Conflict in Development, Art and Violence*, Strathtay: Clunie.

Meltzer, D., Bremner, J., Hoxter, S., Weddell, D. and Wittenberg, I. (1975) *Explorations in Autism: A Psycho-analytical Study*, Strathtay: Clunie.

Mendes de Almeida, M. (2002) 'Infant observation and its developments: repercussion within the work with severely disturbed children'. Paper presented at the Sixth International Conference on Infant Observation, Krakow.

Miller, L. (2001) *The Brontë Myth*, London: Jonathan Cape.

Miller, L., Rustin, M.E., Rustin, M.J. and Shuttleworth, J. (1989) *Closely Observed Infants*, London: Duckworth.

Miller, S. (1984) 'Some thoughts on once-weekly psychotherapy in the National Health Service', *Journal of Child Psychotherapy*, 10, 2: 187–198.

Mitrani, J.L. (1998) 'Unbearable ecstasy, reverence and awe, and the perpetuation of an "aesthetic conflict"', *Psychoanalytic Quarterly*, 67: 102–107.

Money-Kyrle, R. (1947) 'On being a psychoanalyst'. In D. Meltzer and E. O'Shaughnessy (eds) (1978) *The Collected Papers of Roger Money-Kyrle*, Strathtay: Clunie.

Moore, M. (1968) *Marianne Moore: Complete Poems*, London: Faber and Faber.

Moore, M.S. (2004) 'Differences between representational drawings and re-presentations in traumatized children'. Paper presented to the Association of Child Psychotherapists' Annual Conference, London, June.

Murray, L. (1991) 'Intersubjectivity, object relations theory and empirical evidence from mother–infant interactions', *Infant Mental Health Journal*, 12: 219–232.

—— (1992) 'The impact of postnatal depression on infant development', *Journal of Child Psychology and Psychiatry*, 33, 3: 543–561.

Murray, L. and Cooper, P.J. (eds) (1997) *Postpartum Depression and Child Development*, London: Guilford Press.

Music, G. (2009) 'Neglecting neglect: some thoughts on children who have lacked good input, and are "undrawn" and "unenjoyed"', *Journal of Child Psychotherapy*, 35, 2: 142–156.

—— (2011) *Nurturing Natures: Attachment and Children's Sociocultural and Brain Development*, Hove: Psychology Press.

Negri, R. (1994) *The Newborn in the Intensive Care Unit: A Neuropsychoanalytic Prevention Model*, London: Karnac.

Newson, J. (1977) 'An intersubjective approach to the systematic description of mother–infant interaction'. In H.R. Schaffer (ed.) *Studies in Mother–Infant Interaction*, London: Academic Press.

O'Shaughnessy, E. (1964) 'The absent object', *Journal of Child Psychotherapy*, 1, 2: 34–43.

—— (2006) 'A conversation about early unintegration, disintegration and integration', *Journal of Child Psychotherapy*, 32, 2: 153–157.

Ogden, T.H. (1997) *Reverie and Interpretation: Sensing Something Human*, Northvale, NJ: Jason Aronson.

Panksepp, J. (1998) *Affective Neuroscience: The Foundations of Human and Animal Emotions*, Oxford: Oxford University Press.

Panksepp, J. and Biven, L. (2011) *The Archaeology of the Mind: Neuroevolutionary Origins of Human Emotion*, New York: Norton.

Papousek, H. and Papousek, M. (1975) 'Cognitive aspects of preverbal social interaction between human infants and adults'. In *Parent Infant Interaction*, CIBA Foundation Symposium No. 33, Amsterdam: Elsevier.

Perry, B.D. (2002) 'Childhood experience and the expression of genetic potential: what childhood neglect tells us about nature and nurture', *Brain and Mind*, 3: 79–100.

Perry, B.D., Pollard, R.A., Blakeley, T.L., Baker, W.L. and Vigilante, D. (1995) 'Childhood trauma, the neurobiology of adaptation and "use-dependent" development of the brain: how "states" become "traits"', *Infant Mental Health Journal*, 16: 271–291.

Pessoa, F. (1981) 'Cease your song'. In *Selected Poems* (2nd edn), London: Penguin.

Phillips, A. (1993) *On Kissing, Tickling and Being Bored*, London: Karnac.

Pick, I. (1985) 'Working through in the counter-transference', *International Journal of Psychoanalysis*, 66: 157–166.

Pine, F. (1985) *Developmental Theory and Clinical Process*, London: Yale University Press.

Racker, H. (1968) *Transferencence and Countertransference*, London: Maresfield Reprints.

Reddy, V. (2005) 'Feeling shy and showing off: self-conscious emotions must regulate self-awareness'. In J. Nadel and D. Muir (eds) *Emotional Development*, Oxford: Oxford University Press.

—— (2008) *How Infants Know Minds*, London: Harvard University Press.

Reid, S. (1988) 'Interpretation: food for thought'. Paper presented to the Annual Conference of Child Psychotherapists, London, June.

—— (ed.) (1997) *Developments in Infant Observation: The Tavistock Model*, London: Routledge.

—— (1999a) 'Autism and trauma: autistic post-traumatic developmental disorder'. In A. Alvarez and S. Reid (eds) *Autism and Personality: Findings from the Tavistock Autism Workshop*, London: Routledge.

—— (1999b) 'The assessment of the child with autism: a family perspective'. In A. Alvarez and S. Reid (eds) *Autism and Personality: Findings from the Tavistock Autism Workshop*, London: Routledge.

Resnik, S. (1995) *Mental Space*, London: Karnac.

Rey, H. (1988) 'That which patients bring to analysis', *International Journal of Psychoanalysis*, 69: 457–470 [also in J. Magagna (ed.) (1994) *Universals of Psychoanalysis in the Treatment of Psychotic and Borderline States: Henri Rey*, London: Free Association Books].

Rhode, M. (2001) 'The sense of abundance in relation to technique'. In J. Edwards (ed.) *Being Alive: Building on the Work of Anne Alvarez*, Hove: Brunner-Routledge.

Riviere, J. (ed.) (1952) *Developments in Psycho-analysis*, London: Hogarth Press.

Rizzolatti, G., Craighero, L. and Fadiga, L. (2002) 'The mirror system in humans'. In M. Stamenov and V. Gallese (eds) *Mirror Neurons and the Evolution of Brain and Language*, Philadelphia, PA: John Benjamins.

Robarts, J. (2009) 'Supporting the development of mindfulness and meaning: clinical pathways in music therapy with a sexually abused child'. In S. Malloch and C. Trevarthen (eds) *Communicative Musicality: Exploring the Basis of Human Companionship*, Oxford: Oxford University Press.

Robertson, R. (2005) 'A psychoanalytic perspective on the work of a physiotherapist with infants at risk of neurological problems: comparing the theoretical background of physiotherapy and psychoanalysis', *Infant Observation*, 8, 3: 259–278.

Robson, K. (1967) 'The role of eye-to-eye contact in maternal–infant attachment', *Journal of Child Psychology and Psychiatry*, 8: 13–25.

Rodrigue, E. (1955) 'The analysis of a three-year-old mute schizophrenic'. In M. Klein, P. Heimann and R.E. Money-Kyrle (eds) *New Directions in Psycho-analysis: The Significance of Infant Conflict in the Pattern of Adult Behaviour*, London: Tavistock.

Rosenfeld, H. (1964) 'On the psychopathology of narcissism', *International Journal of Psychoanalysis*, 45: 332–337.

—— (1987) *Impasse and Interpretation: Therapeutic and Anti-therapeutic Factors in the Psychoanalytic Treatment of Psychotic, Borderline, and Neurotic Patients*, London: Tavistock.

Roth, P. (2001) 'Mapping the landscape: levels of transference interpretation', *International Journal of Psychoanalysis*, 82: 533–543.

Rustin, M. (1997) 'Child psychotherapy within the Kleinian tradition'. In B. Burgoyne and M. Sullivan (eds) *The Klein–Lacan Dialogues*, London: Rebus.

Rustin, M.E. (1998) 'Dialogues with parents', *Journal of Child Psychotherapy*, 24: 233–252.

Salo, F. (1987) 'The analysis of a well-endowed boy from an emotionally impoverished background', *Journal of Child Psychotherapy*, 13, 2: 15–32.

Sander, L. (1975) 'Infant and caretaking environment: investigation and conceptualization of adaptive behaviour in a system of increasing complexity'. In E.J. Anthony (ed.) *Explorations in Child Psychiatry*, New York: Plenum.

—— (2000) 'Where are we going in the field of infant mental health?', *Infant Mental Health Journal*, 21, 1–2: 5–20.

—— (2002) 'Thinking differently: principles of process in living systems and the specificity of being known', *Psychoanalytic Dialogues*, 12, 1: 11–42.

Sandler, A.M. (1996) 'The psychoanalytic legacy of Anna Freud', *Psychoanalytic Study of the Child*, 51: 270–284.

Sandler, J. (1960) 'The background of safety', *International Journal of Psychoanalysis*, 41: 352–356.

—— (1988) *Projection, Identification, Projective Identification*, London: Karnac.

Sandler, J. and Freud, A. (1985) *The Analysis of Defence*, New York: International University Press.

Sandler, J. and Sandler, A.M. (1994a) 'Phantasy and its transformations: a contemporary Freudian view', *International Journal of Psychoanalysis*, 75: 387–394.

—— (1994b) 'The past unconscious and the present unconscious: a contribution to a technical frame of reference', *Psychoanalytic Study of the Child*, 49: 278–292.

Sanville, J. (1991) *The Playground of Psychoanalytic Therapy*, Hillsdale, NJ: Analytic Press.

Scaife, M. and Bruner, J. (1975) 'The capacity for joint visual attention in the infant', *Nature*, 253: 265–266.

Schafer, R. (1976) *A New Language for Psychoanalysis*, New Haven, CT: Yale University Press.

—— (1999) 'Recentering psychoanalysis: from Heinz Hartmann to the contemporary British Kleinians', *Psychoanalytic Psychology*, 16: 339–354.

Schore, A. (1994) *Affect Regulation and the Origin of the Self: The Neurobiology of Emotional Development*, Hillsdale, NJ: Lawrence Erlbaum.

—— (1997) 'Interdisciplinary developmental research as a source of clinical models'. In M.M. Moskowitz, C. Monk, C. Kaye and S. Ellman (eds) *The Neurobiologcal and Developmental Basis for Psychotherapeutic Intervention*, London: Jason Aronson.

—— (2003) *Affect Regulation and the Repair of the Self*, London: Norton.

Searles, H. (1959) 'Oedipal love in the countertransference'. In H. Searles (1986) *Collected Papers on Schizophrenia and Related Subjects*, New York: International University Press.

—— (1961) 'Sexual processes in schizophrenia'. In H. Searles (1986) *Collected Papers on Schizophrenia and Related Subjects*, New York: International University Press.

Segal, H. (1957) 'Notes on symbol formation'. In H. Segal (1981) *The Work of Hanna Segal*, Northvale, NJ: Jason Aronson.

—— (1964) *Introduction to the Work of Melanie Klein*, London: Heinemann.

—— (1983) 'Some implications of Melanie Klein's work', *International Journal of Psychoanalysis*, 64: 269–276.

Shakespeare, W. (1969) *The Winter's Tale*, Harmondsworth: Penguin.

Shedler, J. (2010) 'The efficacy of psychodynamic psychotherapy', *American Psychologist*, 65, 2: 98–109.

Shiner, R. and Caspi, A. (2003) 'Personality differences in childhood and adolescence: measurement, development and consequences', *Journal of Child Psychology and Psychiatry*, 44: 2–32.

Siegel, D.J. (1999) *The Developing Mind: Toward a Neurobiology of Interpersonal Experience*, New York: Guilford Press.

Sinason, V. (1992) *Mental Handicap and the Human Condition*, London: Free Association Books.

Slade, A. (1987) 'Quality of attachment and early symbolic play', *Developmental Psychology*, 17: 326–335.

Solms, M. (2000) 'Freudian dream theory today', *The Psychologist*, 12, 1: 618–619.

Solms, M. and Turnbull, O. (2002) *The Brain and the Inner World: An Introduction to the Neuroscience of Subjective Experience*, London: Karnac.

Sonuga-Barke, E.J.S. (2010) 'It's the environment, stupid!', *Journal of Child Psychology and Psychiatry*, 51, 2: 113–115.

Sorenson, P.B. (2000) 'Observations of transition facilitating behaviour: developmental and theoretical implications', *Infant Observation*, 3, 2: 46–54.

Spillius, E.B. (1983) 'Some developments from the work of Melanie Klein', *International Journal of Psychoanalysis*, 64: 321–332.

Spillius, E.B. and Feldman, M. (eds) (1989) *Psychic Equilibrium and Psychic Change: Selected Papers of Betty Joseph*, London: Routledge.

Stein, D. (1985) *The Interpersonal World of the Infant*, New York: Basic Books.

Steiner, J. (1993) 'Problems of psychoanalytic technique: patient-centred and analyst-centred interpretations'. In J. Steiner, *Psychic Retreats: Pathological Organizations in Psychotic, Neurotic and Borderline Patients*, London: Routledge.

—— (1994) 'Patient-centered and analyst-centered interpretations: some implications of containment and counter-transference', *Psychoanalytic Inquiry*, 14, 3: 406–422.

—— (2004) 'Containment, enactment, and communication'. In E. Hargreaves and A. Varchevker (eds) *In Pursuit of Psychic Change: The Betty Joseph Workshop*, London: Brunner-Routledge.

Stern, D.N. (1974) 'Mother and infant at play: the dyadic interaction involving facial, vocal and gaze behaviours'. In M. Lewis and L.A. Rosenblum (eds) *The Effect of the Infant on its Caregiver*, New York: Wiley.

—— (1977) 'Missteps in the dance'. In D.N. Stern, *The First Relationship: Infant and Mother*, Cambridge, MA: Harvard University Press.

—— (1983) 'The early development of schemas of Self, Other and Self with Other'. In J.D. Lichtenberg and S. Kaplan (eds) *Reflections on Self Psychology*, London: Analytic Press.

—— (1985) *The Interpersonal World of the Infant*, New York: Basic Books.

—— (2000) 'Putting time back into our considerations of infant experience: a microdiachronic view', *Infant Mental Health Journal*, 21: 21–28.

—— (2010) *Forms of Vitality*, Oxford: Oxford University Press.

Stern, D.N., Sander, L.W., Nahum, J.P., Harrison, A.M., Lyons-Ruth, K., Morgan, A.C., Bruschweilerstern, N. and Tronick, E.Z. (1998) 'Non-interpretive mechanisms in psychoanalytic psychotherapy', *International Journal of Psychoanalysis*, 79: 903–921.

Sternberg, J. (2005) *Infant Observation at the Heart of Training*, London: Karnac.

Stolorow, R.D. and Lachmann, F.M. (1980) *The Psychoanalysis of Developmental Arrests*, Madison, CT: International University Press.

Strachey, J. (1934) 'The nature of the therapeutic action of psychoanalysis', *International Journal of Psychoanalysis*, 15: 127–159.

Strathearn, L., Gray, P.H., O'Callaghan, M.J. and Wood, D.O. (2001) 'Childhood neglect and cognitive development in extremely low birth weight infants: a prospective study', *Paediatrics*, 108, 1: 142–151.

Striano, T. and Rochat, P. (1999) 'Developmental links between dyadic and triadic social competence in infancy', *British Journal of Developmental Psychology*, 17: 551–562.

Sylva, K. and Bruner, J.S. (1974) 'The role of play in the problem-solving of children 3–5 years old'. In J.S. Bruner, A. Jolly and K. Sylva (eds) (1976) *Play: Its Role in Development and Evolution*, Harmondsworth: Penguin.

Symington, J. (2002) 'Mrs Bick and infant observation'. In A. Briggs (ed.) *Surviving Space: Papers on Infant Observation*, London: Karnac.

—— (2004) 'Mrs Bick, infant observation and the question of un-integration'. Paper presented to the International Infant Observation Conference, Tavistock Clinic, London.

Symington, N. (1980) 'The response aroused by the psychopath', *International Review of Psychoanalysis*, 7: 291–298.

—— (1993) *Narcissism: A New Theory*, London: Karnac.

—— (1995) 'Mrs Bick and infant observation'. Paper presented on the 75th Anniversary of Tavistock Clinic, London, August.

Thelen, E. and Smith, L.B. (1995) *A Dynamic Systems Approach to the Development of Cognition and Action*, London: MIT Press.

Tompkins, S. (1981) 'The quest for primary motives: biography and autobiography of an idea', *Journal of Personality and Social Psychology*, 41: 306–329.

Tremelloni, L. (2005) *Arctic Spring: Potential for Growth in Adults with Psychosis and Autism*, London: Karnac.

Trevarthen, C. (1993) 'Playing into reality: conversations with the infant communicator'. In L. Spurling (ed.) *Winnicott Studies*, Vol. VII, London: Karnac.

—— (2001) 'Intrinsic motives for companionship in understanding: their origin, development, and significance for infant mental health', *Infant Mental Health*, special issue: *Contributions from the Decade of the Brain to Infant Mental Health*, 22, 1–2: 95–131.

Trevarthen, C. and Aitken, K.J. (2001) 'Intersubjectivity: research, theory and clinical applications', *Journal of Child Psychology and Psychiatry*, 42: 3–48.

Trevarthen, C. and Hubley, P. (1978) 'Secondary intersubjectivity: confidence, confiding and acts of meaning in the first year'. In A. Lock (ed.) *Action, Gesture and Symbol: The Emergence of Language*, London: Academic Press.

Trevarthen, C. and Marwick, H. (1986) 'Signs of motivation for speech in infants, and the nature of a mother's support for development of language'. In B. Lindblom and R. Zetterstrom (eds) *Precursors of Early Speech*, Basingstoke: Macmillan.

Tronick, E. (2007) *The Neurobehavioral and Social-Emotional Development of Infants and Children*, New York: Norton.

Tronick, E.Z., Bruschweiler-Stern, N., Harrison, A.M., Lyons-Ruth, K., Morgan, A.C. and Nahum, J.P. (1998) 'Dyadically expanded states of consciousness', *Infant Mental Health Journal*, 19: 290–299.

Trowell, J., Rhode, M., Miles, G. and Sherwood, I. (2003) 'Childhood depression: work in progress', *Journal of Child Psychotherapy*, 29, 2: 147–169.

Tuch, R.H. (2007) 'Thinking with, and about, patients too scared to think: can non-interpretive manoeuvres stimulate reflective thought?', *International Journal of Psychoanalysis*, 88: 91–111.

Tustin, F. (1980) 'Autistic objects', *International Review of Psychoanalysis*, 7: 27–39.

—— (1992) *Autistic States in Children* (rev. edn), London: Routledge and Kegan Paul.

Urwin, C. (1987) 'Developmental psychology and psychoanalysis: splitting the difference'. In M. Richards and P. Light (eds) *Children of Social Worlds*, Cambridge: Polity.

—— (2002) 'A psychoanalytic approach to language delay: when autistic isn't necessarily autism', *Journal of Child Psychotherapy*, 28, 1: 73–93.

Uzgiris, I.C. and Hunt, J.M.V. (1975) *Towards Ordinal Scales of Psychological Development in Infancy*, Champaign: University of Illinois Press.

Van der Kolk, B. (2009) 'Proposal to include a Developmental Trauma Disorder diagnosis for children and adolescents in *DSM-V*'. Paper presented at the UCLA Trauma Conference, California, July.

Viding, E. (2004) 'Annotation: understanding the development of psychopathy', *Journal of Child Psychology and Psychiatry*, 45, 8: 1329–1337.

Vygotsky, L. (1978) *Mind in Society: The Development of Higher Psychological Processes*, London: Harvard University Press.

Waddell, M. (2006) 'Integration, unintegration, disintegration: an introduction', *Journal of Child Psychotherapy*, 32, 2: 148–152.

Wakschlag, L.S., Tolan, P.H. and Leventhal, B.L. (2010) 'Research review: "Ain't misbehaving": towards a developmentalized specified nosology for preschool disruptive behaviour', *Journal of Child Psychology and Psychiatry*, 51, 1: 3–22.

Waska, R.T. (2002) *Primitive Experiences of Loss: Working with the Paranoid-Schizoid Patient*, London: Karnac.

Williams, A.H. (1960) 'A psycho-analytic approach to the treatment of the murderer', *International Journal of Psychoanalysis*, 4: 532–539.

—— (1998) *Cruelty, Violence and Murder*, London: Karnac.

Williams, G. (1997) 'On introjective processes: the hypothesis of an omega function'. In G. Williams, *Internal Landscapes and Foreign Bodies: Eating Disorders and Other Pathologies*, London: Duckworth.

Wing, L. and Attwood, A. (1987) 'Syndromes of autism and atypical development'. In D. Cohen and A. Donnellan (eds) *Handbook of Autism and Pervasive Developmental Disorders*, New York: Wiley.

Winnicott, D.W. (1945) 'Primitive emotional development'. In D.W. Winnicott (1958) *Collected Papers: Through Paediatrics to Psycho-analysis*, London: Tavistock.

—— (1949) 'Hate in the countertransference', *International Journal of Psychoanalysis*, 30: 69–74.

—— (1953) 'Transitional objects and transitional phenomena: a study of the first not-me possession', *International Journal of Psychoanalysis*, 34: 89–97.

—— (1954) 'The depressive position in normal emotional development'. In D.W. Winnicott (1958) *Collected Papers: Through Paediatrics to Psycho-analysis*, London: Tavistock.

—— (1960) 'The theory of the parent–infant relationship'. In D.W. Winnicott (1965) *The Maturational Processes and the Facilitating Environment*, London: Hogarth.

—— (1963) 'The capacity for concern'. In D.W. Winnicott (1965) *The Maturational Processes and the Facilitating Environment*, London: Hogarth.

—— (1971) *Playing and Reality*, London: Tavistock.

Wittenberg, I. (1975) 'Primal depression in autism – John'. In D. Meltzer, J. Bremner, S. Hoxter, D. Weddell and I. Wittenberg, *Explorations in Autism: A Psycho-analytical Study*, Strathtay: Clunie.

Wolff, P.H. (1965) 'The development of attention in young infants'. In L.J. Stone, H.T. Smith and L.B. Murphy (eds) (1974) *The Competent Infant: Research and Commentary*, London: Tavistock.

Wollheim, R. (1971) *Freud*, London: Fontana.

Woods, J. (2003) *Boys who Have Abused: Psychoanalytic Psychotherapy with Victim/ Perpetrators of Sexual Abuse*, London: Jessica Kingsley.

Wrye, H.K. and Welles, J.K. (1989) 'The maternal erotic transference', *International Journal of Psychoanalysis*, 70: 673–684.

Index